Praise for Orrin Grey's *How to S...*

"*How to See Ghosts & Other Figment...*
more monsters, ghouls and ghosts th.... ..., ...........t ........ ......
in memory, but with real emotional depths to back them up. It's like peering through the eye holes of a cheap Halloween monster mask to see the tangible and very human sadness lurking just beneath."
—Trevor Henderson, Illustrator

Praise for Orrin Grey's *Guignol & Other Sardonic Tales*

"In this career-spanning collection, Grey assembles 14 peculiar tales of horror into a veritable smorgasbord of horrific thrills and chills. [...] This collection is a must-read for hardcore fans of horror..."
—*Publishers Weekly*

"In his third and arguably best collection, Orrin Grey spreads his black wings and takes us on a thrill ride into his limitless imagination. Through musty attics and mist-shrouded crypts, down soot-choked chimneys and into mysterious portals to faraway planets we ride, emerging at the end buzzing, a little dizzy, and most certainly changed. Cinematic, dark, and daring, *Guignol* is a book that will bring out the monster in you...and let it feed."
—Matthew M. Bartlett, author of *Gateways to Abomination* and *Of Doomful Portent*

"To say that Orrin Grey is a phenomenal writer is like saying the Phantom of the Opera knew his way around a pipe organ. Nobody evokes classic terrors while simultaneously offering a melancholy, beautifully macabre world as brilliantly as Grey."
—Christopher Slatsky, author of *Alectryomancer and Other Weird Tales*

Praise for Orrin Grey's *Painted Monsters & Other Strange Beasts*

"*Painted Monsters & Other Strange Beasts* is a fantastic follow-up to Grey's first collection, *Never Bet the Devil*. This is the kind of writing that shows what can still be done with the classical weird."
—Laird Barron, author of *The Beautiful Thing That Awaits Us All*

"This is an outstanding collection, one to which you will return again and again long after the house lights have come up."
—Daniel Mills, author of *The Lord Came at Twilight*

"The horror genre is a many-splintered thing. Grey collects those splinters, mixes and matches them, concocting a beast of a collection that is as fun as it is scary, as charming as it is chilling."
—Philip Gelatt, director of *They Remain*

"In his latest collection, Orrin Grey not only pays homage to the classic horror films of yesteryear, he tears down the silver screen to reveal the true horrors that lurk on the other side. Fans of H. P. Lovecraft, Vincent Price, and the Hammer horror films will feel right at home."
—Ian Rogers, author of *Every House Is Haunted*

"If you're looking for something between Ray Bradbury's headlong genre-bending fabulist glee and the *Insidious* movie franchise's unapologetic vaudeville creep, then Grey's your man."
—Gemma Files, author of *Experimental Film*

"Orrin Grey's roots (or should I say tentacles?) run deep, squeezing the best from horrors both classic and obscure, twisting them in his own particular way. He's a fine storyteller who'll pull you in, and so will *Painted Monsters*. Don't miss it!"
—Norman Partridge, author of *Dark Harvest*

# GLOWING IN THE DARK

Writings on the Horror Film

Other books by Orrin Grey

Anthologies:

*Fungi* (with Silvia Moreno-Garcia)

Chapbooks:

*Gardinel's Real Estate* (with M. S. Corley)
*The Mysterious Flame*

Collections:

*Never Bet the Devil & Other Warnings*
*Painted Monsters & Other Strange Beasts*
*Guignol & Other Sardonic Tales*
*How to See Ghosts & Other Figments*

# GLOWING IN THE DARK

## Writings on the Horror Film

## ORRIN GREY

WORD HORDE
PETALUMA, CA

*Glowing in the Dark* © 2024 by Orrin Grey
This edition of *Glowing in the Dark* © 2024 by Word Horde

Cover art and design © 2024 by Yves Tourigny

Edited by Ross E. Lockhart

All rights reserved

First Edition

ISBN: 978-1-956252-07-1

A Word Horde Book
www.wordhorde.com

# TABLE OF CONTENTS

Introduction: Light and Shadow ........................................................... 1
Cosmic Horror in John Carpenter's "Apocalypse Trilogy" ................... 7
*House of Wax* (2005) .......................................................................... 15
Hammer Frankenstein-athon ............................................................. 18
*Pacific Rim* (2013) ............................................................................. 23
Dark Angels: Insects in the Films of Guillermo del Toro .................. 27
The H Word: But Is It Scary? ............................................................. 34
"Each one of these things comes from an egg, right?" ........................ 38
Life in the Monster Squad ................................................................. 41
Monsters in *Kong: Skull Island* ......................................................... 46
Toho's "Bloodthirsty Trilogy" ............................................................. 50
*Dark Intruder* (1965) ......................................................................... 56
*The World of Vampires* (1961) ........................................................... 60
*Suspiria* (2018) .................................................................................. 64
Fulci's *Zombie* Lives On .................................................................... 67
Of Giallo and Gore—*Torso* (1973) and *The Wizard of Gore* (1970) ... 71
*Maniac* (1980) ................................................................................... 77
*Audition* (1999) ................................................................................. 81
*The Andromeda Strain* (1971) ........................................................... 85
The American Horror Project Vol. 2 .................................................. 89
*Alice, Sweet Alice* (1976) ................................................................... 97
*Cruising* (1980) .................................................................................. 101
The Norman J. Warren Collection .................................................... 106
*The Prey* (1984) ................................................................................. 114
*Nightwish* (1989) ............................................................................... 118
An Ardent Defense of the *House on Haunted Hill* Remake ............... 122
*Us* (2019) ........................................................................................... 127
The *Ringu* Collection ........................................................................ 131
*Man of a Thousand Faces* (1957) ....................................................... 140
Famous Monsters ............................................................................... 147
Mission Statement ............................................................................. 151
*Underwater* (2020) ............................................................................ 153

*The House by the Cemetery* (1981) .................... 157
*The Mad Magician* (1954) .................... 161
Black Balloons: Cosmic Nihilism in *Gags the Clown* (2019) ............ 165
*Beyond the Door* (1974) .................... 169
Grey's Grotesqueries: The Crestwood House Monster Books ...... 174
*Tremors* (1990) .................... 178
The H Word: Victims and Volunteers .................... 182
"An elegance approaching the supernatural." .................... 187
*Cthulhu Mansion* (1990) .................... 190
*Shadow of the Cat* (1961) .................... 192
*The Cannibal Man* (1972) .................... 194
Weird Wisconsin Collection .................... 197
*Malignant* (2021) .................... 205
*Born for Hell* (1976) .................... 209
*Siege* (1983) .................... 212
*The Spine of Night* (2021) .................... 216
*Blind Beast* (1969) .................... 220
The Inadvertent Sci-Fi of Universal's Original *Mummy* Sequels ... 223
*Frankenstein 1970* (1958) .................... 228
*The Snake Girl and the Silver-Haired Witch* (1968) .................... 231
What We Never Saw .................... 233
Here Be Dragons .................... 236
*The Unknown Terror* (1957) .................... 238
Two Early Mexican Horrors .................... 241
Grey's Grotesqueries: Coming Late to *Ultra Q* .................... 246
Stop/Motion:
Ray Harryhausen and the Magic of Stop Motion Monsters ...... 251
The Legacy of *The Dunwich Horror* (1970) .................... 256
The Two Earliest Films Starring the Silver Masked Man ......... 259
*Phenomena* (1985) .................... 264
*The House That Screamed* (1969) .................... 267
Horror Is Where You Find It .................... 270
The Dark Séance .................... 274
100 Movies to See After You Die .................... 281

"Everything exists through its opposite. For pictures of calm and tranquil beauty to have any meaning, even for 'sweet' pictures to have any meaning, it is necessary that the grotesque and the distorted exist. Perfection of form is significant only because the malforms exist also. Those who turn away from the grotesque are losing the richness and completeness of artistic experience."

—William Mortensen

For Adam Cesare, Gemma Files, and Stephen Graham Jones, three great fiction writers who had a huge impact on how I watch and understand movies—and myself.

# INTRODUCTION

# LIGHT AND SHADOW

In my story "Night's Foul Bird," which first appeared in *Innsmouth Magazine* in November 2013 and was subsequently reprinted in my second collection, *Painted Monsters & Other Strange Beasts*, I wrote a description of what it feels like to watch a horror movie, when it all really works. "Terrified, yes, by every creak and flutter, but something else, too. Alive, illuminated. I could feel the beating of my heart, feel the rush of blood in my veins. I felt as if I were glowing in the dark, as if I were giving off light."

I always liked what I captured there, and it has always stuck with me when I think about the effect of a good horror movie, especially one seen in a darkened theater. And, of course, there's a double-meaning at play, when it comes to what became the title of this book you now hold in your hands. While you may, if you're anything like me, feel like you're glowing in the dark when the movie is over, the movie itself is quite literally glowing in the dark while you watch it up there on the screen.

\*\*\*

I'm not sure it would have ever occurred to me to put together a book like this, had it not been for John Langan. Years ago, I had a column at *Innsmouth Free Press*, writing about vintage horror films. It was called "The Vault of Secrets," and it was eventually collected into two small, slim volumes, also from that same press: *Monsters from the Vault* and *Revenge of Monsters from the Vault*.

That process happened organically, though. I already had the column, and I wrote it diligently month after month, year after year. And then, when the column had ended, Silvia Moreno-Garcia, my editor and publisher at *Innsmouth*, approached me to collect them into books. Not much initiative required from me.

It was John Langan who lamented, somewhere on social media, that there was no such volume collecting my various other writings on film, which, unlike those rather carefully-themed columns, ran a wide gamut, even then.

For years, my bios have identified me as, among other things, an "amateur film scholar," but at the time that John made those observations, I don't think I really considered myself a film writer. I was just a hobbyist. My fiction I regarded as worthy of collecting into a book. My musings on cinema? Perhaps not so much.

But the seed was planted, and as the years wore on, I realized that I had probably spilled more ink, over the last decade or so, writing about horror film than I had writing fiction. There were, of course, other factors that fed into this. As I became a full-time freelance writer, I started writing more for various online venues, which meant more opportunities to polish and publish a lot more nonfiction, much of it about horror movies.

Then, I also began receiving review copies of films that were being re-released onto Blu-ray, spanning the decades from the silents to the present. In exchange for these review copies I had to, perhaps obviously, actually *review* them, which meant even *more* film writing.

Of those, most were horror movies, but not all. Still, looking back over the film writing I've done over the past decade or so, the lion's share is about horror cinema. Which makes sense, after all. Horror is what I know. If I am an amateur film scholar, as my bio

# INTRODUCTION: LIGHT AND SHADOW

suggests, the closest I have come to shedding that "amateur" tag is in the horror genre.

\*\*\*

From that snippet in "Night's Foul Bird" I took the title that would ultimately grace this book, and from John's offhand comments I took a bit of the confidence needed to eventually put something like this together, but it still took years to hit upon a form that I thought such a book could take that anyone might want to read. What you hold in your hands now is the culmination of all those disparate pieces coming together.

Inside these pages, you will find film writing of a variety of types, in a variety of lengths. There are deep dives into the cosmic horror of John Carpenter's "Apocalypse Trilogy" and the inadvertent sci-fi in the Universal *Mummy* sequels; there are very personal reminiscences of my first time watching *Monster Squad* and *Aliens*; there are perhaps somewhat rambling thoughts about the monster movie as a form and what it means to be a film critic. Some of these are heavily polished pieces originally published in highly respectable venues. Others are simple musings that originally appeared on my personal blog.

There are also quite a number of reviews. These are nowhere near all of the reviews that I wrote between 2011 and 2023. I tried to select some of the best ones, the ones that I thought best reflected what I am always trying to do when I sit down to write about film. As a result, they are reviews that are spread across a wide range of films and a large span of decades, from the very obscure to the very mainstream, and they are… arbitrary. Not chosen truly at random, but rather informed by which movies I got for review, and which ones I managed to write something about that I have since judged worth reading.

It was hitting upon an organizational principle for all of this disparate content that allowed me to finally put this book together.

When trying to group the reviews all together, or the essays all together, or organize them by the chronology of when the movies themselves were released, I found myself constantly with loose ends, things that defied classification, or didn't seem to belong anywhere at all. So, instead, this book is organized by the order in which the pieces were originally published, meaning that reviews, essays, pieces from my personal blog, and more are jumbled together side by side.

You can, of course, pick through the book, looking for the pieces that most interest you. Or you can read it in order. Sometimes, there will be what I hope are interesting resonances set up by the proximity of one piece to another. Other times, the combination might be a bit jarring. But hopefully, it creates a whole that is more harmonious than not.

***

For most of the years covered by this book, I was working full-time as a freelance writer. This meant writing all kinds of things, some under my own name and others ghost writing. I worked on marketing copy, pitched ideas to publications, and eventually picked up a staggering *four* regular columns, all of which I am still doing at the time of this writing.

My work, during this time, ran the gamut, obviously, but much of it was about films. I wrote about films for venues such as *The Lineup*, *Ranker*, *Unwinnable*, *Signal Horizon*, *The Pitch*, and others. Sometimes, these were assignments I was given, other times they were ideas I had pitched myself. Occasionally I was invited to critics' screenings, allowed to sit in those chairs in the theater that are reserved for members of the press. Somewhere along the way, I began receiving review copies of Blu-rays, usually of older movies that were being re-released on the medium, often for the first time.

These came from a variety of distributors, including Arrow Video, Indicator, Severin, Blue Underground, and many others. Most came to me via a relationship with stateside distributor MVD. Some were nothing more than a disc—what is known in the industry as a "check disc," with no artwork or packaging—while others were the whole deal, exactly as you would buy it in a store.

I had, at best, limited control over which of these I would receive, though most of them were horror films, at least, due to the venues for which I wrote and the imprints with whom I worked. And I reviewed very nearly every one that I got, with one exception—a hardcore sex film masquerading as a giallo-style slasher, something I had neither the expertise to discuss, nor a proper venue for a review.

All this meant that I was often writing about films I had never previously seen, about which I knew very little, and which I was often predisposed not to like much. Other times, it meant that I was writing about old favorites that I needed to look at in a new way. The lion's share of these reviews found print at either *Signal Horizon* or *Unwinnable*, both of which gave me admirable leeway to write as I wished, about whatever movies came my way.

This is an unusual position for a freelancer. Normally, a freelancer like myself would write what was assigned to me—as I did at most of the other venues where my work has seen print over the years. If I received a review copy of a movie, it would be via the *venue's* relationship with a distributor, not my own. I was lucky to have the working relationship I did with the folks at *Unwinnable* and *Signal Horizon*. Without it, this book would probably not exist.

***

Throughout this volume, I will discuss—more than once—what being a film writer means to me. I often resist the word "critic," just as I tried for years to eschew the word "review" to describe what I was doing when writing about a movie. This is not because there is anything actually wrong with either of those words, but because, in our modern parlance, both of these words have come to mean something more reductive than their actual intent.

Film criticism is, in my opinion, meant to help us understand films better, not to tell us whether those films are "good" or "bad." And yet, in a marketplace where commodification is the order of the day, many reviews have been boiled down to precisely that, often at no fault of the reviewers themselves. Look at a site like Rotten Tomatoes, which splits reviews between "rotten" and "fresh," or even the classic "thumbs up" and "thumbs down" popularized by Siskel & Ebert years ago.

I'm not going to argue that there is no value in sites like these, in systems like these, but rather simply state that *my* interest, when writing about a film, is not to tell you whether it is "good" or "bad." I have come to realize, over the years, that there are many nuances between those two polarities, and even if there weren't, I'm not interested in such prescriptivism.

Rather, what I want to do when I write about a film, is to explore the film. When I read about a film, I want to end up understanding it better than I did when I began. I want to look at it in a different way. When I find a film writer whose work resonates with me, I am often overjoyed when they write about films I *don't* like, because I am hopeful that I can learn something about the movie that makes me see it in a new light, or that teaches me something about myself that I had not previously realized.

That's the high I'm chasing when I read about film, and it's what I try to accomplish when I write about film. You will rarely find discussions of "good" or "bad" in these pages, and this is why. But I hope that, when you finish reading, you will think about some films differently than you did before. If so, then I feel like I've done my job.

Originally published October 2011
*Strange Horizons*

# COSMIC HORROR IN JOHN CARPENTER'S "APOCALYPSE TRILOGY"

Over the course of thirteen years, director John Carpenter created three seemingly unrelated films that form what he has dubbed his "Apocalypse Trilogy:" *The Thing* (1982), *Prince of Darkness* (1987), and *In the Mouth of Madness* (1995). Not merely separated by time, they're also disparate in style, subject matter, and quality. They were filmed under different production companies, with different casts, and from screenplays penned by different writers. At first glance, there's nothing to tie them together besides their director, and his designation of them as a trilogy. When you begin to scratch below the surface, however, you find that they are connected by strong thematic underpinnings that could easily be overlooked or underplayed in any one of them alone, but which come strongly to the fore when all three movies are viewed as a linked trilogy.

These thematic underpinnings are basically those of what's known as cosmic horror. Cosmic horror is mostly associated with H. P. Lovecraft, though his conception of it was in turn inspired by earlier writers like Algernon Blackwood and William Hope Hodgson, and can be summed up in a quote from his collected letters where he said, "Now all my tales are based on the fundamental premise that common human laws and interests and emotions have no validity or significance in the vast cosmos-at-large."

In short, cosmic horror is less the horror of some specific bogeyman, and more the horror of a cold, uncaring universe, in which humans are of no importance. Carpenter has said many times that he is a fan of the works of Lovecraft, and two years before he made the first movie in his "Apocalypse Trilogy" he was already working references to Lovecraft into some of the names in his classic ghost film *The Fog*. While Carpenter wouldn't go on to make an overtly Lovecraftian picture until *In the Mouth of Madness*, cosmic horror and Lovecraftian traits form the thematic backbone of all three movies in the "Apocalypse Trilogy," along with threats that are apocalyptic both to human life and to the basic human sense of self.

## *The Thing* (1982)

In the present day, *The Thing* is widely regarded as one of John Carpenter's greatest masterpieces, and I would personally consider it a contender for the title of the best horror film ever made. It didn't always receive such a rosy reception, though. It was released in theatres just weeks after Steven Spielberg's much more blockbuster-friendly *E.T.*, and its theatrical performance and initial critical reception weren't anything to write home about.

Perhaps because it's the first film in the "Apocalypse Trilogy," the themes that tie the three movies together are the most subtle in *The Thing*. The story concerns an alien creature found frozen in Antarctic ice that can absorb, digest, and then imitate perfectly any creature that it comes into contact with. What follows from its discovery is a classic meditation on paranoia, punctuated by some of the best practical special effects ever put on film.

*The Thing* is a remake of the 1951 Howard Hawks film *The Thing from Another World*, which was itself based on a short story by John W. Campbell called "Who Goes There?" While there aren't any direct references to Lovecraft in *The Thing*, there are certainly no shortage of indirect ones, beginning with the Antarctic setting (a nod to Lovecraft's "At the Mountains of Madness"). While the creature in *The Thing* isn't found in a cyclopean ruined city, it *is* discovered in an equally gigantic spaceship, frozen in ice that one of the characters hypothesizes must be "100,000 years old at least." And, in true Lovecraftian fashion, the implications of the creature's nature drives one of the protagonists (played by Wilford Brimley) insane.

Once it is revealed, the titular Thing is almost entirely unknowable. Not only is it alien in the most literal sense, but it's also outside of normally understood biology, genetically dissimilar from all life on earth. When discussing how the Thing can do what it does, or how it can live after being frozen for so long, one of the characters (played by Kurt Russell) says, "Cuz it's different than us, see. Cuz it's from outer space." And that's about all the more understanding of its reasoning the characters ever get. Though the creature can obviously speak perfectly when it is imitating one of the humans, it never explains itself, or attempts to reason once it's found out. In fact, once revealed to be a Thing, it never speaks at all. Like Lovecraft's ancient alien gods, its psychology appears to be as far outside of man's sphere as its biology is.

As the moniker might imply, all three movies in the "Apocalypse Trilogy" concern threats with apocalyptic consequences for the human race. The goal of the titular creature in *The Thing*, as near as the humans can guess, is to get out of Antarctica and into the civilized world, where it can find more hosts to consume and imitate. Early in the movie, Wilford Brimley's character runs a computer simulation of what would happen if the Thing were to succeed, a simulation that ends with the prediction that the entire world's population would be assimilated roughly 27,000 hours from first contact.

In all three movies, however, the threat to the world is less disconcerting than the threat posed to the individual concept of self. *The Thing*'s negation of the individual self is perhaps the most obvious of any of the films in the trilogy. When the creature devours someone, it produces a perfect duplicate, complete with memories and behaviors. So perfect, in fact, that the only way to tell the difference is through a blood test. "If I was an imitation," one character asks another, "a perfect imitation, how would you tell if it was me?" That moment of realizing that everything about a person could be completely subsumed and replaced by an alien imposter and no one would know the difference is more chilling than all the gory carnage that the monster wreaks when it's discovered.

## *Prince of Darkness* (1987)

While *The Thing* is widely considered one of John Carpenter's best films, *Prince of Darkness* is just as widely considered one of his lesser ones. It's also the only one of the three movies that was written by Carpenter himself under the pen name Martin Quatermass, a reference to the character created by Nigel Kneale, a British sci-fi writer whose work shows many Lovecraftian themes and was a big influence on *Prince of Darkness*.

*Prince of Darkness* is the thematic lynchpin of the trilogy, providing more hints to the trilogy's themes than any other single movie taken on its own. The lengthy opening credit sequence shows a series of ominous but unobserved events—reminiscent of the opening sequence of *The Fog*—while a professor (played by Victor Wong) delivers a monologue to his class that pretty succinctly sums up the themes of the movie, and the trilogy, while also acting as a sort of quickie summary of cosmic horror itself. "From Job's friends insisting that the good are rewarded and the wicked punished, to the scientists of the 1930s proving to their horror the theorem that not everything can be proved, we've sought to impose order on the universe," he says. "But we've discovered something very surprising. While order *does* exist in the universe, it is not at all what we had in mind."

The story concerns the discovery of an ancient green liquid in the basement of a church, which was heretofore guarded by a secret sect of priests called the Brotherhood of Sleep. The last member of the sect has died and the secret has finally come to Father Loomis (played by Donald Pleasance), who brings it to the attention of the professor and some other scientists in the hopes that they can scientifically prove the nature of the substance and thereby warn mankind.

The liquid proves to be a demonic force (characters sometimes call it Satan), "A substance, malevolence. Asleep, until now." It possesses insects, worms, homeless people (who stand in nicely for Lovecraft's degenerate cultists), and eventually the scientists themselves in order to bring across from another dimension its imprisoned father, the Anti-God, which all sounds very Lovecraftian once you strip off the Christian theology names. (There's a line in the diary of the last member of the Brotherhood that could have come straight out of Lovecraft: "The sleeper awakens. I have witnessed his stirrings.") Even Jesus gets in on the act, when an ancient tome found near the liquid reveals that Jesus was a member of an extraterrestrial race of human-like creatures who came to warn mankind against the devil-liquid.

Much more than even *The Thing*, *Prince of Darkness* conveys a Lovecraftian sense of slumbering malevolence, and a universe in which mankind is far from the center. While the events that would occur if the Anti-God were released from its dimensional prison are certainly world-endingly apocalyptic, once again it's really the implications for mankind's sense of self that are portrayed as the most terrifying. The devil-liquid is capable of possessing and effectively deleting the identities of those it comes into contact with, but it's mankind's cosmological selfhood as a whole that is in the greatest danger. Father Loomis talks about how the Church made a decision, "to characterize pure evil as a spiritual force, the darkness in the hearts of men," which would allow "man to remain in the center of things." The awful truth, however, is that there's a "universal mind" controlling everything on the subatomic level, the "Anti-God, bringing darkness instead of light."

## *In the Mouth of Madness* (1995)

There are a lot of people who consider *In the Mouth of Madness* to be the best Lovecraftian movie ever made, which is ironic since it isn't actually an adaptation of any of Lovecraft's stories, though it's obviously heavily inspired by them. The story of *In the Mouth of Madness* concerns an insurance investigator named John Trent (played by Sam Neill), a skeptic and cynic, who is hired to locate a phenomenally popular horror author named Sutter Cane (think H. P. Lovecraft by way of Stephen King), who has gone missing before the completion of his latest novel. As Trent delves into the case and travels to the theoretically fictional town of Hobb's End—where Cane sets most of his books—he begins to question the nature of reality.

*In the Mouth of Madness* is certainly the most Lovecraftian movie in the "Apocalypse Trilogy." Lovecraft's prints are all over the film, from the title on down. Though it's inspired by his work in general, rather than any one particular story, almost everything in the movie is a nod back at Lovecraft in one way or another, from the titles of Sutter Cane's books to the names of places like the Pickman Hotel. Whenever a character reads aloud from one of Cane's books, the words are always adapted from Lovecraft's stories, including passages from "The Rats in the Walls" and "The Haunter of the Dark." The picture even opens, in classic Lovecraft fashion, with a lead character in a madhouse, insisting that he's not insane.

There are, of course, also Lovecraftian monsters, "older than mankind and wider than the known universe," waiting on the other side of reality to get in. "When people begin to lose their ability to distinguish fantasy from reality, the Old Ones begin to come back," Cane says near the end of the movie. "The more people who believe, the faster the journey." But the real cosmic horror in *In the Mouth of Madness* comes not from the monsters themselves, but from the flimsy and inconstant nature of reality. One of the characters sums it up neatly when she tells Trent, "Right now reality shares your point of view. What scares me about Cane's work is what might happen if reality shared his point of view."

When all three movies in the "Apocalypse Trilogy" are viewed in order, there's an undeniable progression of scope and scale in the threats of each film. While *The Thing* and *Prince of Darkness* threatened us with possible apocalypses, *In the Mouth of Madness* actually appears to deliver one. It begins, like in *Prince of Darkness*, with an early buildup. In this case, in the form of violent riots and epidemics that are transmitted to the characters (as well as the audience beyond the film's fourth wall) by television news broadcasts, etc. When someone describes the events of Cane's last book (not surprisingly titled *In the Mouth of Madness*) they describe "people turning into things. The end of everything." And that looks to be what the movie actually delivers, as it closes on views of a depopulated city, with a lone voice on the radio talking about a "worldwide epidemic of mass violence." Not only that, but the barriers between reality and fiction have obviously broken down (if they were ever really there at all) as Trent makes his way to an empty theatre to watch the movie version of *In the Mouth of Madness* which (again unsurprisingly) turns out to be the movie that we've just finished.

It is perhaps the ultimate expression of cosmic horror, and the capstone of Carpenter's "Apocalypse Trilogy." While *The Thing* threatened the annihilation of the human species, and *Prince of Darkness* posited an illogical universe in which god was malevolent, *In the Mouth of Madness* paints a picture of a world in which there is no objective reality at all. The creature from *The Thing* could replace you and mimic you perfectly, and the devil-liquid in *Prince of Darkness* could override your free will, but *In the Mouth of Madness* shows that you never really had any free will to begin with.

**Author's Note:** This was the second of two essays that I published at *Strange Horizons* more than a decade ago, and it went on to win the magazine's Audience Choice award that year. It has since been cited in books, academic papers, and Wikipedia entries, and translated into other languages, making it probably the most widely-read piece of writing I have ever done.

While the goal was to focus on cosmic horror—and specifically Lovecraftian cosmic horror—in these three John Carpenter films, if I had this one to write over again, I would have spent more time on the connections to Nigel Kneale's Quatermass stories in these three films, as those fingerprints are all over them every bit as much as Lovecraft's, probably more so.

Originally published October 2012
orringrey.com

## *HOUSE OF WAX* (2005)

I really shouldn't like this movie at all. It's a not-very-well-regarded entry into a genre that I don't care for (the mash-up of teen slasher and that backwoods grindhouse *Texas Chainsaw Massacre* stuff that Rob Zombie is inextricably associated with). And yet, and yet... I love it.

The first time I saw it, way back when it was new, you could chalk my reaction up to having my ridiculously low expectations surpassed (I certainly didn't *expect* to like it, I only rented it because it was a *Dark Castle* movie, and because back then I still worked at a video store and watched just about every horror movie that came out), but I've seen it a bunch of times since then, even own a copy, and if anything I probably like it *more* now than I did back then. So what's up?

Well, the fact is, it's just *better* than it ought to be. Very little of that's in the story, which is pretty by-the-numbers, though it gets huge points for the fact that the protagonists, specifically the brother and sister pair played by Elisha Cuthbert and Chad Michael Murray, are fighters who, when they're in danger, immediately attempt to arm themselves, to fight back. There's a scene that epitomizes this just as the violence of the movie is getting going, when Murray's character has no clue what's going on and one of the killers takes a swipe at him from out of nowhere. His character's first response, without so much as a beat of hesitation, is to punch the guy right in the face as hard as he can. That's certainly a nice change of pace from the seemingly weapon-allergic *protagonists* of a lot of similar films.

I think most of what I like comes from the approach of director

Jaume Collett-Serra (whose follow-up *Orphan* I haven't yet seen, but I've heard good things about). He may be making a modest backwoods slasher flick, but he comes at it with the instincts of a *giallo*. *House of Wax* has a distinctive visual palette, and boasts some very nice shots (there's a particularly good aerial shot of a chase out the front doors of a church), and while the wax town idea may stretch credulity somewhat, it's an undeniably *cool* idea, and Collet-Serra makes good use of the sets.

Collet-Serra also draws out the gothic elements of the story. While the good twin/evil twin themes of the movie may be pretty heavy handed, the sense of decay hidden under a veneer of normalcy (as nailed perfectly by the wax figures with rotting corpses underneath) is handled much more deftly. Even the town itself could nicely stand in for a gothic castle, with its washed-out road serving as moat.

*House of Wax* is also a surprisingly slow burn, for a movie of its type, eschewing a traditional "cold opening" (one was shot and is included in the bonus features, but wisely left out of the finished film), and opting instead to hold back on any actual violence until around the forty-five-minute mark. When the violence does finally start, it gets brutal very quickly, and is initially all of the immediately relatable kind that Guillermo del Toro talks about in his commentary track for *The Devil's Backbone*, the kind of pain that you can understand, and wince sympathetically along with. While it doesn't take long for the movie to veer into more standard slasher-style death scenes (that make less and less sense), the first few bursts of violence are about as unbearable as any I've seen.

All of which is not to say that the movie doesn't have its problems. The more it stumbles into clichés, the less well it works, and it's certainly got some male gaze-y issues, though, sad to say, not really any worse than the general run of movies of its ilk. (And much, though by no means all, of the worst of *that* happens when the camera is, literally, in the hands of socially awkward kids or serial killers, which I guess is something.)

HOUSE OF WAX (2005)        17

Still and all, for a movie that I shouldn't like, and that *no* one else seems to, I think *House of Wax* is actually pretty great, and has a lot more going for it than it gets credit for.

**Author's Note:** I've since seen *Orphan* and, indeed, most of Collet-Serra's subsequent films, though this remains my favorite. Someday, I'm going to write a longer, better piece about this *House of Wax* as gothic, but who knows when that will be?

Originally published May 2013
orringrey.com

## HAMMER FRANKENSTEIN-ATHON

When *Frankensteinia* announced their *Peter Cushing Centennial Blogathon*, I knew that I would have to do something to participate, even though I also knew that May was going to be the busiest month I've had in, I dunno, maybe ever. But what could I do with my limited time and resources that would still fit the stature of such a great blogathon? I settled (perhaps not too wisely) on watching all six of the Hammer Frankenstein films starring Peter Cushing in my favorite role he ever essayed, that of Baron Frankenstein himself. (I did not count 1970's *Horror of Frankenstein*, which doesn't feature Cushing anyway.)

It turned out that I already owned all six movies, having acquired them all at various different times and not realizing until that moment that I had "caught them all," as it were. And while watching them occupied the vast majority of my movie-watching time during the month, it was interesting to see them all stacked up together.

The Hammer Frankenstein films, like their slightly-more-famous Dracula counterparts, are not really sequels to one another in the way that we're accustomed to sequels working (with the exception of *Revenge of Frankenstein*, the second movie in the series, which picks up literally right where its predecessor left off). Instead, they're more like, I'm not really sure, alternate universe episodes in the life of Baron Frankenstein, a character who is always more or less the same, but whose history and even personality seem to fluctuate to fit the needs of one script or another. Here he murders a guy in cold blood, there he says he's never killed anyone, here he's almost heroic, there he's as cruel and sadistic a character as you're likely to find.

There's a fascinating quality to all of Hammer's gothic horror films, one of many things that set them apart from their contemporaries and imitators, which is the way they all feel as though they take place in the same universe, while at the same time seldom sharing any continuity from one to the other. And even when they *do* share continuity—in the form, say, of recurring characters like Baron Frankenstein—they play fast and loose with it. It's appropriate that one of the recent Hammer film logos mirrored the Marvel movie logo, since the not-quite-shared universe of Hammer's classic horror films feels like nothing more than it does a comic book universe. And the Frankenstein movies are no exception to this rule.

Of all six movies, the only one that was entirely new to me was *Frankenstein Must Be Destroyed*, which I have seen widely touted as the best of them. Certainly, it was extremely well put-together and dramatically satisfying, but it also features the Baron at his most cruel, and a completely unnecessary rape scene that Peter Cushing himself famously objected to filming, which resulted in my finding it more difficult to enjoy than I did many of the others, in spite of its other virtues.

Of the other films a few I had seen repeatedly (*Curse* and *Evil* for sure), while for others this constituted only my second viewing (*Frankenstein Created Woman*, *Revenge*, and *Monster from Hell*). I found things to like in all of them, of course, and it was a great deal of fun to watch Cushing's characterization of the Baron at once stay true to the basics and at the same time move all over the map, depending on the film.

But that's probably enough generic blathering from me. When I mentioned doing this, I promised to list my favorites from the films, and so I'll get on that, without further ado:

### Favorite Assistant:
The vast majority of the movies feature the Baron being assisted

by one stripe or another of eager young doctor (a couple of them, I believe, named Hans), and while each of them have their own strengths, they do sort of blur together after a while. Standing out more are the Baron's Disapproving Friend Paul (as Gemma Files dubs him) from *Curse* and Thorley Walters's boozy but kind Dr. Hertz from *Frankenstein Created Woman*. Ultimately, Dr. Hertz is the winner for me, with the combination of his bumbling performance and his genuine awe of Frankenstein.

Favorite Lab:

Hammer films pretty much unfailingly feature great sets, and the Frankenstein films are particular standouts of this, with every movie featuring one kind of spectacular laboratory or another. The lab in *Revenge*, in particular, has a great disembodied nervous system, while the lab in the opening of *Frankenstein Must Be Destroyed* is full of green lights and wonderful creepy things in tanks. But the hands-down winner of the best lab, for me, is easily *Evil of Frankenstein*, which contains not only my favorite lab (the one in the mill), but *also* my second favorite (the more extensive castle lab, which, like most of the rest of the movie, is Hammer's take on the Universal version).

Favorite Creature:

Unlike the Universal Frankenstein films, which followed the adventures of the monster, the Hammer films all follow the Baron, who creates a new creature in every film. These range from a beautiful girl with her boyfriend's soul in *Frankenstein Created Woman* to a giant caveman in *Frankenstein and the Monster from Hell*, and just about everything in between. Hands down the best of the bunch has got to be Christopher Lee's iconic interpretation of the classic monster in *Curse of Frankenstein*, but I've got a soft spot for the creature in *Evil of Frankenstein*, with his giant shoebox forehead. He looks a lot like what I imagine would have happened if Jack Kirby had taken a stab at designing the famous Jack Pierce makeup from the 1931 original.

Favorite Baron:
This is probably the most difficult category, since Cushing is always playing some variant of the same guy, even though he wobbles from almost heroic in *Evil of Frankenstein* (ironically) to incredibly and needlessly cruel in *Frankenstein Must Be Destroyed*, with stops off on almost every destination in between. Every performance is basically magnificent, for my money, but the best ones are the ones where Frankenstein is a little tired and a lot acerbic, and so I'm pretty sure *Frankenstein Created Woman* takes the cake. He's also got some of his best lines in that one. "Of course I'm alive. Didn't I say I would be?"

Favorite Movie:
It's an unpopular choice, but my favorite movie of the bunch is *Evil of Frankenstein*, no question. It is the one that's least like the others, in that it really feels like Hammer doing a best-of interpretation of the entire Universal Frankenstein series, from the carnival to the deaf/mute girl to the unscrupulous hypnotist to the design of the creature and the design of the lab. But rather than feeling like Hammer aping Universal, it all feels to me like the best of both worlds, and I love every minute of it, even the monster frozen in a block of "ice" that's obviously just plastic sheeting. My second favorite is probably its immediate follow-up, *Frankenstein Created Woman*, which is way, way less sleazy or exploitative than you'd probably imagine given the title/premise.

**Author's Note:** *Frankensteinia* is a long-running blog dedicated to all things Frankenstein. For a while, I participated in a yearly blogathon they held in which various other blogs posted about Frankenstein-related things, and they rounded them all up. This was my favorite, the year that they celebrated Peter Cushing's centennial and, for the occasion, I watched all of Cushing's Hammer Frankenstein movies—which remain personal favorites of mine.

Originally published July 2013
orringrey.com

## PACIFIC RIM (2013)

I tried really hard not to get too excited about *Pacific Rim*. I've been let down by Guillermo del Toro's big budget movies before (*Hellboy 2*, I am looking meaningfully in your direction) and while I love all monsters and grew up on Godzilla movies, the whole kaiju subgenre is no longer really in my creative wheelhouse the way it once was. But it didn't take more than about one trailer for *Pacific Rim* to overcome my defenses and vault it to the number one spot of movies I was looking forward to this year.

I know that not everyone felt the same way about the trailers, though. When I first got back from the preview screening on Tuesday night, I posted to Twitter that "If you think you'll like *Pacific Rim*, you are probably not wrong." I'll stand by that. If you *don't* think you'll like *Pacific Rim*, well, I don't know what to tell you about it. We probably have very different taste in movies anyway, so you might not want to listen to me.

*Pacific Rim* was everything that I needed it to be. There were lots of monsters, and they looked great. I went home wanting toys of them. The fight scenes were suitably epic, building-crushing things, designed to convey at every turn the sheer size and scope and weight of what was happening. The movie around them wasn't any dumber than it needed to be, and it didn't try to be any smarter than it needed to be either. Probably the best thing you can say about *Pacific Rim* is that there's no cynicism, no guilt apparent in its construction. It is a movie about giant robots punching giant monsters made by people who love that, and who think you should love it too. They're not trying to cash in on a product they don't care about, and they're not ashamed of the big, cartoony aspects of what they're doing. There's something inherently silly about a robot punching a monster with a rocket fist, it's true. But while Guillermo del Toro *knows* that it's silly, he still treats it with respect, not as something shameful, or as an in-joke. The result is a $180-million Saturday morning cartoon, made by a master craftsman. It aspires to no more than that, and it delivers that superbly.

There's a tendency, when talking about movies, to act as if there's one standard that all movies should be held to. One sort of ur-movie, and that we want every movie to be it. But it's not so, at least not for me. I love quiet, thoughtful, introspective movies. I also love city-crushing blockbusters. The only thing I ask of them in common is that they both be done with skill, by people who do their work well, and who obviously care about what they're doing. On that front, *Pacific Rim* certainly delivers.

I've talked before about the movie that we'll hopefully someday get that's a perfect marriage of the heart of del Toro's independent films with the visual potency of his big budget ones. This isn't it, not quite, but it's close. It's technically stunning, as visually rich as any blockbuster I've ever seen, filled with effects shots, and overflowing with del Toro's aesthetics. It's also beautiful in places. There's a moment in a bunker during the kaiju attack on Hong Kong that was so unexpectedly lovely that I wanted it to go on for at least a few frames longer than it did. Maybe forever. Del Toro obviously isn't ashamed of this movie. He's not cashing in, not collecting a paycheck. There's every bit as much of his heart in this as there was in *Pan's Labyrinth*, it's just a different part of his heart, is all.

I've seen the movie compared to just about everything at this point, with varying degrees of accuracy. Structurally, though, its closest relation might be something like *Independence Day*, without the jingoism, and with robots in place of fighter jets and giant monsters in place of giant spaceships. (Which is to say: *better!*) The climax owes a lot to that film, which has apparently given us the template for the climaxes of all invasion films from here on out.

(See also: *Avengers*.) That's fine, though. In some ways, the familiarity is a boon, taking some of the weight of the world building off the shoulders of the narrative and allowing it to spin out in little details in the background. Because we all know how this is going, they don't have to spend as much time explaining it to us, and can instead just get into the monster punching, the monster organ dealing, and so on.

(Seriously, *Pacific Rim* is a busy movie. It could've probably been an hour longer, easy, without feeling bloated in the least, and it probably actually *needed* at least one more extended Jaeger vs. kaiju fight, so we could get a better idea of how things worked before they started to go wrong. The stuff that happens before the opening credits of *Pacific Rim* is where most movies like this would have stopped, and saved the meat of the movie for a couple of sequels. That *Pacific Rim* puts it all in there is another example of its guilelessness and lack of cynicism. It just wants to get to the good stuff, not string you along.)

*Pacific Rim* isn't a perfect movie. There are a few problems, but very few of them actually mean much. The climax may not hold up to repeat viewings as well as the earlier fights. The supporting characters all stepped straight out of an anime or Saturday morning cartoon and are (unfortunately) never really fleshed out. See above re: there needing to be at least one more big fight sequence, and why. But most of what's wrong with *Pacific Rim* are things just like that; places where it could have done *more*, rather than places where it did something wrong. It may not be the perfect giant robots versus giant monsters movie, but it's the best one we've ever gotten, and it's probably a better one than we deserve (especially if the early and disheartening tracking numbers for the movie's box office performance prove true).

We need movies like *Pacific Rim*. Movies that treat entertainment and spectacle as important, and worthy of the same care and craft that you'd bring to a "serious" film. If you think you'll like *Pacific Rim*, then you're probably already going to the theatre this weekend anyway. And if you don't think you'll like *Pacific Rim*, think about whether you like the idea of $180-million movies made by visionary directors who love and care about what they're doing, and consider maybe giving it a shot anyway.

**Author's Note:** If anything, my opinion of *Pacific Rim* has actually increased considerably since writing this. Is it Guillermo del Toro's best movie? Probably not. But it is definitely my favorite. And I do now have toys of several of the kaiju.

**Originally published March 2015**
*Clarkesworld*

## DARK ANGELS: INSECTS IN THE FILMS OF GUILLERMO DEL TORO

It's no secret that Guillermo del Toro loves bugs. Insects and insect imagery play a major role in just about every movie in his filmography, from the fly-in-amber ghosts of *The Devil's Backbone* to the Reapers of *Blade 2* and the vampires of *The Strain*, with their hive-like social structures and insectile proboscises. Even *Hellboy 2* and *Pacific Rim* prominently featured swarming tooth fairies and kaiju skin parasites, respectively.

Most of the time, these insects serve a primarily visual role, lending verisimilitude to a creature design or inspiring a monster's behavior patterns, but del Toro's inclination toward the insect doesn't end with aesthetic appreciation. In several of his films, insects take on a more thematically dense role, their presence assuming an almost religious significance, with connections to divinity, the underworld, and eternal life.

### *Cronos* (1993)

"*Cronos* is about immortality," Guillermo del Toro says in the book *Cabinet of Curiosities*. Shot when he was only twenty-nine, it is the director's first feature film, and also the one that lays the groundwork for many of the insect themes that will appear later in his oeuvre. The titular Cronos Device is a small, golden mechanism in the shape of an insect—with a living insect trapped inside—that grants its user eternal life by transforming them into something that we would recognize as a vampire.

Del Toro has said that his design of the Cronos Device was inspired by the jewel-encrusted Maquech Beetles that were popular as living jewelry when he was growing up in Mexico, but the Device also bears an obvious similarity to a reliquary, used to house the remains of saints. This similarity is only underscored by del Toro's choice to first reveal the Device hidden inside the base of an archangel statue. In the commentary track for *Cronos*, del Toro says that he wanted the Catholic image of the archangel to hold inside itself the promise of a "more prosaic, more tangible eternal life." It's the first time that del Toro juxtaposes insects with Catholic imagery in his films, but it won't be the last.

In his commentary, he describes his inspiration for the Device, which came from alchemy. What most people know about alchemy is that it was the quest to find a way to transform lead into gold, but del Toro talks about the search for the "ultimate depuration of vile matter—be it lead or flesh—and turn it into the ultimate expression of itself. Be it gold or eternal life, eternal flesh." *The Device*—through the living insect trapped inside it—draws out mortal blood, filters it, and replaces it, adding a drop of the alchemical "Fifth Essence" which brings with it eternal life.

Not only does *Cronos* mark the beginning of del Toro's habit of linking insects with everlasting life, it also prefigures several of the themes that will come to play in his second film, *Mimic*, as the villainous industrialist de la Guardia in *Cronos* muses, "Who says insects aren't God's favored creatures?" It's a sentiment that was meant to be echoed by the protagonists of *Mimic* years later, though the lines wound up on the cutting room floor. De la Guardia ultimately takes his reasoning further than *Mimic* was ever meant to, comparing insects to Jesus Christ and pointing out that, "the matter of the Resurrection is related to ants, to spiders," as he describes spiders returning from seeming death after having been trapped in rock for years.

An anecdote from the set of *Cronos* tells as much about Guillermo del Toro the filmmaker as it does about the importance of insects in his films: The original budget for *Cronos* didn't contain enough money to film the shots of the interior of the titular Device. Producers assured del Toro that he didn't need the shots, but del Toro disagreed, and ended up selling his van in order to pay for the construction of a massive animatronic replica of the inside of the device—complete with rubber insect—through which the camera could be slowly passed. What could have been a silly or pointless sequence in less dedicated hands becomes not only a nod to the monster movie origins of *Cronos*, but also a profound moment of cinematic magic, one that shows the insect not as a monster or an angel, but as much a victim as any of the film's human characters. It is perhaps the greatest condemnation of the allure of immortality in *Cronos*, as we see the insect suffering, trapped inside its golden prison, but unable to die.

## *Mimic* (1997)

In the filmography of almost any visionary director, there is bound to be at least one film that represents a compromise between the director's vision and the demands of the filmmaking machine. For Guillermo del Toro, that film was *Mimic*, his second feature and his first studio film. For years it was available only in a theatrical cut that lacked del Toro's seal of approval, but recently a director's cut, fully color-corrected by del Toro himself, was released onto Blu-ray. The director's cut did more than just remove jump scares and action beats shot by the second unit; it returned the picture to something more closely resembling the director's original vision, and brought the film's symbolic elements more to the foreground.

"I wanted to make them God's favorite creatures, angels," del Toro says of the film's giant Judas Breed insects in *Cabinet of Curiosities*. "I wanted very much to indicate that God favored our downfall as a species." On the opposite page is an image from one of del Toro's ubiquitous notebooks, in which a man is "prostrating himself before the godlike figure of the man-shaped insect, a shaft of sunlight sweeping diagonally across them from on high, as if God were passing judgment."

In the original screenplay, one of the characters was meant to take up de la Guardia's chorus from *Cronos*, with lines like, "What if God is fed up with us? What if insects are now God's favorite creatures?" Unfortunately, none of this dialogue made it into the final screenplay, leaving the heavy lifting of the film's thematic concerns almost entirely in the hands of the visuals. The director's cut *does* restore a scene of a woman calling the Judas Breed what del Toro called them in early treatments for the film, "dark angels."

The first time we see the Judas Breed is in and around a rundown inner city church. The film's first on-screen fatality is a priest who falls to his death in front of a huge neon cross that reads, "Jesus Saves." Inside the decaying church, the Judas Breed blend in with the plastic-wrapped figures of saints, familiar imagery for viewers of *Cronos* with its hanging gallery of archangels wrapped in plastic sheeting. In his commentary for *Mimic*, del Toro says that he wrapped the saints in plastic to make them "obsolete, out-of-order holy figures."

"We created the church and the despoiled figures again in the idea that the natural order of the sanctity of the world and our place in creation was being subverted, and that the new fathers and mothers of the world were insects," del Toro continues in his commentary track. As the film progresses, this subversion is driven home again and again through careful visual choices. From the color coding, which makes it feel as if the "humans are insects trapped in amber," to a dramatic change of scale in the film's final acts, in which the humans find themselves in a massive underground subway station, effectively reduced to the size of insects, scurrying around, desperately trying to accomplish menial tasks, while the "dark angels" can climb the walls with ease or effortlessly fly around them.

Among the many struggles that del Toro describes when talking about the making of *Mimic* are his efforts to ensure that the character of Dr. Peter Mann wears glasses. "I like the idea of showing how imperfect mankind is," del Toro says in *Cabinet of Curiosities*. "The insects in *Mimic* were all organic, but mankind needed glasses, artificial limbs. The mimics are the perfect ones, not us." The value of human imperfection is another subject that comes up again and again in Guillermo del Toro's filmography, and the dichotomy of the mechanistic perfection of the insect is one that he also brings up in the commentary track for *Cronos*, where he says, "I do happen to believe that insects, as far as form and function, are the most perfect—albeit soulless—creatures of creation."

## *Pan's Labyrinth* (2006)

If asked to identify the single most recurrent theme in Guillermo del Toro's body of work, "the value of human imperfection and the choices that we make because of it" would probably be a pretty good start. While del Toro's sixth feature and his third—and most widely celebrated—Spanish-language film may not seem to have a lot to do with insects at first glance, it *does* have a lot to do with choice and human imperfection, and it features an insect in a particularly key role.

We are first introduced to the insect in one of the earliest sequences of *Pan's Labyrinth*, where we see it crawling out of the statue of a saint, continuing del Toro's habit of equating insects with Catholic imagery. It's also the last time it will happen in the film, though, breaking the insect free of its previous Catholic trappings in *Cronos* and *Mimic* and eventually equating it with a more pagan conception of eternal life. During this sequence, as the human protagonists arrive at the mill where most of the rest of the film will take place, our focus stays on the insect as it flits between the trees. In his commentary track, del Toro says, "I wanted to emphasize with the camera how important the insect was."

Freed from the Catholic imagery of *Cronos* or *Mimic*, the insect in *Pan's Labyrinth* is also distinct from the more oppressive or ominous themes of the insects in those films. No longer a "dark angel" passing divine judgment, the insect instead acts as a psychopomp, not only literally leading Ofelia into the labyrinth, but also serving as a visual transition device that signals to the viewer a shift from the "real world" of fascist-occupied Spain to the film's fairytale underworld.

In most traditions, the psychopomp's job is not to pass judgment on the dead, but merely to provide them safe passage into the underworld. In this way, the insect in *Pan's Labyrinth* is very different from the Cronos Device or the "dark angels" of *Mimic*, acting as a bridge to eternal life, rather than a means of obtaining it, or an alternative to it.

Over the years since the film's release, much has been made about whether the magical elements of *Pan's Labyrinth* are intended to be objectively "real" within the film, and del Toro himself has called the film a "litmus test" for audiences. By any reading, though, there are obvious parallels between the fairytale world of the film and the afterlife of many religious traditions. Del Toro has pointed to Ofelia's choices at the end of the movie as her "giving birth to herself," a theme that recurs in many of his projects.

It's telling that the last image of *Pan's Labyrinth* is not of Ofelia in the fairy world, but of a flower blooming on the formerly dead tree that she saved from the toad in the "real world." Here we see a purer kind of eternal life than the one offered by the Cronos Device, an immortality in which our choices today promote new life in the future.

**Author's Note:** I originally wrote this for a book of scholarly essays on Guillermo del Toro's filmography that was supposed to come out from McFarland, I believe. However, the resulting essay wasn't long enough for that book, so I eventually sold it on to *Clarkesworld*—to date my only publication in that venerable venue.

At the time this was written, Guillermo del Toro's most recent movie was *Pacific Rim*, but I'm sure someone could easily add an additional section to this essay dealing with Sebastian J. Cricket and the religious iconography of GDT's *Pinocchio*.

**Originally published March 2016**
*Nightmare*

# THE H WORD: BUT IS IT SCARY?

That seems to be the litmus test to which horror is most often held. When you get back from the latest movie about ghosts or serial killers, put down your favorite horror novel, or mention a spooky story on social media, it's the first question that you're likely to be asked. In our eternal struggle to find the boundaries of this vast and often contradictory territory called horror, I've seen more than one writer resort to "it aims to scare you" as a working definition.

Not that long ago, fans and detractors alike were wringing their hands about whether or not Guillermo del Toro's love letter to the Gothic romance genre *Crimson Peak* should be considered a horror movie. The main concern seemed to be that it wasn't particularly scary, and, perhaps more damning, didn't really try to be. Which comes back to the idea that, whatever else it might be, horror should be trying to scare you, and can be judged on how well it succeeds.

Even if we *do* accept "it aims to scare you" as the definition of horror, there are lots of different kinds of fear, and different ways to be scared. When someone asks if something is scary, they're most often talking about the much-maligned "jump scares" that populate the majority of Hollywood's horror output, and which, even at their best, mostly amount to someone jumping out and yelling "Boo!" But while that may be the most obvious kind of scary, it's certainly not the only one.

There are much more cerebral fears to be found in the literature and cinema of horror, from the cosmic nihilism of Lovecraft, Ligotti, and Barron to the "pleasing terror" of M.R. James and

E.F. Benson. Movies like John Carpenter's *The Thing* combine the visceral terror of body horror with paranoia and existential dread. Even *Crimson Peak*, which isn't particularly scary by most measures, carries a heavy freight of inevitability and decay.

The precise difficulty that accompanies any attempt to pin horror down, to fence it in, is also exactly why horror works so well, and part of why we love it. Horror thrives at the edges of every other genre, in the places on the map marked "here be dragons." It's why *Gremlins* is not only in the same genre as *Texas Chain Saw Massacre*, but even contains a nod to it. Horror means different things to different people, and each one brings to it their own interests and obsessions, their own foibles and fascinations. For some, it's simply a matter of what aims to scare you, and how well it succeeds, while for others, it's more a set of touchstones and traditions, something that we can use as shorthand to help fire our imaginations, and fear doesn't even really enter into the equation.

Limiting horror to only what scares us seems like it would rob the field not only of many of its best entries, leaving them orphaned in the storm without a genre to call their own, but would also rob horror itself of many of its resources. Horror is capable of so much—beauty, numinosity, dread, even humor and hope—scaring you is just one trick up its sleeve.

When I first started publishing stories, I struggled with the label of "horror writer," and one of the biggest reasons was because I never write with the express intent of scaring anybody. At most, I aim for a pleasant frisson, James' "pleasing terror," those cold little caterpillar feet up your spine. More often, I'm interested in the tropes and the atmosphere of horror, the phenomena of the supernatural or the uncanny, and being scary isn't really on my mind at all. So I flinched away from calling myself a horror writer, even while horror is the genre that I love the most, and most readily consume.

Just as when I write, though, I'm seldom looking for fear when I crack open a book or sit down in the dark to take in a movie. I'm happy enough when I get it, but it's not my raison d'être. I love all kinds of horror, but some of my favorites are vintage horror films. The creaky stuff from the '30s and '40s, the Universal monsters, Hammer's Gothic horrors, the works of William Castle, the atomic panic films of the '50s, Roger Corman and Vincent Price very loosely adapting Poe in vivid Technicolor. Are those films great? Absolutely. Are they scary? Well, definitely not to us now, not anymore. Do they need to be? Hell no.

When I write and consume horror, I am more likely to be looking for something "to kick open doors to light and shadow and let us view something that otherwise we might not see," as Joe R. Lansdale once put it more eloquently than I ever could. It's why I write about monsters and ghosts and things that probably don't exist.

The things that really scare me aren't that interesting. They're banal, boring, and quotidian. Like most people, I'm afraid of failure, of financial hardship, of getting sick, of letting my loved ones down. The really scary things in life don't put your heart in your throat and get your blood pumping; they just weigh you down, day after day, like being pressed under stones, one stone at a time, any one of which would be nothing at all, all of which added together crushes the air from your lungs and makes every breath an agony. Those are the things that scare me, but I sure as hell don't want to write about them. I'd rather write about monsters.

**Author's Note:** Despite the fact that most of the examples I use in this essay are movies, it's a bit of a stretch to call this an essay on the horror film. That said, I think it belongs here, in no small part because it is my first publication in *Nightmare*, the venerable online horror magazine.

Every issue, *Nightmare* asks a horror writer to pen a nonfiction piece for their regular "H Word" column, and this was the first time I had ever been invited. It definitely felt like one of those

"I've arrived" moments. I've since published a couple of stories with *Nightmare*, and written another H Word column, reprinted later in this book, but this one felt like a big deal.

Originally published April 2016
orringrey.com

## "EACH ONE OF THESE THINGS COMES FROM AN EGG, RIGHT?"

It was March 14, 1989 when I first saw *Aliens* in its broadcast television premiere. (Thanks to Jason McKittrick of *Cryptocorium* for helping me track down the date.) I must have been seven years old—I would turn eight that October—and it hit me the same way that *Star Wars* seems to have hit most everyone else.

To this day, I remember the scenes from the *CBS Special Movie* presentation intro, which included my first glimpse of the famous xenomorph design, and I also remember being confused by my later viewings of the theatrical cut, which was missing several scenes that were added back into the television version, notably the moment when Ripley learns about her daughter. It led to one of those bizarre situations that sometimes happened in the days before DVDs and special editions, where I knew something about a movie that wasn't included in any cut of the movie that I could conveniently find, and so I wondered if I had perhaps made it up.

I had seen other horror movies before, of course. I grew up watching stuff like *Squirm* and *C.H.U.D.*, *The Food of the Gods* and countless Godzilla flicks. I think I had even seen bits and pieces of *Predator* when my brother rented it on video. I remember watching Cronenberg's *The Fly* on network TV while eating a hamburger, and my mom coming into the living room during some particularly gross scene, and asking how I could eat while watching that. I don't know if that was before or after I saw *Aliens*. (I wonder now how heavily edited *The Fly* must have been to even show up on TV in those days.)

## ALIENS (1986)

But when I first saw *Aliens*, it was like nothing else I had ever seen. It felt more complex and more ambitious than I was used to my monster movies being, and I was struck by the design—and, of course, the life cycle—of the eponymous creatures. The alien queen might have been my first introduction to the idea of the boss monster in cinema, and the battle between the queen and Ripley in the cargo-loader exosuit, with its callback to the great stop-motion monster battles of *King Kong* and Ray Harryhausen, and the rubber suit wrestling matches of the Godzilla films, had an enormous impact on my young imagination.

I can't remember a time when I wasn't in love with movies, but seeing *Aliens* was, without a doubt, a turning point in that fascination. The *Alien* franchise became my first fandom, for lack of a better word, a fact that was only reinforced by the gradual revelation that the *Alien* and *Predator* films might take place in the same universe—another concept that, while not actually original, was new to me at the time.

When I saw *Aliens* for the first time, I had no idea that it was a sequel to anything, and the opening minutes of the movie felt so amazingly ground-breaking to me. Here was this character we met *in media res*, having survived some strange off-screen ordeal that primed her for the one that was coming. It's an oddly inaccurate experience, but one that has remained lodged in my consciousness ever since, one that I come back to again and again.

I don't remember when I first saw *Alien*, but I saw *Alien 3* and *Resurrection* in the theatre. I bought piles of the *Aliens* and *Predator* toys that Kenner brought out in the '90s, with their various animal-themed xenomorphs. I even got the cloaked (ie, cast in clear plastic) "Ambush Predator" figure that you had to send away for.

Through it all, *Aliens* remained my favorite movie in either franchise, and something very close to my favorite movie period (a slot it probably had to share with *Monster Squad*). And while today other films have usurped that favorite spot, and my affection for the *Alien* and *Predator* flicks is as much nostalgia as not, both franchises are ones I own on Blu-ray and revisit regularly. (Less so the unfortunate crossover films, though I've seen both of them more times than they probably deserve.)

Their influence was so formative that I can't really identify all the ways that the *Alien* films made inroads into my creative output. Besides obvious places like the near-closing line of "Painted Monsters," that big, haunting, H.R. Giger-designed ship with its ancient astronaut and its payload of mysterious eggs, the grotesque and bizarre life-cycle of the aliens themselves, that line from the CBS intro, "so who's laying these eggs," that shot of the xenomorph rising up out of the water behind Newt, the alien queen, the enormous ships that were like floating industrial blocks, all of it feels like my gateway to so many of my later obsessions, from the grim future of *Warhammer 40K* to weird fiction.

To this day, the films hold a special place in my pantheon, and they remain one of a *handful* of franchises for which I would love to one day write licensed fiction. So in honor of "Alien Day" (4/26, get it?), I figured it was high time to do something to pay tribute to one of the most important cinematic experiences of my life. So here's to you, *Aliens* CBS Special Movie Presentation. You may not have started it all, but you sure as hell started a lot.

**Author's Note:** I've still never written licensed fiction set in the *Alien* universe. I'd still love to.

**Originally published October 2016**
*Unwinnable*

# LIFE IN THE MONSTER SQUAD

In one of my earliest memories, I am sitting on a bale of hay in a darkened barn, looking at monsters.

The year was 1988 or '89 (I've never been able to figure out which) and it was Halloween. In those days, I lived in a tiny southern Kansas town called Sedan; the birthplace of famous circus clown Emmett Kelly, county seat and largest population center of Chautauqua County. Today, Sedan's population sits at around a thousand souls. In that year, the entire *county* had a population of only around four thousand.

We lived on the edge of town, just down the street from the county fairgrounds. Every Halloween, the 4H Club put on a haunted house in the cattle pens there, tacking up sheets of black plastic to form a labyrinth through which screaming kids groped blindly while volunteers in rubber werewolf masks leapt out, brandishing chainsaws with the chains removed. My first experience with a Halloween haunted house was in those cattle pens, the beginning of an addiction that I would carry with me to this day.

But not that year. That year I sat in the dark on a bale of hay in a long, low 4H barn and watched a projector throw the lighted image of the 1987 Shane Black/Fred Dekker film *The Monster Squad* up onto the wall. I've seen the movie many times in the years since, so it's hard to say what that first experience was really like. Was I scared? I'd already seen plenty of much scarier movies by that tender age, so probably not. I know that I was in love, and I keenly remember that walk home from the fairgrounds, down the long, barely-lighted streets on the edge of town, the night suddenly electric around me.

When it comes to truly formative influences, it's always difficult to imagine how differently life would have turned out without them. They come upon us while our molten surface is still cooling, and they change forever the shape that we will ultimately assume. Did I already love monsters and scary stories before I ever saw *The Monster Squad?* Absolutely. Would I have grown into the person and the writer that I am without that Halloween night in the 4H barn? That's much tougher to say . . .

I was born in 1981, too late to be a true Monster Kid. By the time I was around, most of the horror hosts were off the air and we didn't have cable or a satellite dish, so the handful of TV channels that we *did* get didn't show classic fare like the Universal monster movies, Hammer's Gothic chillers, the big bug movies of the '50s or the schlocky shockers of William Castle. When I got monster movies at all, it was stuff like *Squirm* and *C.H.U.D.* and *The Food of the Gods.*

So *Monster Squad* became my gateway to those old Universal monster movies, those classic monsters. Years later, my older brother would record a showing of *Monster Squad* off HBO onto a VHS tape along with two other movies—*Aliens* was one of them, if memory serves, *Creepshow* may have been the other—and I watched it until the wheels fell off. Until I could reliably quote the film in its entirety and could probably have accurately reproduced it from memory. If Ray Bradbury's *Fahrenheit 451* future had come to pass and had included movies, I could have been the kid who safeguarded *The Monster Squad* for future generations.

In so many ways, *Monster Squad* was tailor-made for me. Here were kids who thought and acted and talked like the kids I knew; who cussed and were obsessed with monsters and speculated about the things that movies would never show us. I recognized myself in these kids. I even owned the exact same knock-off Godzilla toy that sat on Eugene's desk. More than that, though I didn't fully understand it at the time, I recognized myself in these filmmakers. I saw that there were other people who thought and felt the way

I did. Not just in terms of loving monsters, but in the ways that I saw connections between them, layers in stories laid down by the sediments of preceding narratives.

Here was a jokey, self-referential horror movie years before *Scream* or even *Wes Craven's New Nightmare*—and it treated the monsters with seriousness even while it made a joke out of most everything else. Here was a movie completely mired in the '80s, yet with an absolute reverence of the past.

I didn't actually see any of the original Universal monster movies until I was in college. Before then, the closest I came were those Crestwood House monster books, with their orange and purple covers, filled with evocative black-and-white stills from movies that I had never seen, but that I could imagine with such vivid clarity.

Maybe it was thanks to those books that I realized, even as a kid, how much of *Monster Squad* nods to its predecessors. The armadillos standing in for rats in Dracula's crypt, the old dark house in the swamp, Drac himself going by the anagram Alucard, his wolf-head cane a reference to the walking stick that kills poor Lon Chaney Jr. in the original *Wolf Man*. (Was that also, I always wondered, a part of the whole "only one way to kill a werewolf" joke?)

At the same time, what I *didn't* realize as a kid was how carefully the filmmakers had to skirt around the actual Universal monsters. Universal didn't originally release *Monster Squad*; Tristar did. This meant that Stan Winston's (incredible) monster effects had to walk the tightrope of evoking the original monsters perfectly, while never actually stepping across the line of copyright infringement.

The more I learn about what goes on behind the scenes of the movies that I love, the more I come to think that "movie magic" actually means, "We couldn't do it the way that we originally wanted to, so we had to come up with something else, instead." In this case, the reimagining of the Universal monsters led to something better than if they had been able to use their actual likenesses, creating interpretations that are instantly familiar, while also every bit as striking as their more famous counterparts originally were.

Because I came to *Monster Squad* first, its versions of the creatures informed my personal image of each monster. I've argued before that no one iteration of a story or character makes it truly iconic, that it is the repetition of tales with minor (or major) alterations that creates a kind of gestalt entity that *is* Dracula or the Frankenstein's monster in our collective imaginations.

For me, that gestalt entity, for each of these classic monsters, began with *Monster Squad*. Duncan Regehr's menacing and commanding turn as Count Dracula, which *Wizard* magazine once controversially called the greatest cinematic Dracula of all time. (I might not disagree with them.) Tom Noonan's gentle, melancholy version of Frankenstein's monster. The only gill-man suit that could ever possibly compete with the original.

Another thing that I didn't understand as a kid was the tradition in which *Monster Squad* was operating. Back then, I never questioned the idea that Dracula, Frankenstein's monster, the mummy, the wolf man, and the Creature from the Black Lagoon would all coexist in the same world, the very real world that we all inhabit. Of course they would! I was unaware that, decades before Marvel would dominate the box office by creating a shared cinematic universe populated by all of their various comic book superheroes—inspiring pretty much every other movie studio to attempt to recreate the phenomenon—Universal Studios had already done the same thing with their monsters.

Beginning with *Frankenstein Meets the Wolf Man* in 1943, Universal attempted a string of what came to be called "monster mash" films, in which their various monster franchises crossed paths. They followed up *Frankenstein Meets the Wolf Man* with *House of Frankenstein* and *House of Dracula* in quick succession. Comedy duo Abbott and Costello even got in on the act, starting with *Abbott and Costello Meet Frankenstein* in 1948, and going on to meet Boris Karloff, the Invisible Man, Dr. Jekyll, Mr. Hyde, and the Mummy.

Universal would try the same trick again after the success of their 1999 remake of *The Mummy*, by putting that film's director in charge of the 2004 creative and financial failure *Van Helsing*, which mashed up Dracula, the Frankenstein monster, a hunchbacked assistant, werewolves and even a brief appearance by Mr. Hyde.

There are even plans now for another attempt to climb aboard the "shared universe" train that they seemingly created way back when, with a series of interlocking monster movies on the drawing board, slated to follow *yet another* remake of *The Mummy*, out next year and starring Tom Cruise (sadly not as the mummy). Even so, it seems unlikely that they will ever manage to capture the lightning in a bottle that was *The Monster Squad*.

These days, I probably couldn't quote *quite* all of *Monster Squad* from memory anymore, and I may have developed a greater appreciation for Dekker's previous directorial debut, *Night of the Creeps*, but *Monster Squad* still holds a special place in my cinematic pantheon and I doubt if that Halloween memory of the darkened barn and the larger-than-life monsters will ever fade.

**Author's Note:** This was my first contribution to *Unwinnable*, the beginning of what would become a long and profitable association. You'll notice, as you read through the rest of this book, that quite a large number of the movie reviews and essays in these pages first appeared in *Unwinnable*.

**Originally published April 2017**
orringrey.com

# "YOU CALL THEM WHATEVER YOU WANT."

## MONSTERS IN *KONG: SKULL ISLAND*

I recently got back from a trip to Atlanta for the first (annual?) Outer Dark Symposium on the Greater Weird, where I was one of a handful of panelists who talked about "The Weird Monster." While the panel (and, indeed, all of the Symposium) is intended to show up as a part of *The Outer Dark* podcast sooner or later, I wanted to share a few thoughts that came about independent from but related to the panel.

For one thing, the discussion of the subject among the panelists began (as such things so often do) at the bar the night before the Symposium actually started, and continued throughout the weekend, ranging far and wide. On the flight to Atlanta and back, I started reading John Langan's *The Fisherman*, and had I finished it then, I could certainly have brought it up as a modern novel that tackles the "weird monster." (Not to mention a great contemporary example of the "weird novel," which was the subject of another panel at the Symposium.)

As is often the case, however, while we talked about monsters in literature, many of our examples were drawn from movies. Because, while we have sometimes read the same books, we have almost all seen the same movies. Throughout the weekend, subjects returned with an almost uncanny regularity, including (probably because of the proximity of *Alien: Covenenant*) how angry we all still were at Ridley Scott's *Prometheus* for being so unforgivably terrible (with the exception of a handful of dogged defenders).

One subject that came up a couple of times was *Kong: Skull*

*Island*, which I had recently seen, and which we discussed, along with the whole backlog of Kong and Godzilla and other kaiju cinema through the lens of the weird monster. I'm not really here to regurgitate any of our theories on that, though no less a personage than Caitlín R. Kiernan has made a pretty good argument in the past for consideration of the original 1933 *King Kong* as a Lovecraftian tale.

One thing I didn't get to talk much about, except with kaiju enthusiast and Symposium co-organizer Anya Martin on the car ride back to the airport, is a subject that I have been meaning to bring up in re: *Skull Island*, but that I wanted to wait until the movie had been in theatres for a few weeks so as to avoid spoilers. Still, fair warning, there will be a few in what follows, so heads up.

I liked *Skull Island* well enough, but one thing that really struck me about it is something that I haven't seen anyone else talking about, though I'm sure they have. *Kong: Skull Island* was packed to the gills with monsters, and while those monsters may have varied somewhat in execution, I saw in most of them a sort of kinship with monsters from previous Kong and Godzilla movies.

The big spider that shows up in *Skull Island* looks an awful lot like Godzilla's sometime-nemesis Kumonga, while the scene of Kong fighting the squids or octopi could easily be a nod to the scene when Kong fights the giant octopus in *King Kong vs. Godzilla*.

Those are pretty minor, though. More significant are the skull crawlers. These bipedal lizard-like creatures are the main antagonists of *Skull Island*, the subterranean horrors that Kong's presence helps protect the rest of the island from. Their design has received both praise and derision, depending on the person, but virtually everyone I've seen talk about them has discussed them as though they are a wholly new addition to the giant monster canon, but for me, at a glance, I saw something else entirely.

As anyone who is reading this probably knows, the first cut of the original 1933 *King Kong* contained a famous (and famously lost) sequence in which the protagonists fall into a "spider pit" and are attacked by all sorts of weird creatures. Over the years, a couple of shots that are supposedly from this sequence have surfaced, but the sequence itself remains one of the most famous pieces of lost film in history. When Peter Jackson remade *King Kong* in 2005, he not only added the "spider pit" sequence back into his narrative, he also "restored" a version of it using stop-motion animation and incorporating footage from the original film.

Apart from Peter Jackson's recreation, the closest we're ever likely to come to actually seeing the original "spider pit" sequence from *Kong* is a cave sequence in the 1957 film *The Black Scorpion*, for which Willis O'Brien did the special effects. According to rumor, the models used for the cave sequence in *The Black Scorpion* were repurposed models from the original "spider pit" sequence.

Like all of the original *King Kong*, the "spider pit" sequence was heavily influenced by the artwork of Gustave Dore. You can see some obvious "spider pit" seeds in a couple of Dore's illustrations for *Don Quixote* and *Orlando Furioso* in particular. In Dore's illustrations and Jackson's recreation of the "spider pit" sequence, you'll find odd lizard-like creatures that have only front legs, which transmutes, in *The Black Scorpion*, to a sort of giant worm with bifurcated tentacles mounted near its head. These bipedal lizards are, I would argue, at least potentially, perhaps subconsciously on the part of the monster designers, the ancestors of the skull crawlers from *Kong: Skull Island*.

This isn't really an attempt at a defense of those critters. If they didn't work for you on screen, chances are they still won't, and I'll be honest when I say that I'm not entirely sure how I feel about them, even now. (Their design seems at once boringly modern while at the same time oddly weirder than it needs to be; it took me a while to notice that they had eyes mounted *behind* the eye sockets of their skull-like heads.) But it was something that I noticed and (obviously) wanted to write like a thousand words about, so there you go.

[Edited: Thanks to Outer Dark host Scott Nicolay for reminding me that the weird bipedal lizard does, in fact, show up in the original *King Kong*, and that I hadn't just hallucinated it there because I knew about all this other crap.]

**Author's Note:** The Outer Dark Symposium *did* turn out to be annual, though COVID threw something of a wrench into those works. The discussion in question *did* eventually show up on the Outer Dark podcast, where I believe you can still listen to it. And this post originally included several links to places to view the recreated spider pit sequence or the cave sequence from *The Black Scorpion*, which are both well worth watching. It also included links to some further information about Gustave Dore's influence on the original *King Kong*, a subject I've long been fascinated by.

**Originally published July 2018**
*Unwinnable*

# "IF THE DEVIL IS TO EXIST IN THIS WORLD, IT CANNOT LOOK LIKE A DEVIL." TOHO'S "BLOODTHIRSTY TRILOGY"

I've said before that nothing could be more on-brand for me, personally, than a trio of Toho movies aping Hammer movies. After all, Hammer's line of gothic chillers is probably my favorite category of films, full stop, and many of Japan's forays into the horror genre are not far behind. But implying that these movies are merely imitating Hammer is also unnecessarily reductive. As the booklet insert that comes with the Arrow Video Blu-ray eloquently points out, while the Hammer horror films may be the most obvious inspiration acting on the so-called "Bloodthirsty Trilogy," these films are best understood by placing them within their *own* cultural and historical context, as well.

Of course, we already knew that, right? That's a big part of the appeal. If these were just Hammer movies recast with Japanese actors, that wouldn't be nearly as much fun as movies that actually bridge a couple of different horror traditions. *Matango* is one of my favorite movies for a reason: because there are rubber suit mushroom people in it. But, if that weren't reason enough, it's also a phenomenal adaptation of William Hope Hodgson's "The Voice in the Night" *and* inescapably an Ishiro Honda film, made on the heels of *King Kong vs. Godzilla* and released right in the midst of Toho's Showa-era kaiju flicks.

I first heard about the "Bloodthirsty Trilogy"—specifically *Lake of Dracula*, the second film in the unofficial set—several years ago, possibly from Kenneth Hite, who was working on *The Thrill of Dracula* at the time. But I didn't get to actually *see* any of these movies in any form until Arrow Home Video released an *amazing* Blu-ray set of the whole trilogy. Which means that I got to enjoy the somewhat disappointing experience of watching the films in order, working my way from what is, without a doubt, the most inspired and possibly best of the three (*The Vampire Doll*) to the one that most resembles that reductive log line of Toho simply aping Hammer (*Evil of Dracula*). (Your mileage may vary, of course, and over at *Birth. Movies. Death.* Jacob Knight calls *Evil of Dracula* the best "or, at the very least, the most purely entertaining" of the three films.)

One thing to understand is that the "Bloodthirsty Trilogy" isn't really a trilogy. Triptych is probably a more honest description. No plot elements, characters, or settings carry over from one film to the next, though they all share a director (Michio Yamamoto), screenwriter (Ei Ogawa) and composer (Riichiro Manabe), who help to give them a sense of unity, even while their story lines diverge pretty drastically.

Now might be a good time to talk about Riichiro Manabe's scores for the three films, which I have seen described elsewhere as "often maligned," but which were, for me, one of the most effective and memorable parts of an almost universally effective and memorable set of movies. Of the three, *Lake of Dracula* may have the best score, with suspense sequences that are accompanied by a weird and dissonant noodling on instruments that really shouldn't work but does anyway. By *Evil of Dracula*, the incidental music has turned to jazzy riffing reminiscent of *Manos, the Hands of Fate*, while scenes of tension are backed by screeching static and Theramin.

*The Vampire Doll*, released in 1970, *should* have represented the director and the studio still getting their feet under them in this new European gothic vein, but instead it is perhaps the strongest film of the bunch, thanks in part to its tight running time, atmospheric direction, and genuinely unsettling ending, which brings in elements of Poe and reveals a capacity for human evil as bottomless as anything that Dracula himself could ever bring to bear.

Even as it opens in suitably gothic fashion, with a young man being driven through the rain to meet his girlfriend at her distinctly Western-style family manor out in the middle of nowhere—only to find, upon arrival, that she has met an untimely end—*The Vampire Doll* is already distinguishing itself from its Hammer predecessors, in no small part by being set in the present day, rather than some costumed past.

Not that the past doesn't hang heavy over *The Vampire Doll*. In true gothic fashion, the return of the repressed is very evident in the story here, as a terrible crime which befell the household years ago still informs the strange and sinister goings-on within its walls. This early installment "feels Japanese" in ways that the other two gradually move away from and, both aesthetically and narratively, I was reminded as much of the horror manga of Kazuo Umezu as I was the Eurohorror of Hammer or its imitators.

Sure, there are old dark houses, dramatic lightning bolts, late-night disinterments, strange sounds coming from the off-limits basement and even a few bats, but there is also the wind whispering through tall grasses and the film's "vampire," with her long black hair falling around her downturned face, prefiguring the soggy ghosts who would haunt J-horror screens in decades to come.

(It bears mentioning that the word "vampire," when used to describe these movies, is fraught with some translational complexities. These are explored with greater care than I could ever manage in the liner notes for the Arrow Blu-rays, written by Jasper Sharp. But nowhere is the term more of a potential misnomer than in *The Vampire Doll*, where the titular "vampire" lacks the traditional fangs, instead killing with a knife.)

Yukiko Kobayashi, who was in *Yog Monster from Space* (AKA *Space Amoeba*) that same year, plays the vampire here and she does so about as eerily as any vampire to ever creep across the screen, her smile every bit as haunting as the golden contacts which help her stand out from her European counterparts. A comparison has been made elsewhere between the look of her character and the "Blind Girl" photograph by Christer Stromholm, showing a Japanese girl who was blinded and scarred when the atomic bomb was dropped on Hiroshima.

Whatever their ultimate purpose, the golden eyes are a striking motif, and one of the only ones that repeats between movies, showing up again in *Lake of Dracula*, which takes the stylistic touches of *The Vampire Doll* and adjusts them one notch closer to the gothic chillers from which these movies are taking their cue. The vampires in *Lake of Dracula* share those golden eyes, but they also have the fangs that we're used to seeing. Screenwriter Ei Ogawa is joined by Masaru Takesue on both this film and the next one, which may help explain why they feel more of a piece with their Eurohorror counterparts.

According to Toho's international marketing department, "even vampires, when not at work sucking blood, probably enjoy sexual activity," leading them to "doubtless foster offspring, albeit illegitimate ones. Dracula himself would have been no exception. It was thus during the early years of this century that one of Dracula's bastard sons made his way to Japan, liked it and settled down." However, none of the movies ever actually use the D-word in their original Japanese incarnations.

In the English version of *Lake of Dracula*, Shin Kishida's character is simply credited as "the vampire," but his physicality in the role is obviously influenced by Christopher Lee's performances in the Hammer films and when the character perishes, he does so in a way that is clearly influenced by Lee's iconic death scene in the first Hammer *Dracula*.

Shin Kishida is also one of the few familiar faces to show back up under pancake makeup in *Evil of Dracula* some three years later, though by then he has lost those iconic golden eyes and is used, unfortunately, to worse effect. Much of his silent physicality is missing, though he remains suitably sinister and suave during scenes when he isn't done up in corpse paint with his mouth jammed full of vampire teeth. While the plot is a fairly clever bit of "vampire in a girls dormitory" shenanigans, *Evil of Dracula* was, for me, the low point in the triptych, even while it is also the movie that feels most like a direct lift of, if not the Hammer films themselves, then any of their various European mimics.

Bringing in an origin story for its "Dracula" that involves a Christian missionary shipwrecked in Japan and forced to renounce his faith and spit on the cross—not to mention some great imagery including a giant, unburied coffin—*Evil of Dracula* still isn't content to rest entirely on European vampire tropes. During a particularly lurid third-act ritual, *Evil of Dracula* abruptly introduces an odd twist on the methodology of the vampires that not only makes them stand out from the crowd but also manages to visually call back to *The Vampire Doll*.

At the end of the day, it probably doesn't really matter much whether the films of "Bloodthirsty Trilogy" are good or not. They are interesting, which, for fans of these kinds of obscure horror oddities, is more important. The fact that they are also mostly good—from the taut and effective *The Vampire Doll* through the lyrical *Lake of Dracula* to the occasionally shaggy *Evil of Dracula*—is just an added bonus.

**Author's Notes:** Beginning around 2018, I started writing film reviews, first for *Unwinnable* and then for *Signal Horizon*. Though I had dabbled in film criticism from time to time over the years, I had mostly resisted the temptation to engage in it because I was still feeling my way forward when it came to *how* I wanted to engage in criticism.

As you'll see from many of the subsequent reviews in this book, I don't approach the act in the same way that many of my contemporaries do—I am rarely interested in whether a movie is "good" or not. Instead, I try to explore what the act of watching the movie was like for me, and give the reader something to think about as they watch it, or after.

This essay bridged a gap, of sorts. My previous Monsters from the Vault column on vintage horror cinema, which had run for years at *Innsmouth Free Press* and has since been collected into two volumes from that same publisher, had come to an end, and I actually folded this essay into the second of those two books. This is the only reprint from those books in this one, though, so if you already have those volumes on your shelves, you don't have to worry about a lot of repetition.

**Originally published October 2018
Classic Horrors Club**

## "YOU SEEM TO SPECIALIZE IN OBSCURE ACQUAINTANCES."—*DARK INTRUDER* (1965)

I first heard about *Dark Intruder* from artist Richard Sala, which makes sense, as its eponymous "Intruder" looks every bit the part of some creeping brute from a Richard Sala comic. Fellow comic artist Stephen R. Bissette apparently wrote a two-part essay on the film for the magazine *Monster!* (issues 27 and 28, to be precise) which I have not yet read, in which he apparently delves into a lot of the stuff that I'm probably about to discuss. So, if you Want To Know More, I recommend seeking that out.

What I learned from Sala was more than enough to convince me to track down the film. *Dark Intruder* was originally shot as a pilot for a TV series that was going to be called *Black Cloak*, but the show never went to series and instead *Dark Intruder* got (rather unceremoniously, I gather) dumped onto screens in 1965 and then largely disappeared from the horror scene.

It stars a pre-comedy (but post-*Forbidden Planet*) Leslie Nielsen, has creature makeup by Universal stalwart Bud Westmore, and features a screenplay by Barre Lyndon, who also provided scripts for a number of better-known horrors including the 1953 *War of the Worlds* and *Hangover Square*. While Leslie Nielsen is the big name, the most distracting casting for me was that of his friend Robert Vandenburg, played by "your dad's alcoholic golfing buddy as *Agent for H.A.R.M.*" who I recognized from watching way too much *Mystery Science Theater 3000*.

Aside from all of this, *Dark Intruder* is notable for very nearly being the first film to feature names and ideas taken wholesale from

H.P. Lovecraft's mythos fiction. While you won't find any Cthulhu or *Necronomicon* here, the main character does drop mouthfuls like "Azathoth" and "Dagon" pretty early on, and there's a lot of talk about religions and gods and demons that were "ancient before Babylon" and things of that nature. The plot also hinges on the kind of identity swap that was a staple of Lovecraft's weird tales.

The first widely acknowledged adaptation of Lovecraft's work hit theatres just a couple of years before, when Roger Corman, Vincent Price, and Charles Beaumont made *The Haunted Palace*, ostensibly an entry into their then-popular cycle of Poe adaptations, but actually a retelling of Lovecraft's *The Case of Charles Dexter Ward*.

While *Dark Intruder* isn't a direct adaptation of any particular Lovecraft story, in many ways it feels more like one of his tales than most of the other adaptations that have come around since, and the reveal of the twisted killer's origins and motives feel like they could have been wrenched from some unpublished Lovecraft manuscript—or maybe from a Robert Bloch story in the Lovecraft vein.

However, *Dark Intruder* also slots neatly into another narrative tradition within the field of weird fiction: that of the occult investigator. In keeping with its planned-for-series nature, Leslie Nielsen plays a bon vivant in 1890 San Francisco, a time and place chosen, no doubt, partly for its association with Jack the Ripper, as the fog-shrouded San Francisco streets stand in nicely for London, and an early shot of the murderer at the beginning of the movie calls to mind any number of Ripper pictures, including *The Lodger*, also from the pen of Barre Lyndon.

Of course, while Nielsen's character plays at being a rake who takes nothing seriously, he is, in fact, a deeply serious student of the strange and occult, who keeps a mandrake plant in his room which moves when supernatural forces are nearby, employs a diminutive servant who knows his "secret identity," has a secret laboratory hidden behind a bookcase, and covertly assists the police on strange cases like the one at the center of the film.

There have been plenty of characters of that stripe in the history of film and fiction, but this one stands out for several reasons, one of them probably coincidental but striking nonetheless. Put a white streak in his hair, and Nielsen's character would be the spitting image of Jason Blood, the human alter-ego of the Demon Etrigan, created by Jack Kirby for DC Comics in 1972. What's more, the plot of *Dark Intruder* involves body-swapping and transformations into a hulking monster.

Am I suggesting that there was any borrowing going on here? It seems unlikely, given how much has been written over the years about Jack Kirby and his creations. If there was any actual concrete connection between *Dark Intruder* and Jason Blood/Etrigan, someone would surely have found it by now. But the idea that Kirby maybe saw *Dark Intruder* on late-night TV and jumbled up the villain and protagonist into one character, adding more than a soupcon of Arthurian legend to get Etrigan, well, it makes for fun pondering, even if it isn't necessarily true.

For a movie that runs a mere 59 minutes, there's a lot to discuss in *Dark Intruder*, and I've spent most of my 800+ words talking around the film rather than directly about it. More than anything, when the final credits rolled following an ending that felt altogether too jocular on the heels of the film's rather tragic climax, I was mostly left lamenting the fact that we didn't get at least a season or two of *Black Cloak* just to see where it all might have gone from here…

**Author's Note:** I was invited to contribute this piece for a special "countdown to Halloween" that was happening at the Classic Horrors Club, the blog of Jeff Owens, who was my boss at the first video store I ever worked at and, as such, a formative influence on my burgeoning cinephilia. I was happy to contribute, especially since I got to write about a particular favorite made-for-TV oddity that had been burning in my brain for a while.

**Originally published October 2018**
orringrey.com

## "[RUBBER BAT NOISES]"—*THE WORLD OF VAMPIRES* (1961)

My quest to watch *The World of Vampires* began with a gif on Twitter. A delightful image of a flying rubber bat cast in a verdigris sheen with glowing orange eyes, it quickly became my favorite rubber bat of all time. With a little digging, I was able to find other gifs from the same film and, eventually, to track down that film's title, thanks to the help of the Facebook hivemind.

Finding the film initially took me to the Tumblr of Rhett Hammersmith, who had a wonderful collection of gifs from the movie, including the ones I had already seen. Where he got the oddly color-cast images I still have no idea, but his page gave me enough information to track down the film. Once I had found it on IMDb under its Mexican-language title *El Mundo de los Vampiros*, I was surprised to discover that my local library actually had a DVD copy in English.

Released by Beverly Wilshire Filmworks and/or Telefilms International, the menu for the DVD had two options, "Bite Me," which played the film, and "Bite Me Harder," which took me to scene selections, for some reason. The movie was an American cut produced by K. Gordon Murray, à la *Mystery Science Theater 3000* classic *Samson vs. the Vampire Women*, which, like tonight's film, was also directed by Alfonso Corona Blake, who obviously knows how to do vampires up right.

The version I watched was dubbed and featured plenty of long monologues about the night and the power of vampires and the kind of stuff that you wouldn't be surprised to hear if you've ever seen *Samson vs. the Vampire Women*. What it *didn't* feature was much in the way of ambient noise, to the extent that a scene of people clapping was absolutely silent. It also looked like it was recorded off television half a century ago, complete with missing frames and plenty of visual noise.

All of which is a shame, because the movie is kind of a goofy delight, as you might imagine if you've ever seen the gifs that led me to it in the first place. It opens, as these movies so often do, with our lead vampire, Count Subotai, who looks like he just stepped out of a telenovela, rising out of his coffin. As most of us like to do when we first wake up, he goes down into the gigantic cave under his house and plays an organ made of bones and skulls, which would have been right at home in a playset from *He-Man and the Masters of the Universe*.

His playing wakes up the film's various other vampires, who would absolutely be its best feature if those adorable rubber bats weren't about to show up. While Subotai and the requisite lady vampires all look about like you'd expect vampires in an old black-and-white horror movie to look—which is to say, like people with fake vampire fangs—the incidental vampires are all just people in capes wearing completely immobile vampire masks. It is a conceit made all the more charming by its absolute lack of necessity. It would have actually been *easier* to just give them vampire teeth, but no, it's exaggerated vampire masks from hell to breakfast.

Subotai talks at length, if occasionally contradictorily, about his plans to get revenge on the Colman family who apparently killed him a hundred years ago, and also killed his ancestor three hundred years ago in Hungary, I guess. The Colman family has been busy, and I like to imagine them as precursors of the Belmont clan in *Castlevania*. As luck would have it, the only three remaining Colmans in the world, the older Sr. Colman and his two predictably lovely nieces, happen to live right nearby and are already acquainted with Count Subotai, who shows up at their house unannounced to interrupt some piano playing and then immediately leave again.

The piano playing in question is being performed by Rudolfo Sabre, who has some sort of romantic attachment to one of the Colman nieces. He studies music that produces "peculiar effects" and, wouldn't you know it, happens to know a song that drives away vampires.

From there, the film devolves into the usual sequence of vampires showing up at peoples' bedsides, those wonderful rubber bats, underground rituals complete with sacrificial altars, and long vampiric monologues. One of the nieces, Leonor, falls almost immediately under Subotai's sway and becomes a vampire, while the other, Mirta, takes on the role of the film's damsel in distress. Rudolfo, our ostensible hero, also gets bitten by a vampire fairly early on, and for the rest of the film undergoes a slow transformation which primarily involves his hands getting progressively hairier.

There's a lengthy fistfight between Rudolfo and the count's hunchbacked assistant, who looks more than a little like Gomez Addams, before the film's final reel. In addition to being disabled by that one particular melody, the vampires in *The World of Vampires* seem to be particularly weak against punching, as Rudolfo manages to beat up an entire room full of them in order to rescue Mirta from their clutches. I hypothesized that this was because their masks made it hard for them to see.

In the end, Subotai is defeated and the vampires all disappear, except for Leonor, who looks to be cured, though at the last moment she flings herself down onto the same stakes that destroyed her "master." Our theory was that she couldn't stand to return to her old life after seeing how much better her makeup and wardrobe were as a vampire. Also, who could give up being able to turn into such an adorable rubber bat?

**Author's Note:** This is one of those movies that desperately needs a high-class Blu-ray release from some boutique label like Indicator or Arrow or Eureka. But honestly, only if they also get Rhett Hammersmith to do a colorized version.

Speaking of which, that is something I've learned since this piece originally appeared on my website. Where Rhett Hammersmith "got the oddly color-cast images" I saw is that he made them. For those who aren't already familiar with Hammersmith's Tumblr, it is a treasure trove of weird gifs from old movies.

Also, if anyone has an actual prop of one of those rubber bats, I want it.

**Originally published November 2018**
orringrey.com

## "TODAY WE NEED TO BREAK THE NOSE OF EVERY BEAUTIFUL THING."—*SUSPIRIA* (2018)

No other movie is ever going to be *Suspiria*. The 1977 original is something of a miracle film, and I'm not at all confident that anyone, even the people who made it, have any idea how or why it is what it is. It's the film I always use as an example of a movie that would be worse if it was any better; a movie that transmutes, by some intangible magic, its own weaknesses into strengths.

To its credit, Luca Guadagnino's remake never tries to be the original *Suspiria*. From the earliest scenes, we are told quite clearly that he is using the blueprint left behind by the original film to fashion a very new edifice. As I said right after seeing it, the differences between Argento's film and Guadagnino's are neatly summarized by the distinctions between the buildings in which the two films take place: The candy-colored art deco interiors and Haus zum Walfisch exterior of the '77 version replaced with dimly-lit Brutalist architecture facing directly onto the Berlin Wall.

The 2018 *Suspiria* knows that we already know that there are witches in the walls, and so it doesn't play coy, dumping us into the reality of the witchcraft early on, even if it still takes most of the film for anyone to react to it. Guadagnino also ties the witchcraft and the dancing much more closely together than Argento's version ever did. In this *Suspiria*, dances are spells, and they have very real consequences. In one of the strongest (in most senses of the word) scenes in Guadagnino's version, the effects of one such spell are graphically, grotesquely displayed in a bit of gruesome body horror that the film never really tops.

The academy in Guadagnino's *Suspiria* is also a house divided. That view of the Berlin Wall is more than just a reminder of the times, or the different tones of the two movies. It serves as a metaphor for the divide among the witches themselves, with some wishing to continue following Mother Markos, while others want to throw their lot in behind Tilda Swinton's Madame Blanc.

It is this division that drives most of the film to its climactic moments, where a plot twist that can be seen coming like a slow-moving freight train chugging down the tracks leads to an extremely bloody denouement, shot with music video artistic license, one presumes to cover up the fact that the CGI blood splatter effects which it leans on heavily are nowhere near ready for prime time.

Ultimately, Guadagnino's film is a (sometimes) beautiful one and an ugly one; at times smart but never subtle; filled with horror touches that it doesn't seem to know what to do with. There were audible gasps from the theatre I saw it in, hands covering eyes, shrinking back in seats, but the images on the screen were often more exploitative than scary. Gasps were more likely to be gasps of disgust than fear. While sitting in the theatre, I scribbled down comparisons to other things, including the video to "Invisible Light" and *120 Days of Sodom*.

I will need time to sit with my feelings about this new *Suspiria*, and something tells me they won't necessarily get better with distance. But whether the end result is good, bad, or indifferent, Guadagnino took this film's relationship to the original and used it to forge something almost totally different using the same floor plan. That's worth something, anyway, regardless of how the finished product may have turned out.

**Author's Note:** I actually got to go to a preview screening of the 2018 *Suspiria* for work, which is always a nice thing, even if you don't enjoy the movie. As of this writing, I've not actually watched it again since. My estimation of it certainly hasn't improved in the intervening years, but I still stand by the things I said in this piece.

Originally published November 2018
*Signal Horizon*

# "WE ARE GOING TO EAT YOU!"—FULCI'S *ZOMBIE* LIVES ON

Like a lot of horror nerds, I went through a period of time in high school when I was pretty into zombie movies.

Of course, this was a few years before the zombie movie really skyrocketed to mainstream popularity, so the only ones I had available to me were things like George Romero's original *Dead* trilogy, *Return of the Living Dead*, *Evil Dead*, Peter Jackson's *Dead Alive*, *Re-Animator*, that sort of thing. One time, I was watching a movie called *The Dead Hate the Living* and I saw that one of the characters had a bumper sticker that read "FULCI LIVES."

Even then, I knew that Lucio Fulci was an Italian splatter director, but I hadn't seen any of his films. In fact, until the 40th anniversary Blu-ray of *Zombie* landed in my mailbox, I had still only seen two Fulci films: *The Beyond* and *The House by the Cemetery*. So I was excited to check out one of his most famous flicks, especially in a package as attractive and feature-packed as this one looked to be.

Among the features on this new disc is a (very brief) introduction by Guillermo del Toro, in which he promises "visceral satisfaction," which is perhaps unsurprising, given the film's pedigree and subject matter, as well as "some of the most graceful, poetic images" in genre filmmaking, which might be a bit harder to swallow. Somewhat to my surprise, however, *Zombie* delivers nicely on both promises.

The opening and closing sequences, filmed in New York, help to give the movie an apocalyptic tenor that goes well beyond its budgetary limitations, even if the famous bridge scene is undercut a bit by traffic flowing along normally below.

While most of the actual action involves just a handful of actors in an isolated locale, this bookend, Fulci's handsome direction, and, of course, the score by frequent Fulci collaborator Fabio Frizzi help to make even otherwise mundane scenes feel iconic.

A friend once described Fulci's particularly gross brand of gore effects as, and I am paraphrasing a bit here, "like someone took a mannequin and stapled a rancid piece of mutton to its face."

While this isn't *factual*, it is *true*, and it gives a good idea of what you can expect from at least my experience of a Fulci movie, which is, of course, part of the draw. After all, how many directors have a gore style that is so unmistakably identifiable?

There is certainly no shortage of rancid mutton-style gore in *Zombie*, even if it takes a little while to really get underway.

While I hadn't seen a lot of other Fulci films prior to this, I also hadn't been living under a rock for the past few decades, so I knew at least a little about *Zombie* going in. Mostly, I was familiar with the cover image of a rotted skull with worms pouring out of one eye—which is immortalized on a lenticular slipcase in the version of the Blu-ray that I got—and I knew that the film featured an underwater zombie fighting a shark. Because everyone knows about that, right?

(What I did *not* know was that the underwater zombie vs. shark fight interrupts a bit of topless scuba diving which, I don't know a lot about scuba diving, but that seems like an uncomfortable proposition, at best.)

Strangely enough, not more than a month or two before I sat down with *Zombie*, I had actually watched the 1957 flick *Zombies of Mora Tau*, which may be the earliest example of the "underwater zombie" subgenre.

To say that Fulci (and/or screenwriter Dardano Sacchetti) must have at least been aware of *Mora Tau* when making *Zombie* is the understatement of the century, even if the underwater zombie of the latter is relegated to that one scene in which a surprisingly limber zombie wrestles an actual, live shark.

In fact, as someone who watches a whole lot of *old* horror movies from the '50s and before, I have long been fascinated by the way in which the zombie film experienced a sea change (no pun intended) following the release of Romero's *Night of the Living Dead* in 1968.

In spite of never actually using the z-word, *Night* changed the face of the zombie movie forever. Prior to that, zombies in cinema were not the undead flesh-eaters of Romero's version, but somnolent products of voodoo.

There are several films that serve as bridges between these two styles. Hammer's *Plague of the Zombies* from 1966 is a good example, keeping intact the voodoo zombie proceedings while prefiguring the look of Romero's shambling zombie hordes. Add to that list Fulci's *Zombie*.

Released in Italy under the title *Zombi 2* in order to position it as a sort of "unofficial sequel" to *Dawn of the Dead*—which was just called *Zombi* over there—Fulci's *Zombie* is also surprisingly aware of the genre's pre-Romero roots.

While its aesthetics and story notes may be purely in the Romero camp, its island setting, voodoo drumbeats, and graveyard full of decayed conquistadors all hearken back to an earlier age of zombie films—and many of them could have been ripped straight out of a movie like *Zombies of Mora Tau*.

Like Romero's films, while it attributes the spate of reanimated corpses to a local voodoo curse, *Zombie* is wise enough to leave the actual cause ambiguous. Ultimately, its best explanation of what's going on is an echo of *Dawn of the Dead*'s famous "no more room in hell" line, "When the earth spits out the dead, they will rise to suck the blood of the living."

Though this is mostly Fulci's show—him and his gross zombies—he needs a living human cast, too, made up of a handful of familiar faces from Italian horror (and Mia Farrow's sister) alongside *The Haunting*'s Richard Johnson, who adds a dash of respectability to the proceedings that the chewy gore might not otherwise allow.

For the 40th anniversary disc, Blue Underground has done a new 4K restoration from the original camera negative, and the end product looks pretty great, giving plenty of nice, clear views of all that outlandishly fetid gore.

How much better it might be than previous editions I will have to leave to those more familiar with the film in its other incarnations, but I can say that the Blu-ray comes loaded with special features, including a couple of commentary tracks and interviews with just about anyone and everyone even tangentially related to the making of the film.

The slightly-oversized case also comes with a booklet by author Stephen Thrower talking about the film's critical reception and a third disc—a soundtrack CD of Fabio Frizzi's score, including that delightfully jaunty island theme, which I spent most of the movie hoping I would find on the soundtrack.

**Author's Note:** This was one of the earliest reviews I did after getting in with various distributors, who would send me discs for review. Many—indeed, most—of the reviews that follow this were written under similar circumstances.

As would be the case with many of my subsequent reviews, I am as concerned with understanding the film's history and positioning it in the context of its genre and when and where it was made as I am with the film itself.

Originally published December 2018
*Unwinnable*

# OF GIALLO AND GORE—*TORSO* (1973) AND *THE WIZARD OF GORE* (1970)

*"You will live through an experience that you now think no living creature can survive."*

When I watched *The Editor* (2014) at a midnight screening at Panic Fest (this is going somewhere, I promise), it took me a while to get the joke of the film's *copious* incidental nudity. At the time, I had seen only a handful of giallo films. (And, as of this writing, I've really only seen a handful more.) By about the mid-point of the film, I had figured out the joke, but I'm not sure that I ever *really* understood it until I sat down to watch Sergio Martino's *Torso* for the first time.

For those who haven't seen it, I described *The Editor* on Twitter as "if *Anchorman* had been a *giallo*," and I still think that's pretty accurate. One of its best gags is that, as the film goes on, background (and foreground) characters are just constantly naked at seemingly random times. The point at which I finally realized it was a joke and not just a stylistic choice was, I believe, when women were doing some light filing in the nude in the background of an office scene.

While *Torso* doesn't have quite as much incidental nudity as *The Editor*, watching it definitely shows you why an homage/send-up of this kind of film would feature a joke like that. Which is a (very) long way of saying that *Torso*'s victims-in-waiting spend a whole lot of time in the altogether.

The days of squinting at pirated pay-TV channels in the hopes of catching a glimpse of flesh are long behind us, however, and a movie needs more than some bare skin to hold up in the modern day. Fortunately, *Torso* has a lot going for it besides its generous nudity.

Those who know me would probably assume (as I did for many years) that giallo films would not be my particular brand of poison. I tend to prefer my horrors more existential or supernatural; I'll take monsters over murderers any day of the week, and, frankly, I have little patience for films that exploit suffering or make a point of victimizing women. Yet the best giallo films carry an air of weird menace that I find entirely mesmerizing and that always makes me completely overlook any of the elements that might otherwise turn me off. *Torso* is no exception.

In fact, there's a quote early on in *Torso*, said during an art lecture taking place in an old church, that acts as a pretty neat summary of what draws me to the giallo genre: "Everything is bathed in an elegance approaching the supernatural." While *Torso* may not quite reach levels of elegance that approach the supernatural, it makes extremely good use of its picturesque filming locations to create atmosphere out of little more than buildings and landscapes—and, of course, the music for which *gialli* are well known, in this case supplied by Guido and Maurizio De Angelis.

It doesn't hurt that *Torso* is kind of a misleading title—the Italian original, which translates to "the bodies show traces of carnal violence," is a little more accurate. In the insert booklet of the Arrow Video Blu-ray, there is an informative essay about Joseph Brenner, the distributor who brought films like *Torso* to grindhouse theaters in the states, not to mention giving them punchy, marquee-ready titles like, well, *Torso*.

Giallo films in general—and *Torso* in particular—are often held up as precursors of the slasher movie, and you can definitely see it in the structure of this picture. The obligatory kill shots are all here, and were probably shocking enough for 1973, but don't seem like much compared to the kinds of gore most horror fans are used to by now. Actually, a surprising number of the kills in *Torso* happen off camera, and even the infamous scene of bodies being dismembered via hacksaw—from which, most likely, the film draws its American title—is more suggestion than show.

What is more apparent in *Torso* is the link between slasher films and voyeurism. Sure, there are the killer's POV shots that we've all come to expect, but the themes of voyeurism come into play in many other ways, from the casualness with which the female characters treat Peeping Toms to the film's opening scene, which features a threesome intercut by the clicking of a camera shutter.

While *Torso* may not draw too many particularly novel conclusions about the male gaze, a *Variety* review quoted in the insert booklet points out that, "By the time the film is half over, Martino has strongly suggested that the dastardly deeds could have been done by just about every male in the cast…"

The film's genuinely nail-biting third-act game of cat-and-mouse, which is more Hitchcock than splatter, also prefigures many elements of the home invasion films that would become horror staples in the aughts. Though, admittedly, most home invasion flicks don't end with knock-down, drag-out fights between the rescuing hero and the killer—including jump-kicks!—so maybe *Torso* has them beat.

\*\*\*

If *Torso* is a subtler film than you might expect from the title, *The Wizard of Gore* is pretty much what it says on the tin. Since I'm told that 1965's *Monster a-Go Go* "doesn't count," this was my first real exposure to the legendary "Godfather of Gore" Herschell Gordon Lewis, who could just as easily wear the *Wizard of Gore* moniker as could the film's eponymous murder magician.

While Lewis's career includes a variety of grindhouse fare—and even a couple of children's movies—he is best known today for his pioneering work in gore effects, which, per *AllMovie.com*, "prob[ed] the depths of disgust and discomfort onscreen with more bad taste and imagination than anyone of his era."

Where *Torso* seems, at a glance, like a movie I wouldn't like, but isn't, *The Wizard of Gore* seems like a movie I wouldn't like, and is. But I also learned a long time ago not to let a movie not being my thing stop me from enjoying what it *does* have to offer. Even famously bad movies like *Manos: The Hands of Fate* can have moments of unexpected effectiveness when you know how to look for them, and Lewis is a favorite *auteur* of my very good friend and fellow author Adam Cesare, for whose sake I would happily keep my mind open through much worse. Besides, any movie that prominently features a restaurant called "Chicken Unlimited" can't be all bad.

In some ways, juxtaposing *Wizard of Gore* against *Torso* is an extremely good way to appreciate this film's modest charms. Lewis didn't earn that "Godfather of Gore" appellation by being understated, and *The Wizard of Gore* pours on the red stuff, with homebrew gore effects made up of actual raw meat, bright red "blood," and obviously fake mannequin heads. The result is disorienting and, at times, genuinely distressing, helped along as much as hurt by the fact that the amount of carnage wrought by the "tricks" of the titular magician doesn't stay consistent from one shot to the next.

The grue in *Wizard of Gore* would probably already be striking, if not shocking, even to the most jaded modern viewer, but when you realize that it was made a full three years before *Torso*, and only a couple of years after Hollywood dropped the restrictive Hays Code, the full import of a film like this—and a filmmaker like Herschell Gordon Lewis—becomes even more apparent.

By far the best special effect that *The Wizard of Gore* has at its disposal, however, is Ray Sager as Montag the Magnificent. His confrontational stage performances not only provide most of the film's suspense, but they are also filled with the thematic underpinnings that give the buckets of blood whatever heft they manage to have.

From the film's opening moments, Montag practically berates the audience—both in his low-rent theater and, by extension, the audience watching at home—for their bloodlust *and* for their unwillingness to get their hands dirty for it, providing a kind of meta-commentary on the sort of picture that he's in.

"Today, television and films give you the luxury of observing grisly dismemberments and deaths without anyone actually being harmed," he says, sometimes looking straight at the camera. There's even a little nod to the way horror has changed over the years, when the film's female lead says on her television talk show (*Housewife's Coffee Break*) that Montag's show made her more afraid than she's been since "the *Wolf Man* left me quivering beneath the seats of the Bijou."

Aside from Sager, Lewis populates the film primarily with non-actors with no other films to their credit, and the sets have the one-angle drabness of someone shooting on a shoestring budget. But "no budget" doesn't mean "no imagination," and *The Wizard of Gore* does a lot with a little. Montag's guillotines and punch presses are bedazzled with glitter and little stars. There are sequences of red-filter night where a coffin rises from the ground at his bidding. And Montag's hypnotism is conveyed, in grand old movie tradition, with a close-up of his eyes—or, in this case, mostly his eyebrows.

The Arrow Blu-ray of *Wizard of Gore* warns of scratches and audio flaws that are the result of the print not being in the best shape, but these anomalies serve to help the film's bargain basement aesthetic more than they hinder it. The Blu-ray also comes with another feature film, a sleazy 1968 romp called *How to Make a Doll*. I'll confess that I haven't yet watched the whole thing. So, as of this writing, I still haven't seen any other Herschell Gordon Lewis movies. I trust Adam's opinion when he tells me that *Monster a-Go Go* really doesn't count, but I can't help noticing a surprising twin obsession present in the two otherwise pretty dissimilar pictures.

*The Wizard of Gore*'s surprisingly ambitious and almost apocalyptic ending takes some of the same ideas that were being listlessly batted around in the "as if an eye had been blinked" ending of *Monster a-Go Go* and runs them much more effectively home, transforming a simple enough gore picture into something that at least rubs up against the uncanny. While no one would ever accuse *The Wizard of Gore* of being "bathed in an elegance," there's no denying that the proceedings not only approach the supernatural, but probably go careening half-drunk across that line.

**Author's Note:** Gathering so many of them together in one place like this, it becomes apparent that my reviewing style, while always unorthodox and sometimes hampered by the editorial dictates of the various venues in which I published, was also constantly at least making some effort to evolve.

The form in which I would pen most of the subsequent reviews I wrote for venues like *Unwinnable* and *Signal Horizon* was still in its nascent state here, but this is still one of my favorites from among these "early" reviews, working from a double-feature that existed only because I happened to receive both of these titles for review at around the same time.

**Originally published December 2018**
*Signal Horizon*

## "THERE'S NO WAY YOU CAN POSSESS SOMEONE FOREVER."—*MANIAC* (1980)

At the World Horror Convention in Salt Lake City—so this must have been back in 2012—I was on a panel about horror films. I don't remember the names of everyone else who was on that panel with me, but one of them was someone who had worked in the makeup or special effects or something department of the then-unreleased 2012 remake of *Maniac* starring Elijah Wood.

Intrigued by what my panel-mate had to say about the making of the film, as well as its gimmick that the entire movie was shot literally from the killer's POV, I watched the 2012 version when it came out and remember liking it well enough. Until the new Blue Underground Blu-ray arrived in my mailbox, that is as close as I had ever come to William Lustig's (in)famous 1980 original.

As Monster Ambassador here at *Signal Horizon*, I am straining the edges of my beat in reviewing *Maniac*. With the exception of one brief nightmare sequence near the end of the film (in which Tom Savini gets to really go to town), there is nothing spectral about *Maniac*'s thrills, and while the titular killer is certainly a monster, after his fashion, he is by no means the squamous, too-many-eyeballs kind that is my usual bailiwick.

In fact, while *Maniac* is well-positioned to be an early-era slasher film, coming out in the U.S. less than a year after Tom Savini had also provided gore effects to the original *Friday the 13th*, it's really as much a character study as it is a horror flick.

From a story by Joe Spinell, who also plays Frank Zito, the

film's titular *Maniac*, in what is probably a career-defining performance—impressive, for a guy whose filmography also includes stuff like *Rocky*, *The Godfather*, *Taxi Driver*, and others—*Maniac* lacks most of the usual horror movie beats.

There is no "hero" in this film, no real "final girl." According to the booklet by Michael Gingold that accompanies the Blue Underground release, there was originally a subplot about a detective—a role that was to have been played by *The Exorcist*'s Jason Miller—but it was left on the cutting room floor for budget reasons.

The result is a movie that is all about the eponymous *Maniac*. From the film's earliest, voyeuristic scenes, we are in his shoes more than those of his victims.

We see him commit his vicious crimes, but we also see how those crimes haunt him, hear his own internal monologue, a running conversation between himself and an imagined version of his abusive (and now dead) mother, both in his own voice. Playing Zito, Spinell goes from lethargic to jittery to pop-eyed, sweaty, teeth-bared murder without warning. It is a chilling performance, and a powerful one.

Helping Spinell along is the score by composer Jay Chattaway, which, as with the Blue Underground release of *Zombie*, is included as a CD bonus disc with the Blu-ray.

In the booklet that accompanies the film, Lustig talks about how he tried to convince Chattaway to ape the sound of Goblin, but Chattaway chose to "ignore everything I had spoken to him about, and create music that he thought was correct for the movie. It turned out to be brilliant, because what he did was, instead of playing the horror of the character, he played empathy for him."

In 2018, we may question whether or not we really *need* or *want* a movie that empathizes with a serial killer who brutalizes women. After all, there's no subtext whatsoever in *Maniac*'s psychosexual themes. By scalping his victims and nailing their bloody hair to mannequins, Zito literally transforms them into objects that he can control.

In 1981, when the film hit U.S. theaters, however, that decision to focus on the killer, and the killer's humanity, helped *Maniac* to stand out in a field crowded with incipient slasher flicks and Italian giallo films.

Not that *Maniac* is a movie untouched by the shadow of giallo. According to that same booklet, *Maniac* was originally going to be produced by Dario Argento, with Daria Nicolodi, Argento's frequent collaborator and wife at the time, set to star in the role that ultimately went to Caroline Munro.

As much as *Maniac* is a movie about a killer, though, it is also about a specific time and place—or the *idea* of that time and place. It is an ugly world, one in which beauty exists only as islands amid refuse—mannequins in store windows, fashion shoots in a photographer's loft.

Point-of-view shots are often through grimy windshields; tracking shots pan across piles of garbage, all underscored by infrequent reminders that this is yet another horror film that takes place shortly before Christmas.

Frank Zito may be the film's main character, but its other most important character is the New York City in which it takes place. One of its earliest shots is of a billboard that says, "N.Y., you don't know what love is." This is not the sunny Rome of giallo films; this is the gritty New York of grindhouse theaters—the kind of place where the movies that influenced it would be playing.

**Author's Note:** Some time after I wrote this review, I watched *Maniac* in a crowded theater as part of a monthly event called "Horror Roulette," staged at my local indie theater, the Screenland Armour. Each month's Horror Roulette had a theme, and that month's theme was slashers. All the other choices available were more likely ones—your *Friday the 13th*s and the like—but the idea behind horror roulette was that the movie was chosen at random by spinning a wheel, and that night the wheel landed on

*Maniac*.

I'm not sure I have ever seen a movie suck the energy out of a theater more completely than that one did. *Maniac* may be an arguably great film, but it's not one that's going to fire up a crowd.

I included this review here in part because I think it's a good example of how I incorporate my own unique experience of watching the film into the review itself, for good or ill.

**Originally published February 2019**
*Unwinnable*

# IT'S A SCARY WORLD:
# *AUDITION* (1999) ON BLU-RAY

*"Someday, you'll feel that life is wonderful."*

*Audition* was my first Takashi Miike film. This was nearly two decades ago, when I still worked at a video store. Before movies like *Ichi the Killer* or *Visitor Q* or *The Happiness of the Katakuris* had become common knowledge here in the States.

My wife—who doesn't like horror movies or gore or torture or much of anything unpleasant, really—actually picked it out. I don't remember why. We none of us had anything to go on besides that now-infamous image of Asami with her syringe on the cover. We didn't know what to expect. We were in over our heads. How could we not have been?

The film traumatized us. For years afterward, when someone asked me what the scariest movie I had ever seen was—a common question, when you work in a video store—I would tell them it was *Audition*. I'm not sure that's true anymore—I'm not actually sure it ever was—but I also don't know what would replace it, making it true enough.

Part of what makes *Audition*'s horror sequences so disturbing—even all these years later—is how disarming the rest of the movie is. In the more than one hundred films that Miike has directed over the course of his intimidating career, he has shown himself to be a master at manipulating the expectations of the audience, and nowhere is this more at play than in *Audition*.

It is 37 minutes into the film before we get our first indication that something is wrong; longer still before there is a genuine scare scene—though this is Miike, so when it comes, it is a doozy. Before that, *Audition* could be a Lifetime original movie, or the setup for a romantic comedy—which, of course, when we consider the manipulative and objectifying nature of the film's central premise, provides a pointed skewer to our notions of romantic films in general.

Much has been written and said about *Audition* in the years since its initial release. Its exploration of gender roles both in Japan specifically and in society at large has been the subject of extensive essays by better minds than mine. Yet re-watching it now, in the midst of the #MeToo movement, it seems impossible to discuss it without also writing at least a little about those subjects.

They are inextricably interwoven into the fabric of what could, at a glance, be nothing more than another example of "torture porn"—a phrase which hadn't been coined yet when *Audition* was released, and which Anton Bitel argues, in the booklet accompanying the Arrow Video Blu-ray, could have nothing to do with *Audition*, having "emerged very specifically from Western anxieties over the methods their nations were using abroad in the aftermath of 9/11."

Like so many who saw *Audition* all those years ago, it was the horror scenes which were seared into my brain so that I remembered them vividly—yes, even viscerally—almost two decades later, with an intensity that couldn't be dulled by time or distance or dozens, even hundreds, of other, often much more graphic horror movies.

Yet even in the film's infamous torture sequence, which Robin Wood describes as "almost as unwatchable as the news reels—of Auschwitz, of the innocent victims of Hiroshima and Nagasaki and Vietnam," we actually see very little. The suffering and horror are conveyed to us instead through sound, through Aoyama's flailing and through Asami's singsong repetition.

## AUDITION (1999)

Revisiting *Audition* for the first time in almost 20 years, I was struck by how little of what we see can be considered objectively real. Once the film's horror has been revealed to us, our protagonist's search for Asami takes on the strangely-lit unreality of a giallo film, and many of the picture's horror sequences—such as a surreal shot of a flapping tongue, fingers, and an ear—take place entirely in his mind.

In fact, an argument can be made that the film's entire second half is a dream sequence, an argument bolstered by the ways in which chronologies shift, break down and bleed into one another during the film's climax. Whether or not that is the case, however, it seems undeniable that the horrors of *Audition* are as much internal as external.

Part of the genius of *Audition* is the way in which it makes the audience complicit in Aoyama's wrongdoing. We like him, even while we know that the whole audition idea is skin-crawlingly dishonest and predatory. We allow ourselves to excuse him because *he* seems just as uncomfortable with it as we are. "I feel like a criminal," he says to his friend as they sit down to begin auditioning the girls. He knows that what he is doing is wrong, but he does it anyway.

When he is going through the applications, he turns his deceased wife's photo away. His nervousness is almost boyish—a kid slicking back his hair and fidgeting with his bowtie as he waits on the front step to take his date to prom—but it doesn't stop him from going through with the plan. It doesn't stop him from pursuing Asami and it doesn't stop him from lying to her. He is given opportunities to come clean, to maybe repair some of the damage of his actions, but he never takes them.

Yet the film doesn't judge him harshly for these acts. It leaves that to his own conscience. Through things like his relationship with his son, we see Aoyama as just a person. "All the characters in this are just regular folks," they say on the Blu-ray's commentary track, "but regular folks have dark sides."

Undoubtedly, there has been considerable scholarship dedicated to sorting out the "correct" interpretation of the movie's puzzle pieces, but for me, the question of what is real and what isn't is less interesting than the tension that is created by not knowing. Whether Asami is a vengeful sadist forged by a lifetime of abuse and sexual predation, or whether she is lying in bed beside Aoyama while he is tormented by nightmares of his own making, the horrors of the film are a direct result of his actions and it leaves us with the unshakable feeling that he wouldn't deny that he deserves this suffering.

"Am I allowed to feel so happy?" Asami asks in what might be a dream sequence or a memory or reality intruding on a nightmare. Whatever else may be true in *Audition*, it is clear that Aoyama *isn't* allowed to be happy, not yet, and he has no one to blame but himself. "Aoyama ends up like he does," Miike says in one of the commentary tracks included with the Blu-ray, "and he is responsible for that."

**Author's Note:** I rarely rate *Audition* as one of my favorite movies, for reasons that are probably fairly obvious if you've already read this far, but there's no denying that it's one that has stuck with me like few others have.

**Originally published May 2019**
*Signal Horizon*

# "SORRY, I DON'T GO IN FOR SCIENCE FICTION."
# —*THE ANDROMEDA STRAIN* (1971)

Before *Westworld*. Before *Jurassic Park*. Before that movie where Tom Selleck fights mechanical spiders. *The Andromeda Strain* was the first time a novel by Michael Crichton was adapted to the big screen.

Crichton's name wasn't what drew me to this Blu-ray, though. For that, look no further than director Robert Wise.

While Wise is probably best known as the director of some famous musicals (*The Sound of Music*; *West Side Story*) or even other science fiction pictures (*The Day the Earth Stood Still*; *Star Trek: The Motion Picture*), I knew him from his very earliest films with producer Val Lewton; *Curse of the Cat People* and *The Body Snatcher*, not to mention his 1963 version of *The Haunting*, which remains one of my favorite haunted house flicks.

On *The Andromeda Strain*, Wise was joined by screenwriter Nelson Gidding, who had previously worked with him on *The Haunting* and others. The result is a film that I have seen called "the antithesis of the modern blockbuster," which I think is both accurate and inaccurate at once.

After all, this is adapted from a Crichton novel, so the structure is pretty much *exactly* that of a modern blockbuster: A potentially global threat manifests itself and a handful of people who have just the right qualifications for the job (all of them American, of course) work tirelessly to haul humanity back from the brink of annihilation.

What sets *The Andromeda Strain* apart from its contemporary relatives is that the band of heroes working to save the day aren't soldiers or fighter pilots or even politicians; they are all middle-aged scientists.

And not discredited crackpots who turn out to have been right all along, either. Respected experts at the top of their fields. And with one dramatic exception, all of the "action" in the film is mostly just them doing fairly mundane science, albeit with extremely high stakes, so expect lots of shots of people looking at monitors and adjusting microscopes.

It is this meticulousness that *really* sets *Andromeda* apart. While there are a few lasers before all is said and done, there aren't any explosions, and the science is, if not accurate, then at least all very straight-faced. (It may also be accurate, too, or may have been in 1971. I'm not a scientist.)

In fact, when the movie was released, a study guide was commissioned by Universal and distributed to high schools to help teachers use the film in their classes. This study guide is reproduced in the booklet that accompanies the new Arrow Video Blu-ray, and, of course, when I saw it, I immediately thought of *Signal Horizon*, where horror and the classroom are rarely far apart.

While *The Andromeda Strain* has the skeleton of a disaster film, much of it plays out like a procedural. We *watch* people watching screens intently, going through step after step of sterilization, interacting with things only through layers of containment.

How do you keep such a hands-off movie interesting, let alone thrilling? While some may debate whether or not Wise accomplishes the latter, and certainly you need to have a patience for these kinds of meticulous "grown up" movies in order to really enjoy *Andromeda Strain*, the former seems undeniable, thanks to an array of tools that Wise has for the job, starting with the Oscar-nominated set design.

According to that aforementioned study guide, the Wildfire lab, which serves as the setting for most of the film, was patterned after NASA's real-life receiving lunar lab in Houston, Texas. The result is a top-secret, five-level underground facility hidden beneath a USDA agricultural research center in the Nevada desert. Each level of the facility is a color-coded ring that wouldn't look at all out of place in *2001* or an episode of *Star Trek*.

Besides the set design, *The Andromeda Strain* also received an Oscar nod for film editing. The booklet that accompanies the Blu-ray refers to the film's split-screen effects as "a rare stylistic misstep," yet it seems unreasonable to assume that they didn't go at least some distance towards that Academy Award nomination.

Another tool to help keep *The Andromeda Strain* ticking along is its unorthodox soundtrack. Composed by Gil Mellé, who also worked on such classic horror TV shows as *Night Gallery* and *Kolchak*, the score for *The Andromeda Strain* is composed mostly of the beeps, boops, and whirrs of early computers. According to the booklet, Wise advised Mellé to "avoid any sounds that called to mind actual instruments." If it sounded too much like music, Mellé was supposed to cut it out.

Surprisingly, for a movie that was designed to be cutting-edge in 1971, *The Andromeda Strain* doesn't feel as dated as many science fiction movies that have been made since. This may be because it isn't attempting to portray a far-flung future, but a possible present, where "present" includes 1971.

In addition to discussion topics, the study guide contains some behind-the-scenes information on the film, including a cold-bloodedly casual revelation that may make *The Andromeda Strain* a little difficult for modern animal lovers to watch.

"The animals in this film did not die," the study guide assures us, referring to the lab animals which are exposed to the titular strain of alien microbes. "Their oxygen was briefly cut off during the shooting, and a team of physicians hurriedly revived them after each 'take.'" Probably not an explanation that would fly today.

*The Andromeda Strain* is also a reminder that, along with our ideas about the ethical treatment of screen animals, movie ratings have changed since 1971, too. Given its depiction of many, *many* dead bodies, some of whom died by suicide, not to mention its apocalyptic stakes and repeated discussion of nuclear options, it seems unlikely that *The Andromeda Strain* would get by with its "G" rating if it were released today.

Ultimately, *The Andromeda Strain*'s attempt at straight-faced science keeps it from ever venturing into the weird fictional extravagances that are our bailiwick here at *Signal Horizon,* but that doesn't mean there aren't some moments of cosmic horror to be had.

Mellé's score is always disconcerting, and as the scientists coolly discuss the possibility that intelligent life in outer space may be so dissimilar to terrestrial life that we wouldn't even recognize it as life at all, it's difficult to deny that themes of cosmic horror are in play.

**Author's Note:** Calling *The Andromeda Strain* "horror" is perhaps a bit of a stretch, but claiming that it *isn't* horror is even more of one.

**Originally published June 2019**
*Unwinnable*

## NOW SHE'LL BE ALL ALONE: THE AMERICAN HORROR PROJECT VOLUME 2

"We are all haunted by things other than the dead."
—*Dream No Evil* (1970)

I missed out on the first volume of Arrow Video's *American Horror Project*. There's no story here, I just wasn't aware of it at the time it came out. So, when the opportunity to review the second volume came up, I jumped on it.

The first thing that attracted me to the *American Horror Project* set was not anything to do with the movies inside, which I had never so much as heard of. It was how great the set looks. Shallow confession: I am a sucker for good packaging. It's one of the things that keeps me addicted to physical media in an increasingly digital age.

Arrow always delivers in the packaging department, and this set is no exception. The muddy artwork that is a sort of composite mosaic of scenes from each picture is rendered in such vibrant colors that it knocks that muddiness right out the window. It's a striking aesthetic, to be sure.

Based just on the movies contained in this set, it also fits the series nicely. Nothing in here is ever quite as lurid as those covers may look, with the possible exception of *The Child*, but that was true of their original posters, too, which are available as alternative art on the other side of the sleeve.

## Dream No Evil (1970)

Ever wonder what it would have been like if Tennessee Williams had been tapped to write an AIP shocker in his waning years? I give you *Dream No Evil*. Also known as *Now I Lay Me Down to Die*, this sunny gothic was helmed by John Hayes, whose other directorial credits include low-budget horror pictures like *Garden of the Dead* and *Grave of the Vampire*, but also titles like *Jailbait Babysitter* and *Heterosexualis*.

In the essay that accompanies the *American Horror Project* Blu-ray set from Arrow Video, Amanda Reyes points out that *Dream No Evil* probably played in "sleazy 42nd Street type venues or drive-ins," where the audiences must have been very disappointed in what they saw. Indeed, even more contemporary reviews haven't always been kind to this dreamy and glacially-paced film. *The Video Vacuum*, for example, calls *Dream No Evil* "just another tame '70s psychological horror flick."

Tame it most certainly is, and psychological as well, but that "just another" implies that there were boundless horror movies this fundamentally disinterested in their horror premise being released in the '70s, which doesn't seem to be borne out by at least my experience with the genre. That said, the basic elements of *Dream No Evil* all seem familiar enough:

A young girl grows up in an orphanage dreaming that one day her father will come and rescue her. It is here that the voiceover narration begins, giving *Dream No Evil* the feel of a contemporary fairy tale, telling us that her "innocent dream" will become "a bridge to horror."

She is adopted into a "once-respectable" church which has been turned into a "carnival" by its new proprietor and her adopted brother Paul Jessie Bundy, played fantastically by Hayes regular Michael Pataki. There she grows up into a lovely redhead (Brooke Mills) who performs a high dive act as part of the traveling church's faith healing demonstrations, falling into the metaphorical fires of hell in a skimpy, sequined outfit for the edification of audiences.

In her essay, Reyes argues that the film condemns this sort of charlatanry, but I was actually surprised at how sympathetically it was portrayed. I spent probably half the movie waiting for Pataki's Reverend Jessie to turn into a villain, especially as the film sets up a love triangle—quadrangle, really—with Mills' character engaged to her *other* adopted brother, who has abandoned the church to go to medical school and who is gradually falling for a fellow student and more modern woman.

That sounds like a lot—*and it is*—but really none of it is the film's focus. You see, Mills' character is still obsessed with finding her father, which she thinks she does when the traveling church stops at a town where he once lived.

There, she goes to a frightening flophouse where aged women of the night are dispatched by a polite yet slightly sinister pimp/undertaker to comfort silent old men—it both isn't as weird as it sounds and is even weirder. The undertaker (played by character actor Marc Lawrence) says that he was a friend of her father's, but that he died just the day before.

He takes her to his dilapidated brothel/funeral home—which is located in one of the strangest buildings I have ever seen in a film—so that she can view the body, and there her faith healing powers bring her father (played by Edmond O'Brien, the film's biggest star) back to life in probably the movie's most effective horror moment. Unfortunately, that voiceover narration comes barging back in here, informing you without a doubt that none of this is real and that Mills' character has simply retreated into a world of fantasy.

To a modern viewer, that would probably have become clear soon enough anyway, but there's no denying that the voiceover—apparently added in by meddling producers, to the surprise of no one—makes a mess of what is otherwise a strangely effective film, if not particularly effective at being horrific.

The horror elements come as Mills' character commits

murders—which she thinks are being committed by her father—in order to protect the fantasy that she has created. But the film seems far less interested in those killings than it does in her own fragile psyche; which is probably both why Amanda Reyes can call it "a very special film, indeed," in her essay and why viewers who watched it in a DVD set called the "Psychotronica Collection," where it is available from Amazon, may have been sorely disappointed.

## *Dark August* (1976)

The most striking thing about *Dark August* is its regionalism. So legendary *Swamp Thing* artist Stephen R. Bissette implicitly argues in the essay that accompanies the Blu-ray, the lion's share of which is devoted to discussions of this and other films that were shot in and around his native Vermont.

In this way, *Dark August* actually reminded me a bit of the original *Friday the 13th*, which was filmed in New Jersey, not Vermont, but which nonetheless manages to contain that same sense of regional filmmaking. As the Jersey countryside was in *Friday the 13th*, the Vermont hills are a character in *Dark August*, every bit as much as (and maybe more than) its human protagonists.

*Dark August* is no slasher film, though. Not even a *Psycho*-alike proto-slasher, as was *Dream No Evil*. Instead, it is a full-bore folk horror, every bit as much as its contemporaries across the pond, which eventually gave us the term, though it hadn't been coined yet in 1976 and, indeed, wouldn't be for decades. In fact, *Dark August* has essentially the same plot as the 1988 Lance Henriksen monster movie *Pumpkinhead*, albeit told the other way around and with a lot less monster.

"Flatlander" Sal Devito (J.J. Barry) is an outsider from the big city who has settled in rural Vermont for less than a year when he accidentally runs down a young girl. Her grandfather places a curse on him, and it is the working out of this curse that provides the film's horror.

Though the curse invokes "Baal" and his "demon cohort," the trappings of it are pure folk magic, which we see in a slow pan across resin, wax, spent matches and dried seed husks. All of this is just moments into the movie. In fact, when we meet our ostensible protagonist, the deed has already been done, and he has been acquitted of any wrongdoing. It isn't until almost half an hour into the film that we actually see the accident in flashback.

Where *Pumpkinhead* placed its sympathy heavily with Henriksen's bereaved father, in *Dark August* we are ostensibly supposed to root for Sal—and the film, at least, does a good job of humanizing him, even if, as Bissette points out, Sal still "embodies the worst of 'flatlander' misbehavior and belligerence." Ultimately, it's as much Sal's machismo—what we would today identify as "toxic masculinity"—that undoes him as the old man's curse.

Sal simply lacks the mental or emotional tools to deal with the guilt of his deed—let alone the curse that is that guilt's concrete manifestation—and it lies with the "white magic" of women to provide his only conceivable means of salvation. ("There's a very good woman who is going to help you through this.")

Wrapped around Sal's dissolution is a fascinatingly-wrought if extremely slow-moving regional folk horror that could have been one of the "elevated horror" films that we're getting in the theaters these days, albeit less polished and with a lower budget.

And I haven't even mentioned the amazing soundscape.

### *The Child* (1977)

"What the hell did I just watch?" is a sentiment normally reserved for more gonzo movies than anything that *The Child* ever even strives for, but it's appropriate enough here. One user on *Letterboxd* calls it "a paperback gothic cover come thrillingly alive," which is also a good description.

Slow and dreamy is apparently the order of the day in this particular installment of the *American Horror Project*, and *The Child* is no exception—a picture at once stranger and more traditionally "horror" than either of the films that accompany it. The plot is certainly something straight out of a paperback gothic, with a governess who comes to a big, dark house in the woods to care for the strange and morbid little girl who spends most of her time in the nearby cemetery hanging out with her "friends."

That's not some kind of metaphor or a lonely little girl's imagination, either. This cemetery is haunted by actual ghouls and/or walking corpses, a fact that is apparent before the credits even finish rolling, when we see the little girl handing one of them a kitten. While it takes a long time before the ghouls come bobbing into full sight, their presence is always felt around the edges of the frame, even as the entire atmosphere is eerie and oppressive enough to render them all but unnecessary.

The woods in *The Child* remind me a lot of how vegetation sometimes appears menacing and claustrophobic in old paintings, while the cemetery is blown by a constant pall of the requisite fog. The wind incessantly rattles the leaves and pushes the clouds through the sky overhead. The day-for-night shots add to the visual disquiet and the night shots are so dark and grainy that they take on the quality of found footage.

Filmed mainly on "short ends," the bits of film stock that are left over when another movie is done shooting, *The Child* is one of those films that has an uncanny effectiveness because of—rather than despite—the qualities that would otherwise make it not as good.

Disorienting cinematography, head-scratching close-ups and hand-held shots, dubbed-in dialogue performed as if the characters are repeating memorized speeches in separate rooms, a soundtrack that is mostly a lot of heavy banging on the piano and discordant notes. (The music is credited to Muckandmire Music Company, which sounds about right.) Instead of reducing the power of the film, these things weave themselves into *The Child*'s oppressive atmosphere to give the whole proceeding an air that it would lose if the same stuff was shot "better."

Does that mean *The Child* is good? I'm not here to decide that for you. What I'll tell you is this: Zombie hands grab an old lady's ankle from under the stairs, the young governess dances with a scarecrow and there's a lengthy sequence set on Halloween that features a creepy rotating jack-o-lantern. By now, you're either sold or you're not, and nothing else I can say matters very much.

\*\*\*

If "slow and dreamy" is antithetical to your enjoyment of horror movies, you will want to give this set a wide berth. If it is practically a requisite, then have I got a trio of movies for you! For everyone else, mileage will vary from one title to another and the price tag on this set means that it's probably best reserved for die-hard fans of regional and cult horror cinema.

Even if I didn't love any of the films contained in this set, though—and I might have loved *The Child*, I honestly couldn't tell you—there's no doubt that Arrow is doing the proverbial lord's work by giving such loving, hi-def releases to these kinds of underseen films. While these movies will not be for everyone—or, indeed, probably for most—there's someone out there who is waiting for a film just like each one of them, and they might never have gotten a chance to see them if it hadn't been for releases like this.

**Author's Note:** My reviewing format continues to evolve, as I tackle one of the first boxed sets I ever got for review, utilizing more or less that same format that I would continue to the time of this writing: A few paragraphs of introduction, followed by a separate entry for each film contained therein. The quotes that would later lead into each movie are here just one quote at the beginning, but we're getting there.

**Originally published July 2019**
*Signal Horizon*

# "DID YOU MAKE A GOOD CONFESSION?"
# *ALICE, SWEET ALICE* (1976)

What if *Halloween* was *Carrie* was also a Hitchcockian psychodrama? That elevator pitch might be a little reductive, but it'll also get you pretty close to the ballpark of Alfred Sole's unlikely masterpiece, *Alice, Sweet Alice*.

Shot in 1975 in Sole's hometown of Paterson, New Jersey—a town that had just turned on Sole after the release of his erotic first film, *Deep Sleep*—and set in 1961, *Alice, Sweet Alice* owes a heavy (and acknowledged) debt to the films of Alfred Hitchcock. (See, for example, a shot of a coffin in front of a poster for *Psycho*.)

*Alice, Sweet Alice* has also been called the most "gialloesque" American movie of all time, and Sole himself has admitted to being inspired by Nicolas Roeg's classic *Don't Look Now*. All of these observations help to convey what the experience of watching *Alice, Sweet Alice* is like, help to place the film in a broader cultural context, but they also run the risk of downplaying the unclassifiable originality of Sole's film.

According to the booklet that accompanies the new Arrow Video Blu-ray of *Alice*, Sole's debut was "Little more than a low-budget porno produced by an eager young filmmaker desperate to get a foot in the door." *Deep Sleep* unfortunately did much more than that. It was prosecuted under obscenity charges in Sole's hometown, resulting in a highly publicized court case.

Sole was hit with a weighty fine and a prohibition against filming anything for two years. Perhaps more relevant to the creation of *Alice, Sweet Alice*, he was also excommunicated from the Roman

Catholic Diocese in which he had grown up.

Neither Paterson nor the Catholic church come off very well in *Alice*. The palette of the film is mostly all grays and browns, especially in exteriors, where the city seems almost aggressively dilapidated. Water stains mar the walls, abandoned industrial buildings loom large, and rain beats down but cannot wash the city clean. When the characters aren't being menaced by religious iconography, the backgrounds feature signs for fallout shelters.

The church fares even worse. "From one scene to the next, religious iconography overwhelms the screen," Sheila O'Malley writes at *Film Comment*, "paintings of Mary and Christ, marble statues, crosses on every wall, religion leering at the characters from behind." O'Malley goes on to note that, "Religion is not a refuge in *Alice, Sweet Alice*. It is a rejection of the body itself, but the body—its tongues, its teeth, its menstruation—will not be denied."

Also known by a handful of other titles—in the new 2K transfer on the Arrow Video Blu it goes by the original title, *Communion*—*Alice* has been called overtly anti-Catholic, and it certainly doesn't shy away from portraying religion in an unflattering light. When it was rereleased in 1981, to cash in on the rising popularity of Brooke Shields—who makes her feature film debut here, as the young girl whose murder kicks off the film's horror—it was called *Holy Terror*.

*Alice* frequently gets classed as a slasher film—it was ranked #4 on *Complex*'s list of the best slasher films of all time, where it was beaten out only by the original *Nightmare on Elm Street*, *Black Christmas*, and *Halloween*. The reason for this categorization seems pretty obvious: the killer wears a distinctive mask, in this case a sort of translucent plastic mask with a made-up facsimile of a female face and, at one point, a twist-nudging other mask beneath that one.

For a slasher, though, *Alice* is… not necessarily bloodless, but certainly low on body count. In fact, the movie is more than halfway over before the second murder is committed, though in between there is perhaps the film's most disturbing set piece, a stabbing that doesn't lead to death, though not for lack of giallo-red blood.

While the film wants you to wonder whether a 12-year-old girl could really be the perpetrator of such heinous deeds—anyone who has ever known a 12-year-old of any gender knows the answer to this question already—it is obvious pretty early on that Alice can't be the killer, because Alice as the killer is *too* obvious.

Unfortunately, *Alice, Sweet Alice* is at its best before the identity of the killer is revealed. Afterward, things take an even more Hitchcockian turn, with a few "bomb under the table" sequences where characters don't know that they're in danger while the audience definitely does. But certainties are rarely as intriguing as ambiguity, and *Alice* is a prime example.

Still, even when it has been revealed that Alice isn't the culprit, she isn't entirely cleared, either. One of the most fascinating aspects of *Alice, Sweet Alice* is its portrayal of the title character. Played by then-19-year-old Paula E. Sheppard, Alice is a neglected and almost certainly disturbed young girl who is surrounded by people who are supposed to be more "normal" than her except that, of course, they aren't.

Alice is neither a sociopath like the *Bad Seed* or the killer kids in *Bloody Birthday* nor entirely an innocent victim caught up in sinister events. She is capable of malevolence, even if she isn't the villain of the piece, but she also feels, in many ways, more human than the "normal" people in her life, who are filled with their own repressed feelings and often played with intentional soap opera histrionics.

The film also provides a constantly-simmering subtext of sexual abuse that never quite boils to the surface, but is also never escapable. Even as characters hypothesize that Alice is the killer, they also sexualize and objectify her, both directly and indirectly.

The slobby landlord of their dingy brownstone (this movie isn't very kind to fat people, either) tries to force himself on Alice; she gets her period and doesn't tell her mother; when the police are hooking her up to a polygraph, the technician says, "When I was putting the tube around her, it was like she wanted me to feel her up."

This same kind of objectification and projection plays into the motives of the killer, who is punishing those within the congregation she sees as sinful. "Children pay for the sins of the parents," she says, by way of explanation for her actions.

Everyone in *Alice, Sweet Alice* is simmering in a stew of repression and conflicting psychological—and sometimes psychosexual—impulses, none of which are entirely resolved by the time the film ends on a chilling freeze-frame of Alice looking straight at the camera.

The Arrow Video Blu-ray looks great and comes with a raft of extras including featurettes, commentary tracks, even an alternate TV cut of the film. Besides the booklet and reversible sleeve, the Blu-ray also features a poster with a "killer kit" on the back, including a yellow slicker, white gloves, creepy mask, and bloody knife. "Now you can be the killer you've always wanted to be!!"

**Author's Note:** Receiving Blu-rays more or less at random for review means that I have watched a lot of movies that I might not otherwise have seen. *Alice, Sweet Alice* remains one of the best of them.

**Originally published August 2019**
*Unwinnable*

# ONE DAY THIS CITY'S GONNA EXPLODE: FRIEDKIN'S *CRUISING* (1980) ON BLU-RAY

*Cruising* is one of those films whose legend is far more famous than the film itself. In 1979, when William Friedkin was beginning production on *Cruising*, *Village Voice* columnist Arthur Bell—whose own accounts of unsolved murders in New York's gay nightlife served as partial inspiration for the film—called upon his readers to "give Friedkin and his production crew a terrible time."

A copy of the screenplay had leaked and the city's gay community was up in arms. The featurettes included with the new Arrow Video Blu-ray of *Cruising* describe throngs of thousands of protesters who took up Bell's advice to give the production a "terrible time" by whistling and blasting air horns during takes, standing on rooftops and using reflectors to shine light down onto the set, even renting apartments next door and blaring loud music. Anything and everything to disrupt production.

Even before *Cruising* had finished filming, Bell was already calling it "the most oppressive, ugly, bigoted look at homosexuality ever present on the screen, the worst possible nightmare of the most uptight straight." This was the pall under which *Cruising* was filmed and the controversy to which it premiered—to poor contemporary reviews and disappointing box office performance.

The problems with *Cruising* weren't limited to controversy, either. After its release, it was linked to hate crimes, including a mass shooting targeting patrons of The Ramrod, one of the bars featured prominently in the film.

With all this background in mind, I was nervous to check out Friedkin's *Cruising* all these years later. So, was Bell right? Is *Cruising* homophobic? Of course it is, in perhaps the most literal possible sense of the word. The entire film is like one long, sustained note of gay panic; one that the controversial and ambiguous ending only amplifies. The fact that I'm sure the filmmakers didn't mean for it to be only goes so far to ameliorate its problems.

And yet, while it's impossible to write about *Cruising* without also grappling with the controversy that surrounds it, the film's homophobia is in many ways its least interesting feature and, if anything, *Cruising* probably feels *less* controversial now than when it was released.

Maybe that's because mainstream media is less likely to demonize the gay lifestyle today than it was when *Cruising* came out. Reporting on the controversy surrounding the film, *Time* magazine blithely claimed that "homosexual homicides are frequent—and often gruesome."

The National Gay Task Force, in objecting to a profile that the *New York Times* ran on Friedkin, wrote that "in the context of an anti-homosexual society, a film about violent, sex-obsessed gay men would be seen as a film about *all* gay people."

While it's hard to deny that our society is still anti-homosexual, maybe it says something about the progress we've made that the notion that *Cruising* was ever intended to be representative of the lifestyle seems much more far-fetched now than it probably did then.

Friedkin has always argued that there is nothing anti-gay in *Cruising*. Those same featurettes on the Blu-ray point out that Friedkin's crew hired hundreds of members of the New York gay community to fill out the film's many crowded bar scenes, and shot in gay nightclub landmarks like The Ramrod, Anvil, Mine Shaft and Eagle's Nest—at least, until some of them banned Friedkin and his crew from entering.

Nearly forty years later, *Cruising* remains notable for its frank depiction of gay sex—a sequence of implied fisting stands out as particularly *risqué*—but is perhaps even more striking as a time capsule of a moment, captured almost by accident.

There's a scene in the eighth episode of the first season of the TV series *Community* when Pierce (played by Chevy Chase) says, "I tell you, before AIDS, sex was like shaking hands."

"Hence AIDS," Abed replies.

The first cases of AIDS were clinically reported in the United States in 1981, just over a year after *Cruising* made its theatrical debut. Shooting in real bars in New York City's Meatpacking District, using real locals as extras, *Cruising*'s hot and sweaty, tightly-packed and hedonistically lurid bar scenes feel less like a statement about the gay community and more like the last gasp of an era of heightened sexual abandon. After all, the knife-wielding killer of *Cruising* could never claim as many lives as HIV would in the coming years.

It's also unusual to see the male body so aggressively sexualized in a mainstream movie—even today, when Laura Mulvey's concept of the "male gaze," first explored shortly before *Cruising* was filmed, permeates much of our critical discourse on film.

While *Cruising* never goes so far as to hang dong*, there are acres of sweaty flesh on display, and the camera's lingering gaze is every bit as smoldering as the come-hither looks that are thrown left and right. The fact that this serves to Other and objectify the gay men in the film adds to the film's problematic nature, but also serves as an odd counterpoint to the "male gaze" typically found in movies like this.

If anything, the men who haunt these landmarks are portrayed as hyper-masculine. "Even the most 'female' specimens boast Iron Man bodies under their Marilyn-like cascades of long blonde locks," F.X. Feeney writes in the booklet that accompanies the Blu-ray.

Friedkin had already passed on adapting *Cruising* from the 1970 novel of the same name several years before. It took an unlikely confluence of events to rekindle his interest. One was Arthur Bell's own columns about murders in New York's gay community, but another was Paul Bateson, who had appeared, briefly, as a radiology tech in *The Exorcist*.

In 1979, Bateson confessed to killing film journalist Addison Verrill after what Bateson described as a drunken one-night stand. Bateson was also suspected, but never charged, in a series of "trash bag murders," in which the dismembered bodies of gay men were found floating in the Hudson River, wrapped in garbage bags.

Friedkin obtained permission to interview Bateson in prison, and incorporated elements of his story into *Cruising*. "The unexplained deaths and brutal murders aroused my curiosity," Friedkin said. "The devil was at work."

That line about the devil may be a cheeky nod to the film that Friedkin is best known for, but it also gives you some idea of what you can expect from *Cruising*, if it's possible to watch it out from beneath the oppressive cloud of its homophobia and controversy.

*Cruising* feels almost like a supernatural serial killer flick—something caught midway between the deadly elegance of a giallo and a sleazy proto-slasher like William Lustig's *Maniac*, with which it also shares actor Joe Spinell. (If you want to immediately conjure the 42nd Street vibe of New York at the beginning of the '80s, just cast Joe Spinell.)

There is a taut intensity in almost every aspect of the film that is hard to beat and almost impossible to deny. Whatever else you can say about *Cruising*, it is absolutely stunning in its new 4K scan—beautiful as only lovingly restored films from the past can be. Just look at how gorgeous the lighting is in the park scenes that lead up to the film's final confrontation.

The controversial twist may have been discovered in the cutting room, as Friedkin claims, but it also feels inevitable, echoing, as it does, an anecdote told to Friedkin by Bateson; "If I confess to eight or nine more murders, they'll reduce my sentence."

That ending, which was widely rejected by critics at the time, not to mention star Al Pacino, serves to amp up the film's notes of gay panic considerably, as I said, but it also does something else—it gives *Cruising* a sense of scale that reaches beyond its own events, a dissolute grandeur that helps to elevate it beyond the confines in which it might otherwise have found itself mired.

\* At least, not in the print that exists, though the film's outsized legend claims that upwards of forty minutes was cut to bring the film in at an "R" rating. These fabled cut minutes went on to inspire their own film, Travis Mathews and James Franco's *Interior. Leather Bar.*

**Author's Note:** I was extremely nervous about writing this review, and I spent a lot of time workshopping it, compared to many of the others in this book, entirely because Friedkin's frankly rather phenomenal film is so very controversial—for such very good reasons.

**Originally published September 2019**
*Unwinnable*

# "THAT'S A RECIPE FOR ROMANCE": THE NORMAN J. WARREN COLLECTION

Not that long ago, I was hired to make a list of horror movies that take place on New Year's—turns out there's more of them than you'd think. In the process, I learned a little more about *Bloody New Year*, a film whose box art I recognized from my days haunting the aisles of video rental places but which I had never actually seen, having written it off as another in a long line of seasonal slashers, a subgenre I hadn't yet learned to appreciate at the time.

What I uncovered in my research was enough to convince me that I needed to see *Bloody New Year* right away. So, a few months later, when I learned that Indicator was putting out a boxed set of films by cult director Norman J. Warren—including *Bloody New Year*—I figured this was the ideal time to check it out.

Prior to sitting down with the set, I hadn't ever seen any of Warren's films—not these, nor the earlier sex films on which he got his start. Besides that bit of research into *Bloody New Year*, I hadn't read much about them. So, I didn't really know what to expect, beyond what I could tell from lurid titles like *Inseminoid* and *Satan's Slave*.

What I quickly came to learn was that all five of these films share several unmistakable qualities in common, even while they bounce around from one horror subgenre to the next—cashing in on whatever was popular at the moment they were made.

All of them are British. All of them are shot on shoestring budgets, and it shows. Most of them feature a surprising amount of full-frontal female nudity—possibly a holdover from Warren's early days making softcore films. And all of them are more effective than their limited budgets and cash-grab premises should allow.

Because *Bloody New Year* was the movie that had initially attracted me to the collection, I decided to check it out first, even though it's the most recent film in the set, which spans a decade beginning with *Satan's Slave* in '76, and to work my way backward from there.

### Think About Time Like a River: *Bloody New Year* (1987)

According to IMDb, *Bloody New Year* is Norman J. Warren's last feature film as director. Nevertheless, it seems like a good place to start in his oeuvre because, while it is *definitely* set in the '80s, it also feels like a creature out of time—just like its ghouls.

See, the premise of *Bloody New Year* kicks off simply enough: After stumbling into some trouble at a fun fair by the beach, our teen protagonists make their way to a nearby island where their boat capsizes and sinks.

Once on the island, they find a hotel that's decorated for Christmas and New Year's, even though it's the beginning of July. Everything in the hotel is straight out of the 1950s, but nothing seems old or dusty. Then even weirder things start to happen.

Of course, those of us in the audience know that something is very wrong long before the kids do. After all, we're aware that we're watching a horror movie, while they still think they're in a beach blanket bingo type scenario, pissed-off carnies notwithstanding. But we've also been treated to the black-and-white shots of a New Year's Eve party in the hotel, ringing in the year 1960—a New Year's Eve party where we know that *something* went terribly wrong.

In spite of the "killer POV" shots that start pretty much as soon as the kids get to the island, though, *Bloody New Year* is far from a typical slasher film. There's certainly a body count, along with the kind of shot-on-video gore that you might expect. Arms get ripped or chopped off with some regularity. A guy's head is demolished (offscreen) by a boat propeller. Hatchets chop into mannequin skulls and papier mâché heads explode. But for all that, *Bloody New Year* has more in common with an Italian spook show like *Ghosthouse* than it does *Friday the 13th*.

It doesn't spend much time pretending otherwise, either. A figure that is (to the audience) clearly a ghost shows up by the 20-minute mark. But something more than "just" a haunting is going on here, too. A TV playing a 1950s talk show gives us the background, as much as we'll ever get, anyway. It seems that, on New Year's Eve in 1959, the government tested an experimental anti-radar device. One that had the power to bend light—and also time. The plane carrying the device crash landed on the island and the rest is history. Or isn't, as the case may be.

This delightfully bizarre conceit keeps *Bloody New Year*—which was also released as *Time Warp Terror*—hopping. Even before our leads get to the island, there's a chase through the fun fair that culminates on a ghost train. In the hotel, the kids watch the end of *Fiend Without a Face* before a home movie kicks on and a guy dressed as a sheik leaps out of the screen to attack them before folding himself up and disappearing into the lens of the projector!

There are attacks by film stock (a trick Warren had previously used almost a decade earlier in *Terror*); there's quicksand and a seaweed monster that comes up out of the surface of a table; there's an invisible plane crash and unseen laughter and *Evil Dead*-style camera swoops; there are banisters that come to life and a blizzard indoors. And before all is said and done, there are plenty of sand-faced ghouls. Really, what more could you ask for?

### Internal Disturbance: *Inseminoid* (1981)

Even after the extreme weirdness of *Bloody New Year*, there were plenty of surprises waiting for me in *Inseminoid*. The first was seeing Run Run Shaw's name in the credits—according to IMDb, he "presents" the film, whatever that means.

The next was that *Inseminoid* is *way* less sordid than its sleaze-o-rama title would imply. It isn't even the most graphic movie in this set. (*Horrorplanet*, its alternate title, isn't a whole lot more representative, though I want to borrow it for an album title from some imaginary horror-themed metal band.)

My next surprise was that *Inseminoid* is actually pretty tense and atmospheric, as extremely low-rent *Alien* knock-offs go. Given that they didn't have a lot to work with besides colored lights, some rocks, and a few pieces of corrugated sheet metal, it's pretty impressive.

Sure, there are a couple of largely immobile alien puppets, but they don't get a ton of screen time. Most of the threat comes from the impregnated Sandy, played by Judy Geeson, who has most recently shown up in a couple of Rob Zombie flicks. Here, she gives a delightfully unhinged performance consisting of a lot of screaming, face-pulling, and crying. It's almost enough to make you forgive that you *could* be getting a monster instead.

I'm not going to argue that *Inseminoid* is *feminist* or anything approaching it, but it does have a surprising amount of gender parity. Unfortunately, it *doesn't* have H.R. Giger doing production designs, so the crew does the best they can with rocks and red light, plastic coolers and clunky television monitors.

Other directors attempting to rip off *Alien* with such meager resources might not even try, but Warren throws in everything from a mine car chase to giallo-inspired kills to a surreal impregnation scene that's equal parts *2001* and *Rosemary's Baby*, albeit with about 1/1000th the budget of either.

### Something That Frightened Him to Death: *Terror* (1978)

Someone (or something) is knocking off the cast and crew of a low-budget horror flick—not to mention people only tangentially *related* to said cast and crew—in this amiable British take on the supernatural giallo.

Norman J. Warren has apparently admitted that he had just seen *Suspiria* when he was making this movie, and it shows, even if *Terror* isn't really much like *Suspiria* except in that it only makes a little sense, there's witches involved, and Warren is sure to break out the colored gel before all is said and done. (In one kill sequence, a piece of glass even forms a guillotine straight out of Argento's playbook.)

Like most of the other films in this set, *Terror* is somehow a lot more effective than its meager budget and nonsensical screenplay should allow. It's also surprisingly ambitious in its set pieces, even compared to some of the more expensive films that it's aping—see one bit with a car levitating among the treetops, in particular. (Chewbacca himself, Peter Mayhew, also shows up as a mechanic in one of the picture's more effective stalking scenes.)

*Terror* opens with a period sequence of a witch being burned at the stake that will feel familiar to anyone who has seen *City of the Dead*. Then the closing credits roll, and it turns out that we've just been seeing the end of a cheapie horror feature in the Corman/Price/Poe vein.

Except, of course, in this case the feature was based on the real family history of the film's producer, whose bloodline was cursed to the last member by the dying witch. Also, it seems that everyone associated with his ancestral pile—where, of course, the picture was filmed—has met a tragic and violent end.

Naturally, from there, the bodies begin piling up, along with plenty of wind machines and stalk-and-stab sequences. Sometimes, the people die as a result of clearly supernatural tomfoolery—a man is attacked by a mass of celluloid, a stage light plunges onto a victim, a car attempts to run down a police officer under its own steam—while other times a gloved killer stabs people with knives or strangles them with piano wire. At least, gloved *hands* stab people with knives. Is there a killer attached to them? Who knows?

Does any of it make sense? Not a ton. The witch handily looks just like the one in the movie, and if she's cursed the bloodline, then why do so many random people get killed? None of that really matters, though. We're here for the weird lighting and the levitating cars, not the scintillating dialogue or the intricate plot.

## It Came from the Sky: *Prey* (1977)

I'm going to go ahead and say it right out of the gate: The constable who sees a dog-faced alien and immediately starts punching the shit out of it deserves a better fate than he gets.

In *Prey*, also known as *Alien Prey*, a "deadly alien shape-shifter infiltrates a country house occupied to two lesbians, and proceeds to study their behavior, for a sinister purpose," according to the IMDb synopsis. That's pretty much what happens, it's true, but it doesn't capture how deeply weird *Prey* is.

The lesbian couple are in an extremely dysfunctional relationship, and the alien, who dubs himself "Anders Anderson" and doesn't know what water is, ultimately acts only marginally less human than the film's human characters. Which may be the only reason why his awkwardly ingratiating himself into their otherwise isolated lives is at all credible.

Jessica is a "caged animal," as the alien himself points out. She vacillates wildly between terrified and giggly, while her lover Jo is a man-hating lesbian caricature who is domineering and possessive and almost certainly killed a guy, a conclusion that Jessica seems to come to early on, then keeps forgetting about and re-remembering as the plot gradually unspools.

There are plenty of strange and stilted scenes as the alien eats rabbits and chickens and foxes while acting as a prop to the confusing melodrama of the women's disintegrating relationship. Jo absolutely melts down when she finds the chickens dead; they dress the alien up in drag and have a party where they play hide and seek; the alien falls into the swan pond in a sequence that culminates in an endless slow-mo shot of them all splashing around while music drones.

It may be the weirdest and cheapest movie in the set, but, like all the others, that weirdness is filled with moments of surprising power and effectiveness, even if the alien just has a smushed nose, red eyes, and pointy teeth in his "true form." Basically, if you ever watched *Xtro* and thought, "Wouldn't it be great if this had more lesbians and an *even smaller* budget," then *Prey* is the movie for you.

### Let's Try the Left Hand: *Satan's Slave* (1976)

Thanks to my decision to watch these in reverse-chronological order, I inadvertently saved the most graphic movie for last. (I am as surprised as you that *Inseminoid* is not the most graphic, but here we are.)

It's also the film with the most star power, thanks to Michael Gough strapping on a hell of a mustache for a turn as a kindly uncle-cum-evil head of a Satanic coven.

That's not really a spoiler, as the movie makes the Satanic shenanigans pretty clear from the jump, starting out with a black mass complete with a great Halloween goat head mask, which takes some of the wind out of the sails of the film's later attempts at "is it all in her head" rug-pulling.

*Satan's Slave* establishes a whole lot of the trademarks that I had, by now, come to expect from the filmography of Norman J. Warren. It's a low-rent take on a subgenre that was in vogue at the time (in this case, the Satanism shocker) that's more successful than should be possible given its extremely modest budget and also-ran premise.

It has lots of full-frontal nudity, a few extremely effective scenes, and it gets a lot of mileage out of an English manor house—the same one that had been used a few years earlier in *Virgin Witch* and would be used again, by Warren, a couple of years later in *Terror*.

*Satan's Slave* is also probably the goriest film in this set. It's got a graphic eyeball stabbing, a knife stuck through someone's mouth, and an extremely grisly jump off a building in which the human body breaks apart like a pastry filled with blood and bone.

Plot-wise, there may not be much in *Satan's Slave* that we haven't already seen before, and it may spend more time spinning its wheels than some of the other films in this set, but, like pretty much every other Warren title I've watched here, it's also surprisingly creepy and often much more effective than should be possible on its meager budget.

There aren't any levitating cars in this one, though, so, I dunno, you take what you can get, I guess.

**Author's Note:** I liked these films enough that I tried to program one of them (*Bloody New Year*) for the monthly free screening that Tyler Unsell and I host at a local indie theater, the Stray Cat Film Center. Unfortunately, I tried to program it in December or January, and it got canceled by a blizzard—the only one we've yet had to cancel, knock on wood.

**Originally published October 2019**
*Unwinnable*

# "I WANT TO TELL YOU A CURIOUS STORY."
# *THE PREY* (1984)

Given the prominently-featured big monster hands on some of the newly-commissioned art for the Arrow Blu-ray, as well as the film's breathless tagline, "It's not human, and it's got an axe!" I can probably be forgiven for hoping that *The Prey* was a slasher movie about Bigfoot, even if the Blu-ray's other new art makes that pretty unlikely.

Then, once the film was underway and we were treated to stock footage of a raging forest fire in what we were told was 1948 and then a cold opening in which our slasher's killing spree appeared to be triggered by his seeing a campfire, could I be blamed for crossing my fingers, at least a little, that I would be getting an actual film version of Smokey Bear as a slasher?

Sadly, our antagonist is neither of these things. He is, instead, a giant "gypsy," possibly named Leo, who was badly burned in said fire as a child and has been stalking the woods around Northpoint ever since. Brought to life thanks to makeup effects by the late John Carl Buechler, our slasher is more Frankenstein's monster than Bigfoot, and the closest we get to Smokey the Slasher is a shot of some Smokey stationery with the reminder that, "Only YOU can prevent forest fires."

Heck, we don't even really see the slasher himself until the very end of the movie, in spite of some early shots of his gross monster hands, and there isn't really much slashing to speak of until the final reel and the film's "blistering, fever pitch finale," as Ewan Cant has it in his enthusiastic summation that accompanies the

Blu-ray release. And talk about misleading taglines! Not only is our antagonist, indeed, probably human, but he doesn't even have an axe beyond that opening scene!

Instead, *The Prey* spends the majority of its runtime on three distinct tracks: following the fairly tame misadventures of our obligatory band of horny young hikers, the parallel path of a park ranger played by none other than Captain Marvel himself Jackson Bostwick from the 1970s *Shazam!* TV series, and copious nature photography.

That nature photography is one of the things that helps distinguish *The Prey* from other run-of-the-mill slashers of the era. For one thing, there's a lot of it, including shots of all kinds of animals, from frogs to vultures and from tarantulas to bears. For another thing, it's almost all pretty good. The wildlife shots are credited to animal wrangler Gary Gero, and for the most part they could have been lifted straight out of a nature documentary.

They aren't just there for flavor, either. As it becomes clear that these kids are being stalked by an unseen presence in the woods, their exchanges are intercut with shots of a spider catching a bug, an owl swooping down on a snake, a snake eating a mouse, and a swarm of ants picking apart a centipede. Maybe not subtle, but effective nonetheless.

One of the strangest aspects of *The Prey*—though perhaps not *that* strange, in the annals of low-budget horror filmmaking—is its patchwork release history. Much of the booklet that accompanies the new Arrow Video Blu-ray is dedicated to piecing together when certain shots of the movie were filmed, and to discussing the various different versions that were released.

If you look up the movie on IMDb and Letterboxd, you'll find it listed under two different release years (1983 and 1984, respectively), never mind that most of the film was shot in 1979 with a 1980 copyright.

Put out by Essex, a company that had, up 'til then, focused mostly on 35mm sex films, *The Prey* was distributed by New

World Pictures, who gave it a brief theatrical release before dumping it somewhat unceremoniously onto home video. Somewhere in there someone got the bright idea of "beefing up" the film with a lengthy flashback sequence ostensibly describing the killer's origins—even though the killer himself is hardly featured in the flashback's unnecessarily large cast of characters—that clocks in at nearly half an hour.

It would be one thing if this additional half-hour was just haphazardly dropped into the film—which it is, awkwardly replacing an admittedly somewhat pointless campfire retelling of "The Monkey's Paw," one of several long and head-scratching cul-de-sacs in this fairly brief film—but they also went back in and *cut out* several sequences for this "international" release, most of them that aforementioned nature photography.

Given the rest of the filmography by Essex and director Edwin Brown (and his producer and screenwriting partner Summer Brown), which includes such titles as *A Thousand and One Erotic Nights*, *Naughty Girls Need Love Too*, and *Sexual Outlaws*, the "gypsy" flashback feels like what it probably is—an excuse to add in lots more nudity. Though the flashback scenes were shot long after principal photography had ended, and there's no reason to assume that Brown had anything to do with them. Indeed, the Blu-ray takes great pains to point out that these scenes are not "director-approved."

For fans of *The Prey*, this Arrow Video Blu must be something of a godsend. Not only does it include the original U.S. theatrical cut (clocking in at around 80 minutes) *and* the 97-minute "international" cut, complete with the weird and extended "gypsy" flashback storyline, it also has a composite "fan" cut that combines footage from both versions together into an extended experience containing all known elements from this obscure slice of the '80s slasher boom, not to mention outtakes, audio commentaries, and all the other loaded extras we've come to expect from an Arrow release.

For those who aren't already fans, there's probably little enough here that will convert you, unless you just *really* love melty John Carl Buechler monster effects, ill-fated teens camping in the woods, nature photography, racist backstories, distressing exploitation endings, frantic scores, *and* inexplicable digressions like Jackson Bostwick playing the banjo and pulling faces while telling a go-nowhere story to a deer.

Assuming you *do* love all those things and you haven't seen *The Prey*, well, have I got a movie for you!

**Author's Note:** I mentioned before, in the notes for my review of *Alice, Sweet Alice*, that when you're writing reviews for whatever movies you receive in the mail, without a lot of control over what those are, you sometimes strike upon hidden gems you might have missed. Other times, you end up reviewing films that you remember less fondly. This is one of those latter occasions.

**Originally published October 2019**
*Signal Horizon*

## "RELAX YOUR DEFENSES AGAINST THE UNEXPECTED... THE UNUSUAL."

## *NIGHTWISH* (1989)

So, *Nightwish*.

To begin, let me tell you a story about *Nightwish*. It all started maybe a year ago at Analog Sunday. Someone there had a tape of a movie I had never heard of called *Nightwish*, and the back of the tape was more than enough to convince me that I *had* to see it. So much so, in fact, that I bought the tape off them, even though I didn't have a VCR.

I ended up watching *Nightwish* on YouTube because even once I borrowed a VCR, it turned out that I didn't have the cables I needed to hook it up to my TV and *Nightwish* had already waited long enough. Too long, in fact.

Partway through watching *Nightwish* that first time, I paused to take a photo and post it to Instagram because there was an **ectoplasmic snake**.

If you are not already sold on watching *Nightwish* without me needing to tell you anything more about it, then you and I are two very different people, and you may want to take everything I say from here on in with a grain of salt.

When I learned that Unearthed Films was putting out a new Blu-ray of *Nightwish*, I knew that I had to get this weird movie just as completely as I had needed to get it that first time, when it was just a VHS tape that I couldn't watch.

So, *Nightwish*.

The back-cover copy on that VHS tape made it sound like "The Lurking Fear" by way of *Altered States*—or maybe the other way around. And that's a good enough short summary, if you can concoct a short summary for a movie so committed to being everything at once and so incapable of actually *being* any of it.

Here is a partial list of things that are in *Nightwish*: UFO sightings. Cannibalism. Not just one séance but several. Brian Thompson killing everything that he sees on the road and also listening to the all-bongos station on the radio while he does it. Slug women. A very mad scientist who shouts things like, "Reject your hallucinations!" Lots of crickets. Ghosts.

So, *Nightwish*.

In essence, *Nightwish* is about a professor (Jack Starrett) who takes a bevy of graduate students to an abandoned old house out in the middle of the desert. The house is home to literally every paranormal thing you can possibly imagine.

It was built on top of a mine, in a place where the earth's magnetic fields dip lower than anyplace else on the planet. Séances were held in the house, and a child died there. The drinking water in the whole valley was contaminated which caused mutations and madness. Also, there were UFO sightings galore.

Here's another partial list of things that are in *Nightwish*: Alien parasites that gestate in the skin of human hosts. All the green lights in the entire damn world. Twitching dismembered body parts. A girl who is delightfully horny for almost literally everything. A theme song. Early makeup effects by Robert Kurtzman and Greg Nicotero. Sensory deprivation tanks. An **ECTOPLASMIC SNAKE**.

When the ectoplasmic snake shows up, it starts moving toward the girl who is horny for everything (Alisha Das). She is obviously into it, and I was like, girl, I am right there with you.

"Clearly, this site is frequented by a demonic entity with the power to produce hallucinations," the professor tells his students, maybe only after nailing handcuffs to the support beams in the basement and strapping them all in around a chalk pentagram.

He warns them that the demon will try to trick them by getting inside their minds and preying on their darkest fears. He tells them that they will start to feel paranoia, and that it is just the demon turning them against one another. Then *he* becomes paranoid and stabs one of their number, having his evil Uncle Fester henchman (who comes up through a previously invisible trap door in the dirt floor of the basement) drag off the body and torture the remaining students.

The beauty (and ultimate failing) of *Nightwish* is that it is about everything. It is a haunted house movie that is also a mad doctor movie that is also about aliens that is also… you get the picture. It tries to have all of those cakes and eat them, too, and if its eyes are bigger than its stomach, well, those eyes are *very* big, indeed.

How *Nightwish* is going to resolve this mess is fairly obvious from the setup, in which we see the grad students participating in what essentially amount to guided nightmares where they try to visualize their worst fears and the moment of their own death.

That the film is going to end on an "it was all a dream… or was it?" note helps to explain how it can get away with throwing so many kitchen sinks at the wall (to mix all the metaphors), but only goes so far to alleviate the traffic jam caused by the attempt.

It doesn't help that, while writer/director Bruce R. Cook is good at establishing shots that create atmosphere, he doesn't seem to know how to use them or when, so they are simply littered everywhere throughout the film.

*Nightwish* is far from a good film—at one point, a character's severed finger is on the wrong hand—but there's a lot to love in its patchwork Frankenstein monster body.

If the ectoplasmic snake (!) isn't enough to win your heart, then you'll be on the movie's side by the time everyone is handcuffed around a glowing green pentagram—and if you're not by then, you probably never will be.

# NIGHTWISH (1989)

**Author's Note:** I have since acquired a VCR.

**Originally published November 2019**
*Signal Horizon*

# "FUNKY OLD HOUSE, AIN'T IT?" AN ARDENT DEFENSE OF THE *HOUSE ON HAUNTED HILL* REMAKE

I am loath to pick "favorite" movies for any number of reasons, but when asked to do so with horror films, as I often am, I frequently point to the 1959 *House on Haunted Hill*. This is, in part, precisely *because* it isn't the best movie I can think of, by any traditional measure, which frees it up to instead be so many other things.

There is no doubt in my mind that *House on Haunted Hill* is nowhere near the best horror film ever made, whatever that even means; not the most important, not the most inventive, and certainly not the scariest.

It isn't even the best *haunted house* movie that I can conveniently think of. Instead it is charming, creaky, sardonic, delightful.

It has all the earmarks that we associate with William Castle, no one's nomination for best director, but probably more than a few peoples' favorite, not to mention its noir-with-supernatural-trappings script by Robb White, who is honestly probably every bit as responsible for creating what we think of as a William Castle movie as Castle himself. In front of the camera there is, of course, none other than Vincent Price, at his Vincent Price-iest.

*House on Haunted Hill* (1959) is essentially immune to criticism. Call it silly, or talky, or clunky, and even its most ardent supporters are unlikely to disagree. It's the kind of film that can survive the RiffTrax treatment without detracting, in any way, from your enjoyment of the original.

This may also be part of why the 1999 remake works so well. Released the same year as the unfortunate update of Robert Wise's genuine classic *The Haunting*, William Malone's remake of *House on Haunted Hill* has less to live up to than that misfire, and is, therefore, free to take the bones of the original and build a bloodier, more ambitious, and more absurd edifice atop what came before.

At a glance, that bloody ambition separates the two films by orders of magnitude, but when you scrape away the artifice, they have the very same skeleton, and the same beating heart.

In Castle's *House on Haunted Hill* that heart was Vincent Price and Carol Ohmart, whose chemistry as scheming husband and wife, each angling to knock the other off, provided the lifeblood of the film. "It's a pity you didn't know, when you started your game of murder, that I was playing, too," Price says in the final reel of Castle's 1959 original.

In 1999, Malone and his screenwriter Dick Beebe know what made the original film work. This time, the husband and wife are played to acerbic perfection by Famke Janssen and Geoffrey Rush, whose amusement park magnate character, named Stephen Price as a nod to Vincent, is equal parts Price, John Waters, and more than a bit of William Castle himself. Both of the actors are having a hell of a time, reminding us that, like love, mutual hatred is a kind of chemistry, and here it gives off sparks.

The sardonic wit of the original film also finds a good match in the jaded, cynical, post-*Scream* horror of 1999, as all the characters spend most of the movie acting like they're being "had," and, therefore, like they need to pretend to be in on the gag.

That jokey central premise rubs uncomfortably against the film's other elements. Rush and Janssen bring more to the characters than they need to (Rush had already won an Academy Award and was nominated for another the year this movie was filming), with able support from a cast that includes Chris Kattan, of all people, taking on the Elisha Cook Jr. role from the first film and running it hilariously to the end zone.

But none of that is what anyone remembers. What we remember about the '99 *House on Haunted Hill* is what it looks like, because it looks like nothing else.

The production team creates genuinely unsettling imagery that is constantly at odds with the *Saturday Night Live* skit ensemble piece that the film orbits around. Rather than sinking the enterprise, however, these contradictions play off each other, generating a charge that keeps the film going. The poppy character moments keep the set pieces from becoming too grim and joyless, while the sadomasochistic *Jacob's Ladder* visuals prevent you from ever settling in too comfortably.

In this, 2002's odd-duck horror noir *Feardotcom*, and, to a lesser extent, his *Masters of Horror* episode "Fair-Haired Child," director William Malone and his crew conjure up what may be as close as anyone has ever come to creating a modern analogue to the look of those German expressionist horror films of the silent era.

I'm not the only one to think so, either. Roger Ebert, in his review of *Feardotcom*, said, "If the final 20 minutes had been produced by a German impressionist [sic] in the 1920s, we'd be calling it a masterpiece." He's not wrong.

So, is *House on Haunted Hill* a masterpiece? No, of course not. Like its predecessor, it is too preoccupied with being a spook show to worry about whether or not it is a piece of art, which is just as well. But its visuals very nearly are.

Look at the shots when Dr. Vannacutt, played by Jeffrey Combs, the closest thing the movie has to a "lead ghost," steps out of the film's giant zoetrope of a "saturation chamber" and is rendered in impressionistic smudges, like a Van Gogh come to life.

From the almost-but-not-quite monochrome Warner Bros. logo to the stop-motion title animations which nod to Jan Svankmajer and the Brothers Quay, Malone doesn't make any secret of what he is trying to accomplish. Combs plays Vannacutt in almost total silence. The film's exposition is provided by a "Terrifying But True" TV series hosted by Peter Graves. *Feardotcom* opens with Udo Kier fleeing through a subway decorated with a graffiti reference to *Mad Love*'s Dr. Gogol, while in *House on Haunted Hill* Geoffrey Rush is strapped into a straitjacket and muzzle that could easily nod to Hannibal Lecter in *Silence of the Lambs* but instead chooses to reach for *Mr. Sardonicus* and *The Man Who Laughs*.

The place where the visuals of *House on Haunted Hill* are most often credited with falling down is in the film's final reel, when the "darkness at the heart of the house" is unleashed.

Said darkness takes the form of a CGI composite ghost like a living Rorschach inkblot inspired partially (and perhaps apocryphally) by the Michael Whelan covers of H.P. Lovecraft books.

The effect isn't very good, but it also isn't as bad as its reputation. We all treat it as worse than it is because the movie has built it up so much, and because it suffers so in comparison to the genuinely unsettling practical ghosts that surround it. To see what the effects team was trying to accomplish with the inkblot ghost done better, if still not entirely successfully, see the aforementioned last 20 minutes of *Feardotcom*.

The 1999 *House on Haunted Hill* was released as the first film under the Dark Castle Entertainment banner, which was formed with the intention of remaking William Castle movies before going off in other directions after releasing only two, this and 2001's *Thirteen Ghosts*.

William Malone, who had previously made a couple of schlocky '80s sci-fi monster movies and some *Tales from the Crypt* episodes, followed up *Feardotcom* and his *Masters of Horror* installment with an independently financed film called *Parasomnia*, a problematic take on the Sleeping Beauty story which seems to have (perhaps rightly) landed him in director jail for the last decade.

Nothing that he has done since ever bobbed up to the heights of *House on Haunted Hill*, let alone rose above them, but that's okay. The 1959 original was one of William Castle's best movies, too, and whatever else happens, we'll always have those grotesque, nightmare images of jittery, rubber-faced ghosts, their heads madly vibrating in the depths of a burned out "sanitarium of slaughter." There are worse legacies.

**Author's Note:** Tyler Unsell is the owner and publisher of *Signal Horizon*. In the years since I wrote this—not quite my first interaction with that website, but close—he and I have not merely become fast friends, but co-hosts of a monthly podcast and screening series at the Stray Cat Film Center, a local indie theater in Kansas City.

If memory serves, this essay was written as a result of a conversation Tyler and I were having in which I insisted upon the surprising quality of this film. I stick by that.

**Originally published November 2019**
*Signal Horizon*

# "WE'RE AMERICANS."
# JORDAN PEELE'S *US* (2019)

It is difficult to discuss the promise of *Get Out* because that word, "promise," implies unmet potential, and *Get Out* is indisputably one of the best horror films of the 21st century, full stop. Yet even Peele himself, in a rambling profile of the director in *Rolling Stone*, acknowledged that, "I'm such a horror nut that the genre confusion of *Get Out* broke my heart a little."

While for me there is *absolutely* no confusion or ambiguity about the place of *Get Out* in the horror cosmology, to see Peele use the words, "I set out to make a horror movie," is nonetheless a thrilling feeling. Writing in that same *Rolling Stone* piece, Brian Hiatt makes the distinction thusly: "*Get Out* is existentially terrifying; *Us* is spill-your-soda scary."

Sure, I'll take it, even if the unspoken implication—that *Us* is somehow not also existentially terrifying—is in no way true. That it's also funny throughout, the humor sinking its tendrils deep and sending roots into even most of the film's more intense sequences, further serves to muddy that particular water.

Part of any "genre confusion" that may have hovered around *Get Out* was the impossibility of separating that film's effectiveness from its social message. *Get Out* was inextricably about race, and it was impossible for many people to see how effective it would have been if it was about anything else. For those people, there is now *Us*.

While "the sunken place" in *Get Out* is one of the most potent metaphors to grace cinema since the sunglasses from John

Carpenter's *They Live*, the scene in which we are introduced to it is also one of the most effective horror set-pieces ever committed to film.

That's the "promise" that I was talking about above. Even in *Get Out*, it's apparent that Peele is every bit as much a horror auteur as he is a social provocateur—and if we weren't sure of that, now we have *Us*, his unabashed entry into the horror canon, to prove it.

Which is, of course, not to suggest that *Us* is not just as socially provocative as *Get Out*, in its own way. The central metaphor here is less elegant than "the sunken place," but perhaps no less potent.

The best horror icons operate successfully both as themselves and as metaphors—but some of the *very* best may be metaphors for a lot of different things, their meanings shifting and changing depending on the time, and the lens of the viewer. Peele's Tethered may well fall into that category.

It isn't by accident that *C.H.U.D* is one of the VHS tapes seen framing an old-fashioned tube TV in the film's 1986 opening—something that isn't apparent from the trailers, but is from the opening text crawl, which tells us that there are miles of tunnels underneath the United States.

In fact, not much seems to happen by accident in *Us*, though it also never quite gels as neatly as *Get Out*. There are more frayed edges for us to keep worrying at after we leave the theater. Whether that is a feature or a bug is up to you.

Like the Coagula in *Get Out*—which hinted at a more elaborate mysticism that was never explored in the film and only exposited by Peele in his director's commentary—there is obviously something more than science fictional going on in the central conceit of *Us*. Characters may talk about it in Biblical terms, but the film never feels a need to hand-hold us through it.

As such, there's a lot that doesn't really make sense in the movie—the Tethered apparently have sewing machines but maybe not stoves?—but there was also a lot that didn't necessarily make sense in *Suspiria* or any number of other horror classics. What matters is if it all *feels* right, and in *Us*, at least for me, it almost all does.

Even the final reveal, which seems predictable from early on but is saved for the moment when it will have the most impact, manages to be as satisfying as it is inevitable, and retroactively explains many moments that people in the screening I attended expressed disbelief at as they happened. Props to Peele for pulling that trick off.

I've managed to go this far without writing about how great this film looks, the incredible score and use of diegetic music, and the stunning central performances, especially from Lupita Nyong'o, who probably won't win an Oscar for this, but should.

Even when *Us* isn't delivering on all of its many, many ideas, everything else is firing. The horror set-pieces are effective, and with the Tethered, Peele has delivered a "monster mythology"—to use his words—that will sit comfortably in the horror pantheon alongside the greats.

*Us* won't be nominated for as many Academy Awards as *Get Out*. It isn't a perfect house of cards like that film was. It's messier, more ambitious, and more imperfect. That may occasionally be a shame, sure, but it also gives us something to chew over at as we lie awake and wonder just which America we really inhabit—the one where we take our comforts for granted, or its terrifying funhouse reflection? Or maybe both?

**Author's Notes:** This was my first modern review of a contemporary film for a third-party venue, one that I saw in a theater, that I wrote as an actual film critic. Which is to say that I went to a critic's screening of Jordan Peele's sophomore feature—the night before I was to depart for a convention, I believe—as a critic, and wrote about it for *Signal Horizon*.

As you'll see from the rest of this book, writing about contemporary movies, after seeing them just once in a theater, is not where I have focused most of my energies as a critic. For various reasons,

I primarily write about older films, often as they are re-released onto Blu-ray. Perhaps as a result, I'm often not as satisfied with the reviews I write for first-run movies like this. I remain happy with this one, though.

**Originally published November 2019**
*Signal Horizon*

# IT GOES ON AND ON:

# THE *RINGU* BLU-RAY COLLECTION

Like a lot of people, I watched the American remake of *The Ring* when it hit theatres in 2002. And, like a lot of people, it was pretty much my first exposure—albeit indirect—to Japanese horror cinema, the occasional Godzilla movie notwithstanding. It wasn't until a few years later, when I was working at a video store, that I saw the Japanese original from four years earlier for the first time.

Back then, I liked the American remake much better. For years, I held it up as one of the rare instances in which an English-language remake improved upon its foreign predecessor. But I also didn't revisit the Japanese version (which, for the purposes of this review, we'll stylize as *Ringu*) until I received this set from Arrow Video.

> "I've got a deadline to meet."
> —*Ringu* (1998)

Let me start out by saying that the American version of *The Ring* is still quite good, and it might still be my favorite of the two. The American version has a more active protagonist and brings with it a very specific digital sheen and washed-out color palette that is pretty immediately iconic. It also adds in horses, which I find creepy, so that doesn't hurt.

Yet, for all that their beats are nearly identical, both the American and the original Japanese versions have their own very different strengths, and both are really excellent in their own right.

Hideo Nakata's original film is less stylized than its American counterpart. It aims more for a sense of realism, at least most of the time, and as a result it—like *Dark Water*, which would come out a few years later, adapted from source material by the same novelist—is more of a spooky drama than what we nowadays tend to think of as a "ghost movie."

Sure, there are a few scare scenes, but for the most part the film relies on the simplicity of its set-up to achieve its tension. It's not about ghosts jumping out and saying "boo;" it's about the characters knowing their fate and being all but powerless to prevent it, and how they cope with that.

Whichever approach you prefer, there's no denying that the central conceit of *Ringu* is one of the most ingenious horror ideas of the modern era.

Combining the power of urban legend with viral memes, fears of multimedia communication technology, and the age-old motif of harmful sensation, the idea of the cursed tape is a potent cocktail on its own.

Add to it the nihilism of the film's ending (in either version), which turns the traditional ghost story on its head by providing a grudge that lasts not just beyond death but beyond the laying to rest of some unburied (literally or figuratively) crime—and you have something timeless.

The thing I remembered most about *Ringu* from the first time I watched it was a scene in which the protagonist's ex-husband says something along the lines of, "Remember those psychic powers I've always had."

I couldn't tell you, today, whether what I watched that first time was a bad translation, or I just wasn't paying attention or was pretty stupid back then, but the psychic powers play a *huge* role in the story here—not just in this first installment, but in the subsequent ones, as well.

It's probably the place where this film diverges most sharply from its American counterpart, narratively speaking. Sure, in the American version we get some background on Samara suggesting that she could do things—put images in peoples' minds, project them onto other media.

Here, however, the psychic power motif goes far beyond that. Sadako's mother had powers, and Sadako's are orders of *magnitude* beyond hers. She could make a person die just by willing them dead. If she had such an ability in life, no wonder she could spread such a curse with her death.

Our protagonist's ex-husband Ryuji has psychic powers, too. We're given indications of them almost as soon as we meet him, and it's implied that they're at least some of what drove the two apart in the first place. Through him, we see much of the film's backstory via psychometry. He also passed his abilities to his son, which is why the kid is so precocious—a trait that's not given any attention in the American version, save that little kids in scary movies are always precocious.

Rather than a throwaway *deus ex machina* to get some exposition to the audience—which is how I remembered it—Ryuji's abilities give us an understated link that runs through Sadako and her mother to Ryuji and his son, and shows how isolating such "gifts" can be. As much as later films in the franchise will try to give more attention to Sadako's tragic backstory, it is the way that these extrasensory abilities isolate each individual character that generates the most pathos for Sadako's plight in this first film and the one that immediately follows it.

"You can't link a video that kills to a tumor on a blood vessel."
—***Spiral*** (1998)

Before you even start watching it, *Spiral* is already a whole other weird animal—kin to the genetically engineered glowing rats that show up in the background of the film. While it's ostensibly a sequel to *Ringu*, the two pictures were shot concurrently and released in theaters on the same day. They share some of the same cast but look very different thanks in part to having different directors. Where *Ringu* and its other sequel, *Ringu 2*, which I'll cover next, were directed by Hideo Nakata, *Spiral* is directed by Joji Iida, who had previously contributed the screenplay to a TV movie adaptation of Koji Suzuki's novel *Ringu* in 1995.

Where other sequels to *Ringu*—and even *Ringu* itself, to some extent—deviated from the novels upon which the film was based, *Spiral* hews as closely as it can to the plot of Koji Suzuki's follow-up book. However, because it wasn't nearly the success of its sibling/predecessor, *Spiral* was left behind when another sequel to *Ringu* came out just a year later, this one tracing the events of the first film more closely and abandoning the novels.

To make matters even *more* confusing, the 1998 version of *Ringu* wasn't the first time that Koji Suzuki's novel had been adapted to the screen. The 1995 TV movie version of *Ringu* also hewed more closely to the source novel and incorporated more of the "pinky violence" stuff that was apparently in the book. I haven't seen that movie, but from what I've read about it, at times *Spiral* feels more like a sequel to that adaptation than it does to the *Ringu* of 1998, which makes sense, given that Iida worked on both.

For instance, Sadako here is not the sodden *yurei* that we've come to expect, appearing instead as a normal-looking and even seductive young woman whose face we consistently see. As in the novel, *Spiral* begins with the autopsy of Ryuji, who died in the previous installment. Performing the autopsy is our new protagonist, Dr. Mitsuo Ando, a pathologist who went to medical school with Ryuji. Just before the grisly autopsy scene, we see Ando contemplating slitting his own wrists, distraught at the loss of his young son, who died by drowning. All Ando has left are a few strands of his hair.

To say that the plot of *Spiral* is more convoluted than that of *Ringu* is an understatement. Here, the haunted video tape is all but forgotten in a storm of weird, pseudoscientific explanations.

It seems that what is killing all the people who watch the tape is a virus that is somehow transmitted through the tape itself. One scientist compares it to "optical data exchange" on a computer. "Your retina takes in DNA data from the video and reconstructs the virus in the body," he says, though he immediately scoffs at his own conclusions. What's more, the nature of the ring-shaped virus is essentially smallpox, a reveal that, I gather, makes sense in the book, but seems largely pointless in the movie.

*Spiral* doesn't stop there, though. It seems that, in addition to the ring-shaped virus, there is a "broken" virus that works like sperm cells and allows Sadako to not only be reborn via Ryuji's ex-lover Mai, but also to reproduce perfect clones of other people, who grow in a matter of hours or days to the age they were when they died—all of which is revealed only in the film's breathless coda.

The throwaway line from the first film about how Ryuji regretted having a child—presumably because he had passed along his psychic talents—becomes a major plot point here. And, through Ando, much of the movie becomes a weirdly melancholy meditation on fatherhood and genetics.

Where *Spiral* works best is when it is doing what horror movie sequels so seldom do and exploring the grief and confusion that would follow in the wake of an unexplainable, supernatural death like the ones in *Ringu*—that it does so frequently by veering into melodrama only goes so far toward weakening it.

It's also about the only thing that *Spiral* has in common with *Ringu 2*, the sequel that would come out just a year later. The two films are heavily preoccupied not with the main characters of the first film, but with how their fates affect other characters who knew them, spreading outward from the initial "impact" like ripples in water—a metaphor that is not only thematic, but also apt. By the film's weirdly apocalyptic-yet-laid-back ending, though, it's easy to see why studios would have wanted to go a different route when the franchise took off—especially given that the next step in the novels involved virtual reality.

> "This experiment is dangerous."
> —*Ringu 2* (1999)

Just a year after *Ringu* hit theaters, director Hideo Nakata was back for the new sequel, ignoring both the novel and the 1998 film *Spiral* and instead picking up anew where *Ringu* had left off.

It's particularly weird to watch *Ringu 2* on the heels of *Spiral* because Miki Nakatani is back in both films, playing the same character—Mai Takano, Ryuji's assistant and love interest—but she has *very* different arcs in the two films. While she became sinister over the course of *Spiral*, here she is very much our protagonist, along with a reporter colleague of Reiko's, a police inspector, and an overzealous doctor.

Much of the first part of the film is given over to the mystery of what happened after the events of *Ringu*. Ryuji is dead under mysterious circumstances, the remains of Sadako are in the morgue being reconstructed via photographic overlays and a clay model, and Reiko and her young son, Yoichi, are missing. In her apartment, there is a smashed TV and the burned remains of a copy of the tape in the bathtub.

Trying to figure out what happened to her friend and lover, Mai and Reiko's colleague Okazaki begin investigating the cursed tape. Along the way, they eventually run into Reiko and Yoichi. Mai takes an immediate motherly interest in Yoichi, who has been dramatically changed by the events of the previous film—he is essentially possessed by Sadako, replacing the cursed tape in acting as a medium for her rage and fear.

Here, as in *Spiral*, Mai shares Ryuji's gift of psychometry, which helps us along with some of the exposition and also helps to explain why she seems to survive while the others do not—a question posed to her even by the ghost itself, before the end. Along the way, we spend a lot more time learning about how mysterious and powerful Sadako was in life, with the weirdest revelation being that she appears to have somehow been alive in the well for most of the thirty years that it's been since she was dumped down there, only dying about the time that the cursed tape began to circulate.

Through characters like Dr. Kawajiri, we also see a more pragmatic approach being taken to the phenomenon of the cursed tape. Not the "ring virus" explanation that we were given in *Spiral*, though. Instead, Dr. Kawajiri seems to regard the ghost as nothing more than a form of energy, one that he can channel into a safe medium; in this case, a swimming pool—events once more reaching their climax in water.

The sequence in which Kawajiri hooks Mai and Yoichi up to a bunch of ridiculous electrical equipment next to the pool—along with the tragic and violent denouement that follows—is one of the film's most striking moments. It also showcases the technophobia that has always been a part of the *Ring* franchise, along with something else, a distrust of authority.

After all, it was the paternal doctor figure who killed Sadako in the first film. Here, the police inspector and the doctor both act as though they have matters in hand, when, ultimately, they don't. Faced with the reality of the situation, a rictus-grinning Dr. Kawajiri takes some of his own machinery and dives into the pool—electrocuting himself.

Before the credits roll, we're treated to a longer sequence with Sadako than we got in the previous picture, as her Butoh-inspired movements drag her up the side of the well, where she comes face to face with Mai. Instead of the peeled-open eye that became famous from the first film, however, the face that confronts us this time is the clay reconstruction that was buried at sea earlier in the movie, an uncanny touch rendered all the more strange as Sadako begins to speak.

Fundamentally, it is love, not technology or expertise, that will win the day. Or, perhaps not love, perhaps just empathy—which is, after all, what both Ryuji and Mai's power really is.

"Inside it was pitch-black."
—*Ringu 0: Birthday* (2000)

As it pretty much inevitably must, this prequel expanding on Sadako's tragic origin story waters down the inchoate rage of her curse in its effort to tell a tale that is *Carrie* by way of *The Ring*. In this version, Sadako is a young adult who sees dead people. She joins a theatre troupe as a form of therapy, but cannot find acceptance among their number—partly because people seem to end up dead after they cross her.

The first of the series—not counting *Spiral*—not to be directed by Hideo Nakata (he was apparently offered the project, but turned it down), *Birthday* has an entirely different texture than *Ringu* and *Ringu 2*. I'm not an expert on film texture, but if I had to hazard a comparison, I'd say that it looks and feels like it was shot-on-video—or like it was made for TV.

In order to present us with a version of Sadako that is a misunderstood loner in the Carrie archetype, the screenplay, by franchise stalwart Hiroshi Takahashi, offers the notion that, at some point in her youth, Sadako actually split into two people.

One is the poor girl who we see trying to fit in among the theatre troupe, the other is the black-haired wraith that we're all familiar with from the other movies. Leaning heavily into something that has been implied in every prior adaptation—that Sadako's father is something other than human—this film never really provides us with any more answers about who or what Sadako actually is than we've previously been given.

Naturally, the Carrie-at-prom-night scene of the film is the premiere of the play, where Sadako has gotten the lead due, in part, to the mysterious death of the previous leading lady. Here, she is violently confronted with her past, but the expected telekinetic fireworks don't manifest. Instead, Sadako is beaten to death by the members of the troupe. But we in the audience know that this can't be the end of the story.

That's where the "second" Sadako comes in, as they bring the corpse of the "regular" Sadako with them to confront her evil doppelganger. Which proves to be a mistake in the film's kinetic—at least compared to the sedate rest of the movie—climax, which finally ends up with Sadako in the well, as we always knew it must, but not before racking up a body count much higher than the previous films.

"I'm still scared, a bit."

It bears remembering that even *Ringu 0* was released two years before the American remake hit theatres, as the phenomenon of *Ringu* spread like a virus to kick off the J-horror boom in the United States, an event whose reverberations are still being felt today in movies like the blockbuster *Conjuring* franchise.

As such, perhaps the biggest service being provided by the very attractive Arrow Video Blu-ray set—which features several of these films on the format for the first time in the U.S.—is the ability to do what I did and watch all four of these flicks in close proximity.

This not only lets us appreciate things like the lovely chiaroscuro lighting of Nakata's installments—one of the essays in the booklet that accompanies the box set compares *Ringu 2* to a Val Lewton film, and I wouldn't necessarily disagree—it also lets us look at the films as a vibrant, living tableaux, rather than our own faded memories of a VHS tape we watched years ago. For fans of the form, like myself, what could be better than that?

**Author's Note:** Guillermo del Toro says that the first time you watch a movie is a flirtation, the second time is a date, or something to that effect. I certainly judged the original Japanese version of *The Ring* too harshly the first time I watched it, and I'm very grateful to have been given the opportunity to rectify that mistake in print.

**Originally published November 2019**
*Unwinnable*

# A VERY SPECIAL HUMAN BEING:

## *MAN OF A THOUSAND FACES* (1957)

"You know what it's like to be different. Make people understand."

There are a lot of ways to watch *Man of a Thousand Faces*—the "true" story of legendary silent film actor Lon Chaney that was just released on Blu-ray from Arrow Academy. As Hollywood's first prestige biopic about one of its own. As a "women's picture" whose press kit advised cinemas to "play up the heartbreak angle." As a comeback vehicle for James Cagney, who plays Lon Chaney in the film and retired just a few years later.

Those who are coming to it for a 1950s-style parade of Chaney's "greatest hits" won't be disappointed, but they'll have to wait through a whole lot of primo '50s melodrama to get there—at one point, the isolation of the Chaney home is underscored by actual tumbleweeds.

Billed (before the titles even roll) as "Universal International's Special Release for Hollywood's Golden Jubilee," it makes sense that *Man of a Thousand Faces* would be a movie paying tribute to an earlier age of Hollywood, just before the dawn of the "talkies." But it takes a while to get there.

For its first half, the conflict in *Man of a Thousand Faces* revolves around Chaney's first wife, Cleva. The two seem happy enough until Cleva announces that she is pregnant and wants to go home to meet Chaney's family for Christmas.

While Chaney and his brothers and sister are all hearing, however, Chaney's parents are deaf, a fact that he has kept from Cleva until the moment she meets them. She reacts in typical Hollywood melodrama fashion, rushing away from the dinner table and swooning in her bedroom, concerned that her child might be born deaf and crying, "I don't want to be mother to a dumb thing!"

Though Chaney and Cleva stay together and have the baby—who turns out to be hearing—the incident drives a wedge between the two of them that never heals. Finally, after plenty of melodrama mainstays including perceived affairs, heavy silences, and darkened rooms, Cleva attempts suicide by forcing her way on stage while Chaney is performing—this in 1913, while he is still working in vaudeville—and drinking acid!

The screenplay treats Cleva pretty poorly, but one thing you've got to say for her, she knew how to make a statement. If something isn't worth forcing your way on stage and drinking acid, you've got to ask yourself, is it *really* that important?

The mercuric chloride destroys Cleva's vocal cords—she had been a singer—and the scandal destroys Chaney's vaudeville career. Cleva disappears from the hospital and Chaney files for divorce, only to lose custody of his son in the process, the courts ordering young Creighton Chaney into foster care until his father nails down steady work and a more suitable living situation.

At the advice of friend and PR man Clarence Locan (Jim Backus), Chaney goes to Hollywood, where his aptitude with makeup allows him to get steady work in bit parts until his big breakout in *The Miracle Man*, playing a character with twisted legs who is seemingly cured by a faith healer.

During this part of the feature, the main conflict becomes Chaney's relationship with his son—first, trying to win back custody, and then keeping from him the secret that his mother is still alive, and that she's the woman who stops by the schoolyard to watch the kids play.

It is against the backdrop of this and Chaney's second marriage that we are treated to that inevitable "greatest hits" parade—albeit dramatized for the silver screen. In this version of events, Chaney and Cleva meet again, bitterly, in the midst of filming one of the most famous scenes in Chaney's version of *The Hunchback of Notre Dame*.

The film ends with Chaney's death of a throat hemorrhage in 1930, a scene that it plays fast and loose. While the real Chaney died in the hospital, this one dies at home, surrounded by his family and only after relenting on his earlier desire that his son not pursue acting by symbolically passing on his iconic makeup kit, changing the name on the side to "Lon Chaney, Jr."

\*\*\*

The real Creighton Chaney *did* begin acting shortly after his father's death, but it wasn't until the mid-1930s that he changed his screen name to Lon Chaney, Jr., and that at the insistence of studios who found it easier to market him that way. In interviews, he later said that he was ashamed of taking on the name, and that he was proud of the name "Lon Chaney" but not of "Lon Chaney, Jr."

(Poor Creighton Chaney had it kinda rough. Not only did his dad disapprove of his acting bug, but his reconciliation with his birth mother wasn't as rosy as the movie paints it, either. James Cagney recollected the story that the screenwriters couldn't use because it was too "infinitely sad." When the real Creighton tracked Cleva down, she wouldn't acknowledge her identity to him. "That story seemed both crueler and larger than life itself," Cagney wrote in his autobiography, *Cagney on Cagney*.)

It's far from the only time the movie embellishes the facts. Before the film actually gets underway, we're shown a title card informing us that, "On August 27, 1930, the entire motion picture industry suspended work to pay tribute to the memory of one of its great actors." What it *doesn't* say is that the work stoppage lasted for only two minutes—still an impressive feat, in the busy Hollywood of 1930.

Pallbearers at the real Chaney's funeral included Irving Thalberg,

Lionel Barrymore, and Tod Browning, among others. There was also a chaplain and an Honor Guard from the U.S. Marine Corps, who had made Chaney an honorary member thanks to his portrayal of a drill instructor in 1926's *Tell It to the Marines*. None of that shows up in *Man of a Thousand Faces*, though, even if Thalberg is a character in the picture.

\*\*\*

The movie makes much of the fact that Chaney's parents were both deaf. In the first scene we see of him as a boy, he is coming home bloodied from a fight that he got into because other children were taunting his parents. Later, he tells Cleva that he "paid them back for my father and mother, and I grew up paying them back."

"Ma and Pa don't care if people make fun of them," his sister asks Chaney, "why should you?" But Chaney *does* mind—at least, this film version of Chaney does. And as much as his history of living with deaf parents informs his pantomime acting style, the chip on his shoulder over them informs his desire to sympathetically portray those whom society has cast aside.

"I wanted to remind people that the lowest types of humanity may have within them the capacity for supreme self-sacrifice," the real Lon Chaney wrote in an autobiographical essay for *Movie* magazine in 1925.

In the film, a young Irving Thalberg, producer at Universal and later MGM, asks the movie version of Chaney how he sees Quasimodo in *The Hunchback of Notre Dame*, a passion project of Thalberg's. "I see him as a man deformed, cursed, tormented, laughed at as a freak," Chaney replies, "but his tormentors never see the heartbreak or the tears."

"That's just what I want the audience to see," Thalberg crows. "The soul of a man that God made different. If you can get that on film, we've got ourselves a picture!"

"You know what it's like to be different," Thalberg continues.

"Make people understand. Make them see it the way you see it." (In a bit of casting felicity, Thalberg is played by Robert Evans, chosen for the part by Thalberg's widow, who shortly thereafter left acting and became head of Paramount.)

My wife is hearing, but she studied American Sign Language for years. I never picked much of it up myself, but it's always a joy to see signed language on screen.

Some modern Chaney scholars dispute the impact of Chaney's parents' deafness on his acting and his life, and I can't personally speak for how much prejudice there may or may not have been toward the Deaf community at the turn of the century, but what I *can* say is that the film—and its version of Chaney—are both extremely respectful of the Deaf and almost reverent toward sign language.

In one scene, Chaney is shown praying in sign. Cleva, his wife at the time, demands to know why he has to "cut her out of it." Chaney replies that he "wouldn't know how to mean it any other way."

\*\*\*

The film's version of Lon Chaney is played by James Cagney, himself a veteran character actor whose "best years" were already well behind him. As many critics then and now have pointed out, Cagney was almost woefully miscast in the film. At nearly sixty years old, he was tasked with portraying Chaney in his 20s and 30s—indeed, Chaney was only 47 when he died, fully ten years and more the junior of Cagney.

What's more, Cagney's pugnacious face and boxy body look nothing like Chaney. And yet, Cagney delivers a powerhouse performance. He's tasked with the same kinds of melodrama as all the characters around him, but that's not where he shines.

It's in the physicality of inhabiting Chaney that Cagney gives it his all. The facial mugging, the physical contortions and even the convincing vaudeville acts—which we see more of than we ever do film performances, ironically enough—all sell Cagney as Chaney, even if he doesn't look the part at all.

Something similar happens with Bud Westmore's makeup effects. Intended to evoke Chaney's classic characters, they are achieved with immobile latex, rather than Chaney's simple makeup. The results are Halloween mask versions of the originals—perhaps literally, as I remember reading somewhere that this take on the *Hunchback of Notre Dame* was later used as the basis for a line of masks—which could have come from no other moment in film history than the '50s.

Westmore was Universal's go-to guy for monster makeup in those days—even if we now know that he stole the credit for his most famous design, the gill-man of *Creature from the Black Lagoon*, from Millicent Patrick—and the versions of Chaney's famous faces that he presents are pure *Famous Monsters of Filmland*.

While I had never seen *Man of a Thousand Faces* before, the images were immediately familiar to me, and not just from Chaney's originals. In the same way that my brain had—before I ever saw the original *Frankenstein* or *Dracula*—parsed all the various pop cultural incarnations of those giants into one iconic image that was immediately identifiable as such, whether it was Karloff or Lugosi or Lee or whoever under the varying makeup jobs, these faces *look like* Quasimodo and the Phantom, even when they don't.

The latex masks may be less expressive than Chaney's originals, but they have a certain B-movie appeal that still works. Perhaps the same could be said of *Man of a Thousand Faces* in general, though it's certainly striving to be an A-picture, not a B.

The real-life Chaney was a notoriously private individual, who once famously said, "Between pictures, there is no Lon Chaney." He probably wouldn't have appreciated a biopic that spends so much of its time and energy on the turmoil of his personal life—and gets so many facts wrong.

But while Cagney may be miscast in the lead role, and the

Academy Award-winning screenplay may be more Hollywood fluff than historical accuracy, and the latex makeup jobs are immobile masks, they all work together to make movie magic—that "peculiar magic" that the opening eulogy for Chaney says only a precious few possess.

**Author's Note:** Not at all a horror film, but certainly a film for anyone with an interest in the horror film.

Originally published December 2019
orringrey.com

## FAMOUS MONSTERS

In one of my earliest memories—this would have been sometime before I was in third grade—I'm sitting on the living room floor, eating a hamburger and watching *The Fly* on network TV. Not the relatively benign 1958 version with Vincent Price and David Hedison, either. The incredibly gross David Cronenberg one with Jeff Goldblum and Geena Davis.

In the memory, my mom comes in during some particularly gruesome, gloppy sequence and asks me how I can eat while I watch that, to which I just kind of shrug. Here's the relevance of this memory: It was my first exposure a certain, generally much older, kind of monster movie.

I've said many times in various places that I was born too late to be a true Monster Kid. The days when the *Shock Theater* package was showing on TV were before my time. When I was a kid, though, we got a channel that showed monster movies on Saturday mornings. Not the classics. No *Frankenstein* or *Dracula*, but rather stuff like *Squirm* and *The Food of the Gods*, *Willard* and the occasional Godzilla flick.

From my school library, I checked out copies of those *Crestwood House Monster Series* books, which were my introduction to the old monster movies of the '30s, '40s, and even into the '50s. I pored over those books, imagining the films that would go with those evocative black-and-white photos. It was my only exposure to those old movies for years, until I was in college.

This is all a long preamble to the following: Like all kinds of movies, the monster movie *qua* monster movie has undergone transformations over the years. As Dario Argento once said, "Horror is like a serpent; always shedding its skin, always changing."

And monsters, specifically, are uniquely immune to solid definitions. A monster, by its nature, by the very etymology, is an aberration, a breach of the rules.

Also, like all kinds of movies, the monster movie has always been more than one thing. There is its most simple definition: a movie that has a monster or monsters in it. But then there is also the monster movie as a form, which, I would argue, has transitioned through at least two major shapes over the years.

The "classic" monster movie, as popularized by the Universal monsters like *Frankenstein*, *Dracula*, *The Mummy*, *The Wolf Man*, on up through *Creature from the Black Lagoon*, is a film in which the monster is generally both protagonist *and* antagonist.

The movie follows the monster and those who are in the monster's life (or "life") rather than (or in addition to, or as much as) its victims. The monster, whether by its nature or through hubris, is a figure both tragic and sinister. This is as true of *King Kong* as it is of *Frankenstein*.

The second major formulation of the monster movie is one popularized by the "atomic panic" movies of the 1950s—the big bug movies like *Them!* or *Tarantula*, early kaiju films like *Godzilla*, and even alien invasion flicks like *It Came from Outer Space* or *The Blob*.

In this formulation, the monster is often a growing and existential threat. Maybe it will literally wipe out life if it continues to expand, such as in *The Thing*, or maybe it is a threat to free will and identity, such as in *Invasion of the Body Snatchers* or, hey, *The Thing*.

The thrust of this form of film is an attempt to *stop* the monster, usually with some kind of ticking clock where if it isn't stopped before a certain point it will expand beyond our *ability* to stop it. In *The Thing*, this is keeping the monster contained in Antarctica, for instance.

The monster in this form is not generally a tragic figure. With the occasional exception of alien invaders, it cannot (or will not) usually communicate with humans. It is a force of nature, or an animal. In *The Monolith Monsters*, the eponymous monsters were literally inanimate rocks.

The "big bug" movies of the '50s, as their informal name implies, often featured normal animals (usually but not exclusively bugs) grown to an enormous size. In the wake of the success of *Jaws*, these huge animals were often replaced by normal animals simply run amok for whatever reason.

Whatever particular shape they take, the creatures in these movies tend away from the anthropomorphic, in nature if not in form.

From the '50s on, this second formulation became, in most cases, the default for the monster movie *qua* monster movie. Even Hammer's Gothic chillers, which remade the Universal classics for a new generation, sometimes (though by no means exclusively) rendered their creatures more mute and implacable than tragic.

To bring this back around to where I started, one of the things that makes David Cronenberg's *Fly* so striking is that it is that original kind of monster movie.

The 1958 version was too, of course, and it's far from the only movie from the '80s that is, but it was unusual enough for its time, and, probably more importantly for this discussion, was my first introduction to that style of movie, the monster movie's first major form.

Sure, I was certainly *aware* of the plots of *Frankenstein* or *King Kong* by the time I saw *The Fly*, but I had never seen them. Had never seen the pathos of the monster displayed onscreen so eloquently.

I've watched it many times since. I've also watched the original, and all of its sequels. I've experienced all of the original Universal classics, and their silent film predecessors. But watching the David Cronenberg version on Blu-ray today made me think about all of this, so I wrote it down here.

**Author's Note:** Disguised (perhaps badly) as a meditation on David Cronenberg's remake of *The Fly*, this turned into a decently robust dissertation on the monster movie as a cinematic form, hidden away in a post on my website.

Originally published January 2020
orringrey.com

## MISSION STATEMENT

I have always written a lot about film, but over the last few years I have inescapably also become, among other things, a "film writer." I have two books of essays on vintage horror cinema in print, and I regularly write reviews of both new and retrospective films for venues like *Signal Horizon* and *Unwinnable*.

To the extent, then, that I am a "film critic," or a critic of any other kind of art, my interest is not in whether or not the art in question is "good" or "bad." My interest is in the experience of the art itself; in placing that art within its broader context and learning to understand it better, both for myself and for whoever happens to be reading whatever I write.

This makes the experience of art—and of writing and reading about art—necessarily personal, and somewhat immune to criticism, to the extent that you view criticism as nothing more than a binary of "good" or "bad." Siskel and Ebert, probably the most well-known movie critics of all time, famously simplified it to "thumbs up" or "thumbs down"—not to knock either Siskel or Ebert, both of whom also wrote lengthy, heartfelt, highly personal takes on film all the time.

One of my favorite quotes about the role of art comes from Joe R. Lansdale writing an introduction to a trade collection of the comic book *Baltimore*. "Isn't that the job of all great art," Lansdale writes, "to kick open doors to light and shadow and let us view something that otherwise we might not see?"

He thinks it is, at least in part, and so do I.

As a critic, then, my job is to help art accomplish that goal. To jimmy the door just that little bit wider, to point into the light and shadow on the other side and describe what I see. To walk through the door—or at least peek through it—when others may not have the time or the energy or the inclination or the adventurousness of spirit to do so.

My job is also to keep an open mind. Not just when I sit in the dark and wait for the movie to begin, but long after I've seen the credits roll, after I've composed my careful sentences that night or the next day or the next week. This doesn't mean pretending to like something that I don't. It means being open to changing my mind.

Some of my favorite movies I was lukewarm on when I walked out of the theater. Some movies that I loved the first few times I saw them grew stale with time. Neither of these reactions are *wrong*—they're just descriptive of how I experienced the movies.

As a reader of writing about film, one of my favorite things in the world is to find a thoughtful, engaging appreciation of a movie that I thought I didn't like. One that helps me to view something in the movie that I might not otherwise have seen. Sometimes I *still* don't like the movie when I'm done, but I get the chance to glimpse that otherwise unseen thing, and that's really what I'm always after.

Art can only do so much to kick those doors open, after all. Sometimes we have to be ready to look.

**Author's Note:** Many times, both in this book and elsewhere, I have attempted to pin down what it is I do when I sit down to write about film. I think I did a pretty good job of it here.

**Originally published January 2020**
*Unwinnable*

# WE DRILLED TOO DEEP: *UNDERWATER* (2020)

"We've got big things in store for you."

*Underwater* is a summer movie from the late '90s being released in January 2020 for some reason. Maybe part of the reason is that it was actually filmed a few years ago—back when casting T.J. Miller seemed like less of a bad idea—and the distributors obviously don't know what to do with it, given the complete absence of buzz surrounding its release.

Which is a shame, because *Underwater* is a good monster movie, a good disaster movie, and of particular interest to fans of weird fiction, and it deserves a lot more attention than it's going to get before it sinks unceremoniously out of theaters.

Of the few people who are talking about *Underwater* at all, most are comparing it to *Alien* under the sea (so, *Leviathan*, then)—comparisons that it definitely invites, especially for fans of that scene where Ripley is in her underpants. It shares more of its DNA with the various imitators of those films, though.

This is a sibling to movies like *Deep Rising, Virus, Deep Blue Sea, Phantoms, Pitch Black*, and so on. Like many of those films, it spends more of its running time as a disaster movie than a creature feature, though it drags in plenty of creatures before it's done.

In spite of the difference in setting—and tone—I actually thought a lot about *Pitch Black* while watching *Underwater*, due to the emphasis in both films on crossing an inhospitable stretch of ground while fending off half-seen monsters from the dark. Hell, they're even dragging something for part of this one.

*Underwater* opens with pretty much its only moment of calm

before the storm, as Kristen Stewart gives us a voiceover monologue about pessimism and how, when you're at the bottom of the ocean for months at a time, you lose all sense of day and night. "There's only awake and dreaming."

These opening moments—and moments is literally all they are—feel more like the start of a ghost story than a monster movie. There are strange noises, doors that pop open on their own, all leading up to a sudden tremor that tears apart the underwater station that's there entirely to maintain a deep-water drilling operation, seven miles down on the bottom of the Mariana Trench.

From there, the movie never stops running. *Underwater* is a monster movie, but it feels more like a disaster film. Think of it as *Gravity* on the bottom of the ocean. When not in the water, characters are scrambling to reach it, or escape it. Lights are always strobing; sirens always going off. Water drips from every surface or pours in from above. The frame is always full of movement.

Neither the characters nor the audience get much more than a moment or two to catch their breath once the initial earthquake starts bringing the compromised structure down around their ears. The characters climb into massive diving suits that make the picture feel a bit like a dry run for a *BioShock* movie in order to undertake a perilous trek across the ocean floor in an effort to reach the drill itself, which they hope is undamaged.

This breakneck pace doesn't lend *Underwater* a lot of room for character development or deeper themes, though there's just enough of a blue collar, "corporations are bad, actually" message humming underneath everything to keep it from feeling too weightless.

Under the opening titles, we see snippets of newspaper reports—I told you this felt like a movie from a few years ago—about how the company responsible for the drill has dismissed "rumors of strange sightings" and the unknown dangers of working on the bottom of the sea for so long.

Even as the station comes apart around them, the characters are surrounded—and verbally bombarded from the PA system—by corporate platitudes. "You're not just part of our team, you're part of our family." That kind of thing. Meanwhile, when the film is over, the end credits are *also* accompanied by reports of the company hushing things up and getting back to digging, monsters be damned.

Oh, right, monsters. This is me, after all, the "monster guy," so if you're reading my take on a movie about underwater monsters, you probably want to know how the monsters are. Well, for the majority of the picture, they're scarce. Most of the time, the antagonist isn't the monsters at all—it's the ocean itself. The characters are just trying to survive a disaster that is plenty able to kill them all on its own, even before the monsters show up.

But when the monsters *do* finally show up, folks, do they *ever* show up.

Okay, I don't normally do this, but I am going to ring the proverbial spoiler bell here. *Underwater* has a relatively predictable but really great third act reveal which is going to get talked about a *lot* once people finally see this movie—which, at this rate, may not be until it straggles onto home video and/or streaming. So, if you don't want to know how it ends, stop reading now, because I am going to get into spoilers.

If you saw the trailer for *Underwater*, you know that they run into some monsters down there on the bottom of the ocean. It's what got me into the theater in the first place, after all. The earliest of these is a relatively small, practical effect creature that they find inside a corpse. Most of the rest are roughly the size of humans or a little bigger.

Like the vast majority of monsters in movies in the last decade, they look a lot like the *Cloverfield* monster, but their mouths are pretty cool, opening up large enough to swallow a whole person. The underwater bits are murky with sediment, giving all these sequences a found footage feel, but they are also packed with plenty of monsters. They aren't the end, though.

See, in the film's last leg, we discover the cause of the earthquake. It seems that they have accidentally drilled into R'lyeh and woken up Cthulhu.

No, I'm not kidding. They never say his name, and you never see a sunken city, but there's a kaiju-size, humanoid monster from beneath the bottom of the ocean, with a mouth that is fringed in tentacles and wing-like protrusions on its back. No one has to *call* it Cthulhu.

And before you complain that Kristen Stewart (maybe) kills it by blowing up the drill at the end, may I remind you that, in "Call of Cthulhu," they defeat the big C by ramming him with a boat. Setting off what is essentially a giant bomb seems a lot more proportionate.

As I said before, there's not a lot of thematic depth in *Underwater*. If it's cosmic horror, it's from the point of view of the bystanders, someone who gets swept up in the devastation but never really knows the greater implications.

But not a lot of depth doesn't mean none, and we get a touch of that old transcendent nihilism in the arc of Kristen Stewart's character, a self-sacrificing pessimist who fights hard against the dying of the light but, when the time comes, actually seems like maybe oblivion at the bottom of the ocean is what she's been searching for all along.

**Author's Note:** Though I didn't know it at the time, *Underwater* turned out to be the last movie I saw in a theater before the COVID-19 pandemic effectively shuttered them all for a year or so. There were certainly worse ways to go out.

**Originally published January 2020**
*Unwinnable*

## "THE SMELL OF THE ROOMS TERRIFIES ME—

## AND LURES ME ON"

## *THE HOUSE BY THE CEMETERY* (1981)

The first time—of the two times, now—that I watched Lucio Fulci's *House by the Cemetery* was nearly half a decade ago. I was doing a series of columns called Creature Feature Conversations that I actually miss writing, where author/publisher Jonathan Raab and I would watch some (often B-list) creature feature and Jonathan picked this weird, slow-mo nightmare of a movie.

In the back-and-forth that ensued, we said a lot about *House by the Cemetery*, some of which I'm going to reiterate here. Like the fact that it is the original source of two samples from the Skinny Puppy song "Rivers," or my note that, "There is a lot of product placement for Fiddle Faddle in this movie. Fiddle Faddle is the J&B Scotch of *House by the Cemetery*."

At the time, I had seen exactly one other Lucio Fulci movie. At this point I think that number is all the way up to…two? But *Aenigma* and *City of the Living Dead* are on my list, not to worry!

Another author friend, Jeremiah Tolbert, once described the gore style of Lucio Fulci as, and I am paraphrasing here, "like someone stapled a piece of rotted mutton to a mannequin." And that's…surprisingly apt? Enough so that I have since repeated it pretty much every time I've ever written about Fulci.

And that aesthetic bleeds from these movies into other Italian movies of the same era—or vice versa. *House by the Cemetery* and

*Ghosthouse* have more in common than just exteriors shot at the Ellis Estate in Scituate, Massachusetts, for example, in spite of the latter being directed by Umberto Lenzi instead of Lucio Fulci.

Like those films, to say that *House by the Cemetery* doesn't make a ton of sense is to engage in the worst kind of understatement. It didn't make a lot of sense the first time I watched it, and a second viewing did little to clear the cobwebs. But that's also somewhat beside the point. This is a film that *revels* in its cobwebs.

If *Suspiria* is, perhaps, the best example I've yet found of a movie that would be worse if it was any better—a film that takes its own weaknesses and flaws and transmutes them, likely entirely by accident, into something transcendently powerful—then *House by the Cemetery* is its equal and not-quite-opposite reaction, a Frankenstein's monster of a picture seemingly made up of everything that the filmmakers could think of.

Like the film's Dr. Freudstein—perhaps the most suggestively named monster of all time—*House by the Cemetery* is a collection of ill-fitting parts that don't exactly fit well together. But, like Freudstein, they don't have to fit well to be effective.

What the hell is/was Freudstein researching down in the basement? For that matter, what are the researches that bring his victims into his web? We hear that our ostensible protagonist is there to pick up the work of his dead colleague researching suicides—but to what end, for what purpose? Why does everyone in town insist that the male lead has been there before, with a daughter he doesn't have?

The film never really answers these questions, but it leaves them laying out suggestively enough that we feel like the answers are there, somewhere, even if it didn't deign to provide them.

What it *does* provide are all sorts of weird trappings. There's an old dark house with a spooky history (and a tomb in the floor) that everyone in town knows to avoid. ("This isn't New York," our Extremely Understanding male lead tells his wife when she discovers the tomb. "Most of the old houses in the area have tombs in them." Yeah, guy, not buying it.)

There's plenty of cobwebs and mutton-on-mannequin gore and the eponymous cemetery, which comes right up to the front yard of the house. When the realtor is finished showing it to them and is driving away, she backs into one of the headstones.

Of course, there's a precocious kid with *Shining*-like premonitions and the most annoying dubbed voice in the world, who encounters a possibly ghostly girl. There's a delightfully *Castlevania*-y score by Walter Rizzati. There's even a rubber bat, which leads to the goriest bat murder in film history. For real, that bat had to be, like, 250% blood by volume.

In that earlier Creature Feature Conversation, I had a note about the sinister babysitter (because of course there's one of those) cleaning up the blood from one of Dr. Freudstein's kills that said, "Everyone is weirdly okay with this huge smear of blood on the floor! Do they all just assume it's from the gore bat?"

(Gore Bat, incidentally, is the name of my horror-themed thrash metal band.)

While doing the prep work to write this piece, I read another review of the new Blue Underground Blu-ray, which opened with, "I don't like horror movies." If you, also, don't like horror movies, *House by the Cemetery* isn't the flick that's going to change your mind.

In fact, to appreciate *House*, you need to appreciate an increasingly small *niche* of horror movies—the borderline-nonsensical Italian horror films of the '80s, which are remembered for their maggoty gore, but which appeal to me for their haunting and often oppressive atmosphere of weird menace.

*House by the Cemetery* is neither the best nor the worst example of the breed, but it's a fairly representative one. If you don't have the patience for its singular charms, it won't win you over. If you do, though, the new Blu-ray is a welcome addition, complete with some nice behind-the-scenes features and, as with all the recent Blue Underground releases, a soundtrack CD.

**Author's Note:** I really do miss those Creature Feature Conversations. I think you can still find them online, on the website for Jonathan's publishing enterprise, Muzzleland Press. While you're at it, buy some books. Jonathan is a hell of a writer!

**Originally published March 2020**
*Signal Horizon*

## "THERE'S ONE TRICK YOU'VE NEVER SEEN."
## *THE MAD MAGICIAN* (1954)

"That's all I ever hear, morning, noon, and night: Plots, plots, plots."

Today, we're going to talk about John Brahm. Born Hans Brahm of Hamburg in 1893, he directed movies in Hollywood throughout the '30s and '40s and mostly moved to television in the '50s. His early work has been compared favorably to Hitchcock, and Ignatiy Vishnevetsky, writing for the *AV Club*, called him "the Mario Bava *and* Brian De Palma of the 1940s."

My discovery of Brahm came years ago when I picked up a Fox Horror Classics DVD set that contained three of his films—though at the time I knew only that they were three horror films of the '40s, having no idea that they shared a director. Those films were *The Undying Monster* (1942), *The Lodger* (1944), and *Hangover Square* (1945).

Of those three, *The Undying Monster* became a personal favorite for perhaps obvious reasons—the book upon which it is based is also a treat, if you ever get a chance to read it. *The Lodger* is an atmospheric and effective retelling of a Hitchcock silent of the same name, starring Laird Cregar, who also turns in a career-making performance in *Hangover Square*.

Or rather, it *would* have been career-making, if it hadn't killed him. Cregar went on a crash diet for the film, losing a considerable amount of weight—so much so that he suffered from abdominal problems and died in the hospital a few months before the film was released. Think of it a little like the 1940s version of Heath Ledger's performance as the Joker in *The Dark Knight*.

Why am I writing so much about *Hangover Square* in a review of *The Mad Magician*? If *Hangover* was potentially career-making for Cregar, it should have been for Brahm, as well. While I love *Undying Monster* more for its creaky set-pieces and dapper paranormal investigators and, y'know, actual monster, *Hangover Square* seems pretty indisputable as Brahm's masterwork.

Accompanied by a score from none other than Bernard Hermann—including the original concerto played during the film's astounding pyrotechnic finish—the picture is a legitimate, if underseen, classic, and perhaps the last genuine classic film that Brahm would ever make.

Shortly after, Brahm began working mainly in television, directing several episodes of *The Twilight Zone*, among many others, including the classic "Time Enough at Last," which we've all been referencing a lot lately, as we find ourselves quarantined in the midst of a COVID-19 pandemic.

What makes *Hangover Square* relevant enough to devote some 400 words to it in the midst of a review ostensibly of *The Mad Magician*, newly released on Blu-ray from Indicator, is that Brahm remakes much of his 1945 classic a decade later in *Mad Magician*.

Certainly, the Vincent Price vehicle, released in 3D to capitalize on the success of Price's *House of Wax* from the year before, is nowhere near as serious or psychological as its cousin from the previous decade, but certain elements are carried over wholesale, including one of the most striking scenes in either film, in which a body is disposed of in a massive bonfire.

(The bonfire was part of a Guy Fawkes Day celebration in *Hangover*, which was set in London, while in *Mad Magician* it's the result of a football victory.)

It's one of the biggest set pieces in *Hangover Square*, and is repeated nearly beat-for-beat in *The Mad Magician*, a film which ultimately utilizes it more poorly, as it does most every element that it borrows from its higher-brow sibling, while also cribbing a bit from *The Lodger* and a *lot* from *House of Wax*, with which it shares a screenwriter.

So, now that I am nearly *600* words into ostensibly writing about *The Mad Magician*, let's actually talk about it a bit. It is essentially *House of Wax* again, which was *already* essentially just *Mystery of the Wax Museum* again but in 3D and with Vincent Price (which, normally, makes everything better).

And certainly, *Mad Magician* is *better* than it would have been without Vincent Price, of that there is no question. But is it actually *good?* Sure. It's a delight, as many of these creaky movies are. Those who have seen *House of Wax* and thought to themselves, *Yes, I would like to see that again, but in black-and-white and with a magician instead of a wax museum*, it's the movie for you.

Price plays Don Gallico, a consummate mimic and ingenieur of magic tricks with a yen to become a magician himself, who discovers that his contract means that every trick he designs, even in his own time, belongs to his employer. (His boss has already stolen his ex-wife, played by Eva Gabor, and the contract stipulates, as his new detective friend summarizes, that his employer owns "everything but the air you breathe.")

In a rage, Gallico kills his boss using his newly-designed trick, "the Lady and the Buzz Saw," and then has to commit a handful of other murders to cover up the first. There's a sequence with a switched bag that leads to a brief chase around town in search of a severed head, the disposal of the body atop the massive funeral pyre, and the designing of his latest trick, the Crematorium.

"Where did you get the idea?" one character asks him. "From a crematorium," Price replies dryly, as only Price can.

The *Lodger* elements come into play as Gallico, disguised as his now-deceased boss, rents a room from a couple. The wife of the pair is a writer of murder mysteries who takes a keen interest in her new tenant, especially after Eva Gabor's character winds up strangled in the upstairs room.

She and her long-suffering husband provide much of the film's comic relief, and also ultimately help to solve the mystery, with Price perishing, as he was all but contractually obligated to do, in a conflagration of his own making.

It's all very by-the-numbers, and while Brahm's direction is never anything short of adequate to the task, it is also absent much of the ingeniousness that made his earlier horror films so striking. That it's a film that feels like what it is—a way to line everyone's pockets a bit—does nothing to diminish the fact that it *is* still delightful. We just need to be honest about these things.

**Author's Note:** Having written considerably about these sorts of older films for my two previous books of film essays, *Monsters from the Vault* and *Revenge of Monsters from the Vault*, I cover fewer of them than I otherwise might have liked in this collection. But they're always a joy to revisit.

*Originally published April 2020*
***Signal Horizon***

# BLACK BALLOONS:
# COSMIC NIHILISM IN *GAGS THE CLOWN* (2019)

When you get right down to it, the crux of much of Lovecraft's cosmic horror is that his fiction's conception of the universe is not an anthropocentric one. Humankind does not hold some exalted place in the cosmos. Not only is the universe vastly bigger than us, we are but a rung on an evolutionary ladder, and there are countless beings out there who are older, smarter, and better versed in how things really work than we will ever be.

But while Lovecraft's name may be synonymous with cosmic horror, he didn't invent it, and his formulation of it isn't the only one that has been put forth over the years. Before him, writers like Machen, Blackwood, Hodgson, and others were already exploring these same themes, and since then, plenty of other authors have put their own imprint on the field.

Ligotti's cosmic nihilism, for example, frequently holds forth a different central view than Lovecraft's. For Ligotti, humans *are* unique in the cosmos, in that we are uniquely aware that the universal order is fundamentally meaningless. That there is nothing more to existence than a series of cellular and chemical accidents, and all of our searches for meaning are not only doomed to fail, they are the result of an intrinsic defect in our nature that will make us miserable for as long as we *do* survive.

When we think cosmic horror on film, we tend to err more on the Lovecraftian side. Psychedelic visuals and writhing shapes from beyond the stars. But Ligotti's fiction—and Lovecraft's, if we're fair—is as likely to find terror in our own mirrors and backyards as it is in the dark between the stars. And, given that much of Ligotti's cosmology posits that human consciousness is, itself, all one big joke—albeit one with no author—it should come as no surprise that Ligotti's fiction has its fair share of clowns.

Though born out of a series of real-life viral news stories about creepy clown sightings—remember the fifteen minutes a few years ago when that was going on?—*Gags* is a spiritual successor to the "Scream"-faced "freaks" in Ligotti's "Last Feast of Harlequin," just as one example.

It's tempting to write off the phenomena presented in *Gags the Clown* as a thematically-unique but otherwise routine haunting. The clues are all there—the story about a carnival that burned down back in the '70s, the message that "The forgotten are no laughing matter" scrawled in graffiti on the wall near Gags' inner sanctum.

But if the events of *Gags* are a haunting, they are a haunting that spreads like an illness, infecting people via the white powder (shades of Machen?) contained in Gags' ubiquitous black balloons, driving them to self-mutilation and ultimately to a kind of veneration of Gags himself.

Similarly, Gags' powers are clearly much vaster and more surreal than those of any typical slasher villain. Even the "dream demon" Freddy Krueger saw his powers limited to the realm of Morpheus, where Gags seems to exhibit similarly reality-bending abilities in the waking world. In his scope and his form, he is more reminiscent of Pennywise, the "dancing clown" identity that the eponymously nameless creature takes in Stephen King's doorstopper of a novel, *It*. But while the creature in *It* is given an ultimately more Lovecraftian explanation—it came from beyond the stars, or another dimension—who or what Gags is remains unknown, even as the credits roll.

If he is a ghost, his grudge shares more in common with the sodden specters that haunt J-horror, their own curses spiraling out mimetically to ensnare anyone who has the misfortune of coming too close. Transforming their minds and then their bodies, forcing them to become messengers of this same rot that eats away at the world a bit at a time, for no reason that we are ever allowed to understand.

"Clowns have often had ambiguous and sometimes contradictory roles to play," as Ligotti points out in "The Last Feast of Harlequin," an observation that is reflected in *Gags* in the form of the reactions of the various different characters to the eponymous clown. While most are afraid of him, some regard him with scorn, while others dismiss him out of hand.

Still others react with a kind of idolatry—even before the climactic scene, in which Gags takes center stage in what is both a sideshow ten-in-one and an uncanny tent revival meeting. The TV cameraman Dale, played by Wyatt Kuether, calls Gags a "hero," while the film's teenage cast spend their night dressing up one of their number in a clown costume and playing pranks on people, inspired by Gags' exploits.

"Sometimes," Ligotti writes, "a cheerless jester" is needed to draw our attention to "the forces of disorder in the world." However Gags is perceived by the other characters in the film, to those of us in the audience, he is indisputably this "cheerless jester," his seemingly random acts of senseless devastation all part of the cosmic joke that is attempting to find any order in a fundamentally orderless universe.

It is notable that Gags is far from the antic clown of even King's Pennywise. When he shows up on screen, it is rarely front-and-center. More often, he is spotted for a frame and then gone again. On the occasion that he does linger, he remains almost entirely stock still, standing in the same pose, holding his clutch of black balloons. He could be a snapshot.

His actions, then, convey neither amusement nor malice. He simply is—as inexorable as cancer, as unmotivated as a car crash, as blameless as the slow creep of time.

In the film's final scene of surreal terror, Gags appears before the anchor Heather Duprey, who has been pursuing him for most of the film. He lets go of his black balloons, and hands her, instead, a balloon that's shaped like herself. She begins to laugh before she, rather than the balloon, pops.

That this is both utterly senseless and surreal to such a degree that it becomes laughable is not beside the point—it is the point.

**Author's Notes:** By now, I know my way around Lovecraftian cosmic horror pretty well—I ought to, given how much I've written it, and written about it, over the years. Less so with Ligotti's cosmic nihilism. But I tried to feel my way forward through some of it in this essay connecting it with a surprisingly good little mockumentary clown movie called *Gags* that I saw one year at Panic Fest, our local horror and thriller film festival.

**Originally published April 2020**
*Signal Horizon*

# "LET THE DEVIL HEAR MY PRAYER."
# *BEYOND THE DOOR* (1974)

*"Now I will leave you all alone in the dark and let my little story take over."*

Back in the day, the Italians made an art form out of ripping off more successful Hollywood movies, and nobody did it better. Sometimes, in fact, they cut so close that they got hit with a cease and desist order, as when Universal blocked the U.S. release of *The Last Shark*. Other times they merely echoed their Hollywood counterparts so completely that they *should* have been hit with a cease and desist, as in the case of *Robowar* and *Shocking Dark* (which was actually released overseas as *Terminator 2* in some ports, even though it rips a lot more scenes from *Aliens*).

More often, though, these cash grabs simply produce mystifying and sometimes magical results that are so strange that familiarity with their Hollywood counterparts is almost the only way to *decode* them into any kind of context. Such is, in many ways, the case with *Rosemary's Exorcist* here, by which I mean Ovidio G. Assonitis' *Beyond the Door*, which was also released as *The Devil Within Her*.

(Besides a lengthy booklet filled with behind-the-scenes details and the usual load of other special features, the new Blu-ray from Arrow Video comes with a feature-length documentary detailing the history of Italy's various rip-offs of *The Exorcist*, inspired at least in part by the worldwide financial success of *Beyond the Door*, which also got two sequels-in-name-only, the first of them Mario

Bava's *Shock* in '79, the second *Amok Train* in '89, which were released in some markets as *Beyond the Door II* and *III*, respectively.)

For those who have seen *Beyond the Door*, it will come as no surprise that Warner Bros. immediately slapped it with a lawsuit (and won) over copyright infringement regarding *The Exorcist*. Hell, the movie doesn't even bother to play *remotely* coy, to the point that it verges on parody—one of the children spends the entire movie drinking room-temperature pea soup straight out of the can through a straw, a prospect more disgusting than all the projectile vomiting in the world. He's even got a *print* of a pea soup can hanging above his bed.

(The other kid speaks jive, and carries around a couple dozen copies of the same book, which she is constantly reading. This is a weird movie. We'll get more into that later.)

Once Juliet Mills becomes possessed, she levitates, speaks in multiple voices, drools green vomit, and, at one point, her head spins all the way around, a sequence that is as neatly foreshadowed by one of the kids twisting the head around on a doll as it is inevitable in a movie trying so badly to be *The Exorcist*.

Mills also does other things, though, like eating a rotten banana peel that she finds on the ground or a particularly creepy scene where one of her eyeballs moves independently of the other. The children's toys come to life and move around on their own in a scene straight out of *Pod People* as the room shakes on its foundations and a light shines up from beneath the floorboards.

There's a lot going on in *Beyond the Door*, which owes almost as much of a debt to *Rosemary's Baby* as it does to *The Exorcist*, swapping the young Linda Blair for a mother of two and tying the events of her possession to a problematic pregnancy that also seems to be advancing far faster than it should. There's lots of room for thematic interpretation here, to be sure.

When the back of the box raves that Roger Ebert called the film you're about to watch "disgusting," "maddeningly inappropriate," and "scary trash," you know you're in for something *special*. This is the kind of film that opens with a voiceover by the devil himself (he never says the word) and features a scene where Gabriele Lavia (of *Deep Red* and *Inferno*, here sporting a mustache that makes him look like Dean Stockwell in *The Dunwich Horror*) gets accosted by a guy playing the nose flute.

Joining Mills and Lavia is *The Haunting*'s own Richard Johnson, looking somewhat less haggard than he would a few years later in *Zombie*. Here, he plays the closest equivalent the film has to a priest—a figure that we know to be sinister from the trippy music video opening sequence, but who may also be the only hope for poor Juliet Mills' possessed housewife. That he's also an old boyfriend and both more and less than he seems, well... beggars can't be choosers, after all.

Already an established producer (often of just this kind of— quite literally—derivative schlock), Assonitis made the jump to directing with *Beyond the Door*, which shows the kind of ambitious throw-everything-at-the-wall sensibility that was frequently coming out of Italy at the time.

From early on, *Beyond the Door* makes it clear that it is playing a sadistic game with the audience, every bit as much as Old Scratch himself is playing with his toys in the form of the ostensibly innocent family at the heart of the film, or Johnson's harried occultist.

The opening voiceover from the devil is taunting toward the audience, telling us to "go on thinking" that what we can't see can't exist "for as long as you can" and exhorting us to not forget that "the stranger sitting in the seat next to you could be me."

(The devil's voice is provided by notorious producer and distributor Edward L. Montoro, who was, himself, responsible for a whole host of other B-grade cash-grabs including *Grizzly*, *Day of the Animals*, *Pieces*, *Mortuary*, the *MST3K* "favorite" *Pod People*, and *Mutant*. When his Film Ventures International shingle was on the verge of bankruptcy in the mid-'80s, Montoro vanished with over a million dollars and was never seen again.)

During a montage that plays behind the opening credits, Lavia's

Robert Barrett presides over a recording session that is playing the film's main theme, "Bargain with the Devil," and when he yells "cut"—the opening montage cuts, too.

Throughout the film, the soundtrack, infused by sounds from funk and disco music, swells in to drown out what's happening on screen, and the lyrics of the songs taunt the characters directly, not merely providing non-diegetic accompaniment. As Robert leaves his pregnant and possessed wife alone in the apartment with her old flame and walks the streets, desperate and alone, accosted by street musicians, the soundtrack taunts him that, "No one will help you."

Besides its exploitation pedigree and odd-to-the-point-of-surreal filmmaking choices, perhaps the most interesting thing about *Beyond the Door*, especially in the context of the films it's ripping off, is its nearly complete absence of religion.

The devil is very emphatically real in this film, although, as he points out in his opening monologue, you never actually see him. "Unfortunately," he says, "in recent centuries, that has gone out of fashion, although there was a time when I was always being painted or impersonated in one way or another and, as you know, I've always been given the best lines."

Yet God is nowhere to be found. Absent are a young priest and an old priest, or even the lackadaisical Catholicism of *Rosemary's Baby*. In their place, we have Johnson's Dimitri, himself a puppet of the devil, and a woman on a houseboat holding a cat who tells us that, "You can't stand the thought of there existing beings so powerful and strong as to break through the barriers of time and space, and to take a malignant pleasure in causing suffering to the weak and innocent, thereby fulfilling some mysterious project of vengeance."

It's a portrait of universal malice that feels almost cosmic, and not the least bit comforting.

**Author's Note:** The odd life and even odder disappearance of Edward L. Montoro probably deserves its own book.

**Originally published September 2020**
*Weird Horror*

# Grey's Grotesqueries:

# Kicking Open Doors to Light and Shadow:

# The Crestwood House Monster Books

In his introduction to the second volume of Mike Mignola, Christopher Golden, Ben Stenbeck, and Dave Stewart's wonderful gothic comic series *Baltimore*, no less a horror luminary than Joe R. Lansdale describes the original Universal monster movies, "with their wonderfully gothic sets and shifty-eyed peasants and shambling monsters and fluttering bats."

The comic, he continues, "goes where your mind went when you saw those films as a kid, goes where the film didn't, but you think it did, because at that age your mind is fresh and open and full of light and shadow, all of it moving about in savage flickers, having not yet settled and found its civilized position."

I didn't see the Universal movies that he's describing when I was a kid. I arrived late to the Universal monsters, to Hammer's gothic chillers, and all of their ilk. Born in 1981, I came into the world too late to be a true Monster Kid.

By the time I was watching television, schlock pictures like *Squirm* and *The Food of the Gods* had edged out the Shock Theater package of classic Universal flicks that provided a staple for horror hosts in the late '50s and into the '60s.

In their place, I had the Crestwood House monster books. Anyone of my age and proclivities knows the books well; if not by that name, then by a simple description—orange board books with distinctive fonts and a bat-shaped logo.

Each one of them focused on a monster or a monster movie. There were books for Universal greats like Dracula, Frankenstein, the Creature from the Black Lagoon, and also King Kong, Godzilla, *The Blob*, *The Deadly Mantis*, and so on.

There were actually two series; the better-known orange books, which covered some of the bigger names, and a second series, retitled "Movie Monsters," with purple covers and an orange font that looked like a high school letter jacket. This second series dealt with lesser-known films like *The Mole People, Werewolf of London, House of Fear*, and sequels including *Bride of Frankenstein, Dracula's Daughter*, and *Revenge of the Creature*.

When I was very young, my school library had plenty of both. They are the first books I can really remember reading. The text inside, often by Julian Clare May writing as Ian Thorne, retold the stories of the movies, sure, but it also placed them in context. The *Dracula* one talked about Bela Lugosi and Bram Stoker's novel and other various cinematic adaptations of the Count. Ditto all the others.

I think that's important. I think it helped to establish in me a real curiosity for seeing the connections between movies and text, movies and one another.

The writing was only the beginning, though. What *really* drew me to these books, kept me coming back time and time again, why I still remember them fondly to this day, were the pictures.

The Crestwood House monster books were illustrated throughout with enchanting and atmospheric black-and-white stills from the movies themselves. Movies that I had never seen. That I couldn't even *imagine* except insofar as those pictures provided a doorway through which I could peer at a world alive with "light and shadow, all of it moving about in savage flickers."

I didn't just look at those film stills—I *pored* over them. I fell into them and a part of me has never crawled back out. Some of my earliest storytelling came in the form of looking at those strange, staged, black-and-white photographs and trying to imagine the movie that they must have belonged to.

"For everything you see with your eyes at that age," Lansdale says of the Universal movies, "your mind's eye sees a hundred times more." If that's true of the films you actually *watch*, how much more true must it be of the ones that you *cannot* watch, but only long for, unearthing them piece-by-piece from pictures in library books, like an archaeologist conjuring dinosaurs from the imprints of old bones?

There was a thing that we all did when I was a kid, I don't have a name for it—I'm not sure if it's something people still do, in this age of streaming content and everything on-demand—but we would *tell* each other the movies we had watched, as best we remembered them, on the playground the next day, or as we stayed up far too late at sleepovers.

Of course, we watched movies, too, whenever our parents would allow us to rent them or go to the theater. Some of us could see R-rated movies, others could not. But none of us could ever watch nearly as many as we wanted to.

So, to bridge the gap, we told what we knew, and embellished what we didn't. The films took on a life of their own, outside the confines of the theater or our VCRs. In telling one another about them, we turned them into a mythology, inventing rules that the films themselves were never so clear about—this same tendency was later repurposed and transformed into one of the great horror franchises of *my* time, the *Scream* series.

What we were doing when we told each other about the movies that we had seen, or only *wanted* to see, was what I was doing when I looked at those Crestwood House books as a kid and imagined the movies that they must have been describing. It's what I'm doing every time I sit down to write a story. Lansdale has a phrase to describe it—because of course he does—and he puts it better than I ever could—because, again, of course:

"Isn't that the job of all great art," he asks, "to kick open doors to light and shadow and let us view something that otherwise we might not see?"

He thinks it is, and so do I. And without those Crestwood House books to first force that door open a crack, I might never have gotten here.

**Author's Note:** For someone like me, being asked to write a regular column—in this case called "Grey's Grotesqueries"—for a publication like *Weird Horror*, from editor Mike Kelly and Undertow Publications was something of a dream come true.

For the column, I was given free rein to write about anything I wanted, which means that installments have ranged from the Japanese tokusatsu series *Ultra Q* to the unlikely co-genesis of Man-Thing and Swamp Thing to Hollow Earth theory to the horror of inanimate objects. For my first column, though, I tackled a subject that is as near and dear to my heart as any ever can be: the Crestwood House books that were my introduction to so much of what would be important and formative in my life.

Originally published January 2021
*Unwinnable*

# "FOR ALL YOU KNOW THEY COULD FLY."—
# *TREMORS* (1990)
## ON A VERY FANCY NEW BLU-RAY

I like monsters. It's such a part of my identity that it's usually right there in my bio. Yet even I'm willing to admit that monster movies are all too often dreck. Sure, there are plenty of great ones, but for every great one, there's a terrible one—sometimes the good kind of terrible, more often not.

When I was a kid, I had a short list of favorite monster movies that had come out during my lifetime, and *Tremors* was right at the top. My memories of childhood are scattershot, at best, but one early one involves going to the theater to see these subterranean desert monsters for the first time.

I almost got up to leave after the early, still pre-monster scene when Val and Earl find the severed head in the dirt—that scene scared the crap out of me, for some reason—but my mom wouldn't let me. We had paid for the tickets, by god we were going to watch the whole damn movie.

Lucky for me that she made me stay, because I *loved* every other second of it. Here's the thing about *Tremors:* it has aged better than pretty much any other movie on that very short list. There are a lot of reasons for that, beginning with the practical effects for the massive sand worms that the film names "graboids," which are still jaw-dropping some thirty years later, in the unsparing clarity of HD.

It's easy (and correct) to heap praise on practical effects, speaking broadly, and on the ones in *Tremors*, more specifically, but that's far from all there is here. Half a decade before *Scream*, *Tremors* is a self-aware horror movie, but not in the same Easter egg, knowing wink way that film would popularize.

*Tremors* is aware of the familiar ground it's treading (or burrowing under), tapping into the primal well of '50s monster movies. It's aware of the ridiculousness of its premise but, more importantly, it's aware of how people would actually react to such an event—by monetizing it.

*Tremors* gave rise to a spate of sequels that are still (somehow) going, even though everything after the fourth one should be shot out of a cannon into the sun—and even that one is debatable. There was even a short-lived TV series. For a surprising amount of time, the sequels and spin-off series were all remarkably good, and the thing they got right more than anything else—the thing that *Tremors* understood in a way that maybe no other monster movie ever has—is that this would get merchandized in a heartbeat if it ever actually happened.

*Tremors 2* shows us a graboids-themed arcade cabinet and discusses Val and Earl starring in a Nike commercial where they're running through the desert. By *Tremors 3*, Perfection has become a tourist destination and Walter Chang's store sells mostly graboids memorabilia.

What it also shows is how quickly even the most striking thing in the world will get merchandized, normalized and then forgotten. Perfection may be a tourist trap, but it's more dying roadside attraction than Disney World. Imagine a *Jurassic Park* movie set not when the park is flourishing and new, but twenty years after it has become old news and the funding has dried up. Half the rides are closed, storefronts stand empty and the dinosaurs have started to show their ribs, when they show up at all.

Sure, all of that is in the sequels, but the groundwork for it is already here in the first film, with its blue collar, get-rich-quick protagonists. When Val and Earl first discover one of the graboids after tearing its head (which turns out to be its tongue) from its body with their truck, they sell it to Walter Chang (played by the incomparable Victor Wong) for $15, and he proceeds to start charging everyone in town to get their picture taken with it.

*Tremors* is more than a clever gimmick and some good effects, though. It's the rare monster movie that never takes a single misstep. The pacing is perfect, with its gradual-yet-steady build to the growing reveals of the monsters, and the script is always clever. Even scraping off the scrim of nostalgia, *Tremors* is a flick with almost nothing to complain about.

As someone who writes what I often refer to as "fun horror," I'm always on the lookout for other stuff that fits the bill, and horror doesn't come much more fun than *Tremors*. It's also a movie that's smart enough to not over-explain its monster. Everyone speculates about where the graboids come from, and why no one has ever seen one before, but no one knows, a fact that (mostly) stays true through the majority of the sequels, even as the filmmakers (delightfully) complicate their central creatures.

Chances are, though, if you're reading this, you already know whether you like *Tremors* or not. This review is as much a review of the new Arrow Video Blu-ray as of the movie itself, and I'm happy to say that *Tremors* has never looked (or sounded) better than it does on this new 4K transfer.

The special effects have always held up, despite the fact that they're pretty much always shown unsparingly, in broad daylight. That remains true here. The real selling point of this new Blu-ray is not the new transfer, though, it's all the special features. And the Arrow Video Blu is loaded.

There's a lengthy booklet in the box, along with a double-sided poster, some lobby cards and a mocked-up coupon to Chang's Market. The discs themselves are decked out in commentary tracks, interviews, making-of footage and, in the limited edition, a disc containing (among other stuff) three short films produced by the filmmakers, including S. S. Wilson's short student film

"Recorded Live," which would probably be worth the price of admission by itself.

When I was younger, the version of *Tremors* I watched the most was on a VHS tape that I had recorded off network TV. This meant that the movie had been edited for television, which primarily meant overdubbing all the curse words and, weirdly, the instances of taking the Lord's name in vain.

As such, I have an odd fondness for the awkward overdubs, which meant that my favorite special feature was actually "Pardon My French," a new segment made for the Arrow Blu that featured the original footage and then all of the network TV overdubs. While "fooled you" is probably the most memorable of these, upon watching through the featurette I was most amused by "You gotta be brainwashing me."

**Author's Note:** *Tremors* is one of those films that is a sentimental favorite for many of us, but even those of us who love it tend, I think, to underestimate it, in the way that "fun horror" is so often underestimated.

**Originally published January 2021**
*Nightmare*

# THE H WORD: VICTIMS AND VOLUNTEERS

"My kind of horror is not horror anymore," an aging Boris Karloff laments in Peter Bogdanovich's 1968 film *Targets*. And judging by the rest of the movie—which concerns a mass-murdering sniper taking aim at the patrons of a drive-in as they watch a revival screening of one of Karloff's films—he's not wrong.

"Between 1968 and 1976, all the films that redefined the horror movie were made," Roy Olson of *Booklist* observes in his review of Jason Zinoman's *Shock Value*, the book that first introduced me to *Targets*. In *Shock Value*, Zinoman argues that—alongside the "New Hollywood" of the 1970s that gave us auteur directors like Steven Spielberg and Martin Scorsese—"a few eccentric outsiders" were creating a "New Horror" on the fringes of the studio system.

What sets this "New Horror" apart from the creaky, theatrical horror films of yesteryear—Karloff's "painted monsters" that no one is afraid of anymore? Zinoman examines a number of angles, but I'm just here to focus on one. A stark difference that speaks not just to the changing face of horror cinema from the '60s into the '70s, but to what we *expect* from a horror story altogether, whether it's on the screen, on the page, or anyplace else.

With rare exception, the targets (to borrow Bogdanovich's title) of most modern slashers, serial killers, ghosts, and monsters are *victims*. That is to say, they are frequently—and often pointedly—chosen at random, marked for death or terror at most because they transgressed against some minor taboo that often involved simply being in the wrong place at the wrong time. Read any number of the YouTube comments on the trailer of the 2008 home invasion thriller *The Strangers* and you'll find people saying, again and again, that the scariest thing about the movie is the invaders' stated motive: "Because you were home."

While much has been made of the puritanical morality of '80s slasher films, and flicks like *Scream* and *Cabin in the Woods* have attempted to codify the patterns of mass production into "rules" by which these narratives function, the victims in most horror movies made after the 1970s didn't *ask* to be put into this situation and, once in, they have no hope of escape except to survive the night or, if they are lucky enough to be the so-called "final girl," slay the slayer—at least for a time.

By contrast, let's call the protagonists of the horror films of yesteryear "volunteers" who, more often than not, put themselves into whatever situation they are currently facing and have every chance to leave but opt not to, whether due to greed, curiosity, love, duty, revenge, obsession, or the moral sense that they have to do what is right.

They may be detectives, reporters, scientists, soldiers, or even the friends and family of the monster, but they almost always have the option to walk away, but choose to press onward instead. Even in 1940's jokey *The Ghost Breakers*, cowardly Bob Hope continues to explore the seemingly haunted castle out of love and a desire to protect Paulette Goddard's inheritance.

The most famous and obvious of these is Professor Van Helsing from Bram Stoker's *Dracula*—an inveterate vampire hunter who not only pits himself voluntarily against the eponymous undead, but actually goes *far* out of his way to do so, traveling all the way from Vienna to England.

The echoes of these characters can be seen in some of the banner movies of the "New Horror" of the 1970s, in figures like Donald Pleasance's Dr. Loomis in *Halloween* or the three men in the boat at the end of *Jaws*. By then, however, they were already becoming the exception, rather than the rule.

Early "old dark house" films such as *The Cat and the Canary* frequently featured a cast of eccentric characters who had gathered to hear the reading of a will, only to get knocked off one by one over the course of the night. Yet even those characters, who came expecting an inheritance and not murder, could usually spare themselves the danger by simply leaving at any time.

In many of the Universal monster movies and Roger Corman's Poe films, the "monster" even pulls double-duty as both villain and protagonist, with the audience spending at least as much time tracing the inevitability of their tragic denouement as we do with whoever our ostensible lead is.

When that same approach is taken in the "New Horror" films of the late '60s and beyond, as it is in *Targets* or in George Romero's *Martin*, or William Lustig's *Maniac*, or even, to some extent, Hitchcock's *Psycho*, however, the killer is altogether too pitiably human. We see only a person broken in monstrous but familiar ways, not the Shakespearean tragedy of figures like those Vincent Price so often played in Corman's Technicolor gothics.

So, what changed? In *Wasteland: The Great War and the Origins of Modern Horror*, W. Scott Poole argues compellingly that the First World War gave rise to what we understand now as modern horror—specifically, the horror films of the '20s and '30s. Certainly, the long shadow of the war can be felt in films like 1934's surprisingly vicious *The Black Cat*, in which the villain is a Satanic war criminal whose house is built on the ruins of a World War I battlefield.

If that is true, then something similar can be said about the Vietnam War and the "New Horror" of the '70s. Several films make this overt, such as Bob Clark's *Deathdream* from 1974, a take on "The Monkey's Paw" in which a soldier killed in Vietnam shows up back home with tragic results. Even *Targets* tackles the influence of the war head-on, making its murderous sniper a Vietnam vet.

If the earliest horror films were a direct response to the horrors of World War I and II, then the shift from volunteers to victims that accompanies the formation of the "New Horror" can be seen as a reflection of changing public opinion about the wars themselves.

While World War I and II were horrific events, they were widely regarded as necessary, the people who served in them as heroic. The soldiers who fought and died in the World Wars were perceived as at least *achieving* something. They were facing horror—maybe even perpetrating it—but it was for a greater purpose.

The war in Vietnam was different. For many, it felt pointless, meaningless, far from the "just wars" that had come before. Our troops were no longer confronting some great evil. There was no vampire there to slay, only the faceless horrors of American imperialism run rampant. As near as anyone could tell, we were simply feeding children into a meat grinder for no reason other than because it was there.

While the draft had been implemented in World War I and II, as well as Korea, it became notoriously unpopular during Vietnam. The monster was inescapable, and those who had grown up in its shadow found themselves consumed by it, whether they volunteered or not.

At the same time, photographers and TV cameras brought the horrors of the war into the living rooms of America in ways that they never had before. And, as the war dragged on and on for decades—four times longer than either of the World Wars—shellshocked troops began to come home while the conflict still raged and we started to understand, for the first time, some of the real implications of things like PTSD.

The horrors of the World Wars had been faced—at least in America, where the nascent horror film was taking shape—primarily by those who had fought overseas, who were famously stoic about what they had witnessed there. In Vietnam, we saw the images of those wars on our television sets, and we saw the aftereffects on those who had served when they returned home.

Is it any wonder, then, that heroes were harder to find in the

"New Horror" that flowed from the 1970s? Americans had watched intimately as people on both sides of a conflict they didn't understand fought and died for what seemed like nothing—or seen their loved ones come back horribly changed by their experiences—all with no grand morality or greater narrative to explain it all. Like the masked killers who so often populated the films that this "New Horror" would come to spawn, the war seemed pointless, faceless, and inescapable.

If World War I and II were *Dracula*—a terrible and foreign evil that needed brave souls to confront it—then the war in Vietnam was the Sawyer family in *Texas Chain Saw Massacre*: random, indiscriminate, and unshakably American. And the people at the focus of these stories changed accordingly, from the brave volunteers of the old horror to the hapless and luckless victims of the new, who, even when they made it through the night, seldom did so undamaged.

"Who will survive," the tagline of Tobe Hooper's 1974 classic asks, "and what will be left of them?"

**Author's Note:** If my first foray into writing an H Word column (reprinted earlier in this book) was only tangentially about the horror film, this second installment more than makes up for it. This installment is specifically about the transition from the classic horror that is so often my raison d'etre to the more modern "New Horror" that began in the '60s into the '70s, as well as some of my own theories about the changes that came with it—and the reasons behind them.

**Originally published February 2021**
orringrey.com

## "AN ELEGANCE APPROACHING THE SUPERNATURAL."

Why horror? It's a question that anyone who produces—or even consumes—horror in preference to most other forms will run into sooner or later, and probably frequently. Even once you've ensconced yourself among others who share your predilections, you'll find yourself defending the *type* of horror that is your preferred poison. Why monsters over more psychological fare? Why slashers instead of more grown-up stuff? Whatever your tastes, someone will want to know *why*.

Sometimes, that someone will be you.

\*\*\*

For years, I assumed that I wouldn't like giallo films. On paper, they seem like the diametric opposite of what I'm normally after when I come to horror. Infamous for their brutal kills and gratuitous nudity, they make a point of victimizing women and have established problems with misogyny, homophobia, and transphobia, often relying on pseudo-psychological explanations that are simply insulting to anyone with actual mental illness, if taken at face value.

Those are all things I Do Not Like, and they are all emphatically true of many *gialli*. And yet… and yet… and yet… I kind of love them. Not all of them, of course. Who loves *all* of any subgenre? But a large subset—indeed, most of the ones I've seen, especially those by Mario Bava and Dario Argento, recognized masters of the form.

So, if I don't love so many of the things that giallo are famous for, what is it I love about them? Well, I *do* love one thing they're famous for—their scores, which are almost unerringly great, and often used to phenomenal effect. And those scores help to contribute to the larger thing that makes me love them—a sense of weird menace that pervades every frame of the genre's best installments.

While watching Sergio Martino's *Torso*—a movie it seems like I shouldn't like, if ever there was one—I came across a seemingly throwaway line near the beginning of the film that has burned in my mind ever since. "Everything is bathed in an elegance approaching the supernatural." The speaker is describing artwork, but he could just as easily be summing up what I love about giallo.

Sure, some of my favorite *gialli* are ones that are also *overtly* supernatural, the kind that purists would insist "don't really count." Pictures like *Suspiria*, for instance. But even in a film like *Blood and Black Lace*, *Evil Eye*, *The Bird with the Crystal Plumage*, or *Opera*, that "elegance approaching the supernatural" is there, making the films *feel* supernatural, even if their ultimate explanations are more prosaic.

It's this aspect that I think led Ross Lockhart to combine the giallo with another uniquely European tradition in *Giallo Fantastique*, and it's what I think the best of the stories in that volume capture. It's certainly what I was going for in my own contribution, "The Red Church." And it's what I've striven toward every other time I've dipped my toes into the giallo waters, most recently in "Chanson D'Amour," my "timeloop giallo" that's coming in a future issue of *Nightmare Magazine*.

Really, though, it's what I'm after when I come to most any kind of horror. Maybe not always elegance, but always a sense of atmosphere that makes even the mundane feel touched by the numinous.

If there is just one reason "why horror," it's probably that.

**Author's Note:** That "future issue" of *Nightmare Magazine* has since seen print (in September of 2021) and you can read the story in question online there.

**Originally published April 2021**
orringrey.com

## "I HAVE UNLEASHED A MADNESS BEYOND MY CONTROL."—*CTHULHU MANSION* (1990)

Long ago, I owned this movie on VHS, where I had bought it, sight unseen, because it had the word "Cthulhu" in the title. (Those were simpler, stupider times.)

I remembered basically nothing about it besides the cover, which featured a spooky house in the eye socket of a skull, and one half-recollected gloppy makeup effect. What I *did* remember was that it didn't have Cthulhu in it and that it was more than a little disappointing. So, of course, I also picked it up when Vinegar Syndrome recently put it out on Blu.

When I posted shots of the spine and an image of the carnival opening sequence to Instagram, I got a variety of responses, including one person who just replied, "Oof." That was more or less in keeping with what I was *expecting* when I delved into *Cthulhu Mansion*. Adam Cesare, however, in true Adam Cesare fashion, tweeted at me, "This movie rules."

To my own surprise, I found myself more in agreement with Adam than with that "oof." Not that there isn't a lot of oof in *Cthulhu Mansion*—far more of it than there is of Lovecraft, to be sure.

The unlikeable gang of petty criminals who take the aging magician and his daughter hostage in the eponymous mansion (it even has the word "Cthulhu" above the gate) are generally as monodimensional as one might expect, though one guy (Paul Birchard, who had previously shown up in Tim Burton's *Batman* as a reporter and would reappear in *The Dark Knight* as a cop) spends

## CTHULHU MANSION (1990)

pretty much all of his screen time making the weirdest goddamn faces and also, at one point, rubbing a chili dog all over his mouth.

One review on Letterboxd called the flick "all mansion, no Cthulhu," which is also accurate enough. Fortunately, as much as I may like Cthulhu, I probably like mansions even more. And when that mansion belongs to a stage magician (played by Frank Finlay) with a tragic past and a supernatural secret, well, I am far beyond sold.

Is it *good*, though? I was all prepared with an "of course not" kind of response here, but it comes closer than I was expecting. If it doesn't quite grab the brass ring, well, it pretty much does for me, and that's all that really counts. Sure, the film's best creature effect is in a dark ride at the beginning and the closest we get to Cthulhu is a water-damaged book with a drawing of a pentagram inside, but this is a flick that starts out in a carnival and ends up in a magician's creepy mansion during a thunderstorm. How could I do anything *but* love it?

Director J. P. Simon also made *Slugs* (unsurprising), *The Rift* (unsurprising), *Pieces* (not incredibly surprising), *Mystery on Monster Island* (getting a little bit more surprising), and the *MST3K* "classic" *Pod People* (okay, what the hell?), among others, so ... yeah, do with that information what you will. Of that bunch of movies, I haven't actually seen *Pieces* but otherwise this would definitely be my favorite.

Do with *that* information what you will, too.

**Author's Note:** I have since seen *Pieces*. This is still my favorite.

**Originally published August 2021**
*Exploits*

## SHADOW OF THE CAT (1961)

I *really* like Hammer films—those creaky, gothic British chillers of yesteryear. I also *really* like black-and-white, old dark house pictures full of scheming relations. And I really like cats. So, imagine my surprise when I learned that there was a movie that combined all three of those things, and that I hadn't seen it yet.

Fortunately, I was able to correct this injustice with a little help from the latest Hammer box set from Indicator Series. *Shadow of the Cat* (1961), directed by Hammer regular John Gilling and originally released on a double-bill with the (much) bleaker *Curse of the Werewolf*, is a movie whose logline sounds significantly weirder than it is, even while it remains a bit of a miracle that this oddity ever got made at all.

The premise is mostly familiar enough: an old lady gets knocked off by her husband and servants in a relatively brutal opening, and the only witness is the cat. So far so good. But rather than becoming a whodunit (we already know who, after all) or some other old dark house standby, it becomes a sort of proto-slasher, with the vengeful cat taking out the conspirators one by one.

Usually, it does this by leading them into some sort of danger and letting their own clumsiness and growing desperation do the work for it, and we never get anything nearly as, ahem, *direct* as the gruesome cat vengeance in the "Cat from Hell" segment of *Tales from the Darkside: The Movie*—one has to wonder if Stephen King, author of the original story that segment was adapted from, had seen this old chiller.

Part of what makes *Shadow of the Cat* work better than its rather laughable setup is that it is actually more Poe than most of the Poe adaptations that were its contemporaries or successors. We know that the filmmakers are aware of the connection, as the picture opens with the old lady reading "The Raven" to the cat in question.

Even as the cat is literally luring the conspirators to their doom, it also acts as a living—and constant—reminder of their guilt, which is doing them in as surely as any feline cunning.

**Author's Note:** *Exploits* is a sister publication to *Unwinnable*, made up entirely of short "blurbs" and only slightly longer (around 350 words) essays about movies, music, books, video games, etc. This was not my first time writing for *Exploits*, but pretty close.

Since not long after the publication of this piece, I have been movies editor at the magazine, meaning that I haven't written as many essays since then, but I *do* source one every month from other writers, covering a variety of movies from *The Monster Club* to *Hercules in the Haunted World* to *After Blue* and many others besides.

**Originally published August 2021**
*Signal Horizon*

# "THE FLAVOR OF GOOD, RICH MEAT"
## *THE CANNIBAL MAN* (1972)

Decried as a "Video Nasty" in Britain, Eloy de la Iglesia's *The Cannibal Man* is another one of those movies that suffers in part due to its very lurid and misleading title and key art. Yeah, the prominently featured meat cleaver murder does show up in the film, but it's hardly indicative of what you can expect going in, any more than titles like *Cannibal Man* or *The Apartment on the 13th Floor* are.

The print on the Severin Blu-ray has the Spanish title, which translates to the much more apt *Week of the Killer*, which still sounds like you're getting something more grim than what we're presented with here, a character study of an almost accidental serial killer that is really more a camp farce about repressed homosexuality and life under the crushing heel of Francisco Franco and his fascist regime, who were still in power in Spain when this movie got made.

In fact, the closest *Cannibal Man* ever gets to justifying its international title is in the method by which our murderous protagonist eventually disposes of his victims—feeding them into the much-ballyhooed new machine that they recently installed at the slaughterhouse where he works. So, while he's never actually a cannibal, he presumably turns the unsuspecting families who consume the soup that his employer churns out into cannibals without their knowledge, a fact that is acidly foreshadowed by an early-picture commercial of a smiling mom saying, "I always give my family the best food that I can find."

Indeed, though it never reaches the perverse depths of the hellish Pet-Pak Cannery from Russell Mulcahy's *Razorback*, it's also true that nothing Marcos ever does to his victims comes close to matching the horror that he works around every day at the slaughterhouse—a metaphor for Franco's regime if ever there was one.

Before we ever see Marcos butchering his victims, we see the grisly efficiency of the slaughterhouse floor, where twitching cows are strung up by their hind legs, blades plunged into their necks as metal pails are held up to catch the gush of blood, workers milling around everywhere in ways that make the slaughter seem like a spectator sport—echoing the shirtless boys who seem to be perpetually playing soccer in the vacant lot next to Marcos' run-down home, or the starving dogs who roam the area at night.

While there is a certain queasy horror to the killings themselves—how inevitable they seem to become, the way they all circle around the closed-up room where Marcos keeps the bodies until it's time to chop them up and feed them to the machine—much of the film plays like camp, and Iglesia is every bit as concerned with Marcos' budding relationship with his well-off neighbor Nestor, who secretly spies on him from his high-rise apartment, as he is with Marcos' steady decline.

"Legit shocked that something as blatantly homo-centric and anti-fascist as this actually made it past the Spanish censors in 1972," a user named Evan writes at Letterboxd. Five years later, Iglesia would direct *Hidden Pleasures*, which has been called Spain's first openly gay movie. While *Cannibal Man* may not be as open as that later flick, to paraphrase a Letterboxd user describing James Whale's *The Old Dark House*, the gay subtext here threatens to become gay supertext.

There's not just the infatuation with men's flesh—which happens before we are even introduced to any of our principal cast—there's the obvious romance between Marcos and Nestor, a romance that is never consummated but is no less real for it, and which ultimately serves as the former's salvation at the bottom of a pit that he seems otherwise doomed to stack with endless corpses…

**Author's Note:** As I've said elsewhere, when you're receiving films for review without much control over what you're going to receive, you're bound to occasionally get titles that don't seem like they will be your thing. And sometimes, you are pleasantly surprised. *The Cannibal Man* may still not be my thing, but it's surprisingly good—and very much not what it looks like on the tin.

**Originally published August 2021**
*Unwinnable*

# "I CREATED IT AS I WENT ALONG."
# BILL REBANE'S WEIRD WISCONSIN BOXED SET
# FROM ARROW VIDEO

Prior to sitting down with this substantial Blu-ray set, which contains just over half of the feature-length films for whom Bill Rebane is the credited director, the full and complete extent of my knowledge of his filmography came from *Mystery Science Theater 3000*, where a handful of his films had been featured. That's rarely an encouraging place to start from, but in the case of Rebane's notoriously eccentric output, it at least feels like an *appropriate* one.

"This is the 'a go-go' part."
—the 'Bots from *MST3K* re: *Monster a Go-Go* (1965)

Plenty of ink has been spilled over the years speculating on the identity of the worst movie that *Mystery Science Theater 3000* ever covered. While the most popular answer is usually *Manos: The Hands of Fate*, I would suggest that a good contender for that "honor" is this flick, which was cobbled together by none other than the "Godfather of Gore" himself, Herschell Gordon Lewis, using footage left over from several abortive attempts by Bill Rebane at stringing a feature debut together. In fact, Rebane himself has reportedly declared the finished product the "worst movie ever made."

Is that a little harsh? Almost certainly. But while the version included on Blu-ray in this set may look and sound at least a *little* better than the one lambasted by Joel and the 'Bots all those years ago, it's still a far cry from a cinematic masterpiece. And while we're unlikely to *find* a cinematic masterpiece in a boxed set celebrating a director whose greatest exposure probably came via being featured on *MST3K*, it's still unfortunate for Rebane that this set (and his career) starts off with *Monster a Go-Go*, since it is never the movie it was intended to be.

Rebane got his start in features trying to make a "*Twilight Zone* style" movie that was originally going to be called *S*. When that stalled, he moved on to a project called *Terror at Half Day*, named for a now-extinct neighborhood in Chicago. It wasn't long, however, before everything that could possibly go wrong on a first feature, did. The result is not just multiple reshoots cobbled together into a disjointed mess—with actors disappearing and reappearing in the film, once as a deceased character's heretofore-unmentioned twin brother—but a movie that was never actually completed by its original director.

When Lewis bought the footage of *Terror at Half Day* and hung it with a(n admittedly much catchier) alternate title and taglines like, "The picture that comes complete with a 10-foot-tall monster, to give you the wim-wams," it may have been the best thing to happen to the movie, but it would also have been enough to prompt many other first-time directors to throw in the towel.

If there's one thing that we learn about Rebane from this boxed set, however, it's that he's anything but easily discouraged, and in a filmography filled with head-scratching decisions and movies that are defined as much by the adversity under which they were made as by their extremely limited budgets, maybe *Monster a Go-Go* is the perfect way to kick things off…

> "What's so hard about believing that we're not the only ones in this universe?"
> —***Invasion from Inner Earth*** (1974)

Despite what I just said about Rebane not being easily discouraged, more than a decade separates the troubled production of his first feature and *Invasion from Inner Earth*, arguably the first *actual* movie in this set. During that time, Rebane made his living on everything from short films and industrial videos (one of which is included in the special features of this set) to a documentary about the missing arms of the Venus de Milo.

By the time he finally did get back to making features, he had already acquired his 200-acre "shooting ranch" in Wisconsin, and begun to accumulate the traits that would define the rest of his cinematic output, beginning with *Invasion from Inner Earth*, which is basically the movie you would get if *Night of the Living Dead* (or, more accurately, *War of the Worlds*) only followed characters who were nowhere near anything that ever happened.

Those "traits" I mentioned include both good and bad aspects. The regionalism that many point to as the most obvious pleasure of Rebane's filmography is already firmly in place in this snowy and sedate (inner) space invasion flick, along with a resolute commitment to earnest speculation about absolutely off-the-rails "science," such as a particularly great monologue about a giant rose devouring most of the eastern seaboard before blotting out the sun. Of course, they bring with them many not so great aspects, like extraordinarily meager budgets, utterly baffling story decisions, and sound mixing that renders much of the dialogue all but incomprehensible.

As with *Monster a Go-Go* before it and *Giant Spider Invasion* (the other *MST* alum) after, *Invasion from Inner Earth*'s ambitions outstrip its budget by a considerable margin. Indeed, its ideas are, at times, as ambitious as they come. Did you know, for example, that a long time ago, Mars got closer to Earth than the moon is and stayed that way for thousands of years? Did you know that this is why the Martians had to abandon their planet and move to the center of the Hollow Earth? It's apparently fairly common knowledge, so I'm surprised you haven't heard about it…

Of course, with the exception of a couple of pretty decent

no-budget UFO shots, *Invasion from Inner Earth* can't actually *show* any of this, so the "action," such as it is, is relegated to four people sitting around in a cabin and arguing, occasionally broken up by charmingly low-rent sequences of fake newscasts or shots of people running in the streets, fleeing what look to be large smoke bombs.

It almost works some of the time, in spite of all that, even if it is also quite boring. It's much better when viewed as a proof-of-concept for the superior *Alpha Incident*, which would follow it some four years later and on the next disc in this set, and you certainly can't fault it for not taking a big swing, anyway...

"Can you call it an 'incident' when nothing happens?"
—someone on Letterboxd re: ***The Alpha Incident*** (1978)

Bill Rebane made the *MST3K* "classic" *Giant Spider Invasion* in-between *Invasion from Inner Earth* and this flick, but that movie (like several other titles in his weirdo filmography) isn't included in this set, which means that we're watching this and *Inner Earth* back to back, which goes a long way toward reinforcing how much this feels like an attempt, on Rebane's part, to actually pull off what he was going for in *Inner Earth*—and he mostly succeeds!

Apparently, this is Rebane's favorite from among all of the movies he made and, honestly, it's easy to see why. It's probably his best. Sure, the scenes of the scientists talking amongst themselves have all the energy (for good or ill) of *The Incredible Melting Man*—another *MST3K* alum that isn't by Rebane, but the same spirit is certainly there—but Rebane handles the plot of an alien force threatening the world while a handful of people are trapped in a single location where nothing much actually happens much better this time, in part by putting our protagonists at immediate risk from an invisible (and therefore budget-friendly) threat: they've all been exposed to an alien pathogen that will cause them to die gruesomely if they fall asleep.

(It's basically the only special effect in the entire movie, but it's surely a doozy when it finally does show up.)

*The Alpha Incident* is helped along by a tighter screenplay and actual actors, especially reliable character actor and movie drunk George "Buck" Flower, who may be the first one of our limited cast to kick the bucket, but who also milks the most pathos out of his part before he goes. Perhaps no other actor of his era could have quite so successfully sold both the comic relief drunk and the man coming undone by guilt over having inadvertently infected the people around him with an alien virus quite like ol' Buck.

It's also nihilistic in that late-'70s sort of way; claustrophobic and paranoid, weaponizing the very tedium of its central premise in a way that *Inner Earth*'s different logline wouldn't allow. None of which is to say that this is necessarily an A+ effort, by normal metrics, but I can absolutely see why Rebane was proud of it—and I think he was right to be.

"Town's dead."
— *The Demons of Ludlow* (1983)

What do you do when you want to remake John Carpenter's *The Fog* but you don't have any fog or any budget but you *do* have a snowy Wisconsin ghost town, some Colonial-era costumes, and a piano? If you're Bill Rebane and his crew of locals and regulars, you make *The Demons of Ludlow*!

Of all the flicks in this set, this was the one I was most excited about watching, in part because I like haunted pianos better than alien invasions or whatever the hell the next few movies are going to be about. In fact, I like haunted pianos better than most stuff, and if anyone had told me what an obvious riff on *The Fog* this was—complete with actual story beats getting straight lifted—I would have been *even more* excited.

And, to my own surprise, I wasn't let down. Again, *Demons of Ludlow* is no *Fog*, but no one ever expected it to be, probably not even Bill Rebane. What it is, instead, is its own local, low budget, lo-fi, weirdo thing. If *The Alpha Incident* was maybe Rebane's best picture, this might be the first one where all the pieces finally actually come together. For the first time, the movie's ambitions don't outstrip its budget or the talents of the cast and crew, even though *Demons of Ludlow* has less star power than *Alpha Incident* did.

Where that flick was subdued this one… is also subdued, let's be honest, but when it is bonkers, it really commits. There are bloodied hands flickering with optical effect lightning, and the ghostly assaults are low rent but effective, complete with plenty of people in pancake makeup and Colonial wigs licking their lips lasciviously and reaching out bloody hands toward the various (often scantily-clad) townsfolk.

Does it make a lot of sense? Not really, no, though more than the next couple of films in this set are going to. But was that ever really the point? The answer to that is also "no."

"Quite confusing is this story as the tale comes to a close."
— ***The Game*** (1984)

Between *The Alpha Incident* and *Demons of Ludlow*, this set skipped five years and two flicks, including one that I'm really bummed about because of the amazing key art. Oh well, I guess I'll just have to wait and watch *Croaked: Frog Monster from Hell* some other time.

Such is *not* the case between *Demons* and *The Game*, which were released just a year apart. As the (hardcover) booklet that accompanies the set points out, these two films and his Tiny Tim-starring 1987 slasher *Blood Harvest* are also Rebane's only "straight" horror movies, if any of those can truly be considered straight anything. With most of his others, he's at least as interested in the science fiction premises (however outlandish or unscientific) as he is in the horror, usually more so.

Of those three, I haven't seen *Blood Harvest*, because it's not in this set, but I feel like I can still safely say that *The Game* is the one least interested in being a horror flick. Instead, it seems more like Rebane's riff on something like *House on Haunted Hill*, by way of something like *April Fool's Day*. Which is to say that it's less about fear than about setting up gags, continuity or logic be damned.

If you were to do one of those word graph things with all the reviews of *The Game* on Letterboxd, I'm pretty sure the word that came up the most would be "nonsense." And they're not wrong. While the premise is straightforward enough—three eccentric millionaires invite a handful of guests to an abandoned resort to play a "game" in which they have to confront their fears—the unspooling of said events rarely makes much sense, which even the film's own narration acknowledges.

The booklet calls it "a satire of 'mystery plotting' itself," though "nonsense" is just as good a term. *The Game* is nonetheless great fun much of the time, and its most effective element is certainly its three sadistic millionaires, who have a ball creeping around the hallways in scary masks, egging each other on, and getting drunk and singing "Jimmy Crack Corn."

> "This plan cannot fail."
> —*Twister's Revenge* (1987)

Never has a movie from 1987 felt more like a movie from 1978 than Bill Rebane's final directorial feature, *Twister's Revenge*, which also closes out this boxed set as the only non-horror-adjacent movie in the bunch. Indeed, its only nod toward a speculative element is the (unnecessarily) AI-powered talking monster truck from which it derives its name.

In structure, *Twister's Revenge* feels like one of those early live-action Disney movies in which a gang of bickering and bumbling crooks are thwarted by children, pets, or, in this case, a talking monster truck, even if the humor is more sexual and scatological than those flicks would have allowed, and they probably wouldn't have featured a complete musical number by a random local burlesque act.

"This whole film was shot without a screenplay," Rebane is quoted as saying in the booklet that accompanies the Arrow Video set. "Every morning we would take the cast and say, 'What are we going to do today?'" It'd be tempting to say that it shows, but honestly, while *Twister's Revenge* is often jarring and baffling, it's never really more so than many of Rebane's better and more serious flicks, from the head-scratching ending of *Invasion from Inner Earth* to the utter nonsense of *The Game*.

Even Rebane's staunchest advocates generally seem to argue that one of the biggest selling points of his wide array of indie pictures is their regionalism. In many ways, Rebane can be seen as one of the kings of the regional genre movie, and most of the flicks in this set were filmed at his "shooting ranch" in rural Wisconsin.

That regionalism certainly *is* a strength of these films and, perhaps surprisingly, not the only one. Yet, *Weird Wisconsin* is unlikely to bring many new converts to the church of Bill Rebane. If you get to the end of the six films contained here and feel the need for *even more* Rebane, however, the set also comes with a feature-length documentary on the filmmaker, not to mention the aforementioned hardcover booklet, both of which are probably of interest to aficionados of independent and regional cinema, even if you aren't a fan of the filmmaker.

**Author's Note:** At this point, if it wasn't already, I think the format that I'm going to keep using for reviewing Blu-ray sets is fully formed, complete with the separate headings for each film included, opening with quotes from the films themselves. Or, in this case, sometimes quotes *about* them.

**Originally published September 2021**
*Signal Horizon*

# "IT'S TIME TO CUT OUT THE CANCER."
# *MALIGNANT* (2021)

*Malignant*, James Wan's first R-rated horror film since 2007's *Dead Silence*, opens on a shot of a gothic castle perched on a seaside cliff. That the castle is, in actuality, a research hospital in 1993 does little to dampen the message of just exactly what kind of movie we are getting into here—in fact, it may actually amplify it. (At the time of this writing, I had entirely forgotten that the first two *Conjuring* films are actually rated R, because they probably didn't actually need to be. This... definitely does.)

The scene that follows gives us inordinately more exposition than we have heretofore gotten in the film's trailers, which made things sound a lot more like *The Eyes of Laura Mars* than the bonkers supervillain police procedural that we're about to experience. It's filled with lines that land with resounding clunks, delivered with all the melodrama of a TV soap opera. That, also, gives you a solid idea of what to expect from the rest of the film.

In fact, now that I think about it, the three trailers I saw in front of *Malignant* were for the new *Venom* movie, *Last Night in Soho*, and *Prisoners of the Ghostland*, the latest Nic Cage vehicle. That also gives you a pretty good idea of what you're about to experience.

Fundamentally, *Malignant* is not so much the "new vision in horror" that the marketing promises as it is Wan comfortably back in the *Dead Silence* mode. This is a Dark Castle, direct-to-video movie from the early 2000s, given a bigger budget and a director who knows how to make even a miniscule budget seem *much* bigger than it actually is. It's off the rails and ridiculous from the jump, and it never really stops running, despite clocking in at just shy of two hours long.

It's a movie that isn't afraid to be stupid. Burdened with an uninspired script and characters who are paper thin, none of that matters because the train has already jumped the track before the titles even come up, and it never stops going the places you always *hope* movies like this will go but they never do because that would be too ridiculous.

Plenty of people will hate this movie, and that's fine. Like *Dead Silence*, it's a hateable movie. Some will hate it because they are predisposed to, some will hate it because it's just not for them, and some will hate it because it is wild, exuberant nonsense. For those of us who speak this language, though, it is a symphony. As I said on Twitter, "Please hook the ambitious trash directly to my veins."

It is impossible to usefully talk about *Malignant* without getting into spoilers, so there will be *heavy* spoilers from this point forward. I think the film is best watched as cold as possible, however, so if you have *any* inclination to do so, just *watch* it. It's playing in theaters and on HBOMax. You may love it, like I did, you may hate it, but you won't see anything else quite like it anytime soon, and that's probably an experience worth having, anyway.

*Malignant* is many things, and none of those things is "subtle." One of its many identities is that of a giallo. I've been saying since the first *Insidious* that, love him or hate him, James Wan is the closest thing the modern crop of horror filmmakers has produced to early-career Argento, and that's emphatically true here, for good and for ill. Wan has made no secret of his affection for giallo in the past, but this is the first time he has fully embraced the genre on a structural, rather than merely an *aesthetic*, level.

If giallo is, indeed, a genre, rather than a moment in time and space—that is to say, if giallo can be made outside Italy in the late-'70s/early-'80s—then *Malignant* is a giallo in every way that matters. Gory, brutal set piece kills splashed with flat light. A killer who is black-gloved and, for most of the picture, faceless. Police procedural aspects, with a pair of detectives and their supporting cast who could have stepped straight out of a cop show. A civilian who knows the solution to the mystery, but it's buried in her memory, inaccessible until the pieces are all put together. All that's missing is a prominently placed bottle of J&B Scotch.

Much as he did in *Insidious 2*, Wan and his collaborators also carry forward one equally integral part of the standard giallo formula, albeit one that has more problematic resonances in the present day: the explanation for the killer that is both logistically absurd and scientifically unlikely. And, in true Wan style, he cranks that to eleven.

In this case, that takes the form of Gabriel, our protagonist's parasitic twin, who literally shares her brain. Thought to have been excised when she was a child, Gabriel has actually been lying dormant in her body, gaining power through a method every bit as grotesque as the "human puppet" scenes from the end of *Dead Silence*, and he uses their psychic link to render her inert while he uses her body to kill.

So, it's *The Dark Half* if George Stark had superhuman strength and could control electricity. (Others have also pointed out the parallels with *Basket Case*.) Wait what, you're saying, but no, there's not enough time to stop and discuss the superhuman strength and the controlling electricity because we need to talk about the fact that Gabriel literally emerges from the back of our protagonist's skull, meaning that when he kills, she is walking around backward.

And by "walking around," I mean doing parkour up walls. And by "kills," I mean *everyone*. People will tell you that this film's third act is off the rails, and they're right. But this movie was never on the rails. This thing went off the rails before the cold open. By the third act, it's plowing through all the people on the platform.

It's stupid and reckless and bold and breathtaking and it doesn't really seem to care whether you're along for the ride or not. It's going. Grab on if you want to come, too. Otherwise, get out of the way.

**Author's Note:** If anything, my affection for *Malignant* has only grown since I originally wrote this review after grinning my way through a theatrical screening. It is well on its way to being my favorite James Wan film, and one of my favorite flicks of the 21st century so far.

Originally published September 2021
*Signal Horizon*

## "EVERY DAY AND HOUR NOW OUTRAGES ARE TAKING PLACE"—*BORN FOR HELL* (1976)

"You can kill, or get killed, but you've no right to kill yourself."

Released in the U.S. under the much more lurid (and worse) title *Naked Massacre*—imagine, just imagine, having a title like *Born for Hell* at your fingertips and opting for *Naked Massacre* instead—the logline of Denis Heroux's 1976 shocker is pure exploitation.

Based loosely on the real-life crimes of Richard Speck—which were committed only a decade before the film came out—in order to get that "it *could happen* to *you*" inspired by true events text crawl up front, *Born for Hell* tells the tale of a Vietnam vet set adrift who eventually breaks into the home of eight nurses and methodically torments, brutalizes, and slays them. What sets it apart from any number of other movies with similar premises is the decision to shift the action from Speck's Chicago to then-contemporary Belfast in the midst of the "Troubles."

This is all part of a larger effort, on the part of the film, to recontextualize the crimes of its Speck-alike as part of "the spirit of uncontrolled violence at loose in the world today," as one in-camera news reporter puts it. Before we even really meet our killer, he has already been caught in a church bombing and watched a group of children pantomime an execution by firing squad.

Is this intended to suggest that our killer isn't really responsible for his actions? Or is it, rather, an indication that the system has failed to get him the help he needs, as surely as it has failed his ultimate victims by not protecting them from him? Or is it just a way to further sensationalize its tale of brutality and degradation? You can find plenty of people online taking just about every one of these positions, and I honestly couldn't say for sure which one I agree with.

What I will say is this, the movie takes a *long* time getting to the crimes themselves. We spend a lot of time with our antagonist, as he drifts from shelter to bar and back again. We watch him watching the habits of the nurses, see him rescue and then torment an older prostitute. He spends time with a fellow drifter from Vietnam, who suggests that women are all prostitutes, and that our killer is "afraid of women."

Nor does it spend *all* of its time on the killer. We meet all the nurses who will become our eventual victims. They get various subplots and backstories. One is in love with one of the others and is trying to find a way to tell her. One is pregnant. One is engaged but her parents don't approve. One witnesses a death in the street on her way home from the hospital, a result of the violence that is gripping the city.

The film's brutality toward these women doesn't start until around the halfway point, and when it does, it follows the playbook of Richard Speck's actual crimes relatively closely, even while embellishing several points, including the only thing that could possibly justify that *Naked Massacre* title, when he takes the lesbian nurse and her unaware love interest and attempts to force them to have sex with one another.

These sequences are also extremely hard to watch. Not because of any actual violence or gore—there's some of both, of course, he *does* kill eight women before the night is out—but because they are so grounded in a kind of reality. Mathieu Carriere turns in a sweaty, unsettling performance as our killer, alternating convincingly between cold-blooded and pathetic. Among the victims, there are no final girl heroics, and no A24-style histrionics—just people coming apart in various ways, and not always ones that "make sense." Because our reactions to stress and trauma rarely "make sense."

There's no music during these scenes, and precious little to pull you out of the immediacy of the harrowing ordeal the women are undergoing. Off-key dubbing and tempera paint blood can only do so much to break the illusion of this queasy nightmare.

"The tension is repulsive," Bob McCully writes in his *Letterboxd* review. "The violence is incredibly sleazy. There's no music and no hope. [...] You are sinking with these women, deeper and deeper into his throat."

Which is to say that *Born for Hell*—good or bad—is most definitely an *unpleasant* watch. And it should be. We can argue whether films like this glorify their sex predator, serial killer antagonists by humanizing them, and we can debate whether the movie has a problem with women or just accurately depicts men who do, but we should all be able to agree that it should probably not be fun to watch even a fictionalized reenactment of a night of hell in which Richard Speck tormented, brutalized, and killed eight real women.

**Author's Note:** I received a review copy of this movie around the same time as *Cannibal Man*, though I watched them a bit apart. They would certainly make for a feel-bad double-feature.

**Originally published September 2021**
*Unwinnable*

# "I'M TELLING YOU, IF YOU DON'T HAND HIM OVER, YOU'RE GOING TO BE IN A LOT BIGGER TROUBLE THAN YOU BARGAINED FOR!"
# *SIEGE* (1983)

Also released as *Self Defense*, *Siege* is a 1983 Canadian exploitation flick that is one of a long line of movies aping John Carpenter's *Assault on Precinct 13*. It's also probably one of the best ones. A review at *TVGuide.com* calls it "frighteningly effective" and "reminiscent of *Assault on Precinct 13*, though it is not quite as effective," while also (as so many synopses of the movie seem to do) getting the plot details slightly wrong.

The *actual* plot goes something like this: During a (real life) police strike in Halifax in 1981, a right-wing militia calling themselves the "New Order" push their way into a gay bar and start roughing up the clientele. The opening assault is deeply disturbing, even before any violence begins, and violence begins in relatively short order, when the confrontation ends with the bartender dead after a fall onto a broken bottle.

The toughs panic and call their handler, who comes in and methodically executes everyone in the place because otherwise this could be "very damaging to our cause," as he puts it. Only one of the bar's patrons escapes, eventually taking refuge in a nearby apartment, which puts us firmly in *Precinct 13* territory, even if the film's opening titles and pulsing soundtrack hadn't already done so.

Armed with military-grade weapons (complete with silencers) and a sniper with an infra-red scope on the roof across the street, the militia lays siege to the apartment, while the group of folks inside have to defend themselves with nothing but a few homebrew booby traps, a rifle with two bullets, and a bow with a single arrow. From there, *Siege* hits a lot of the usual beats, but manages to maintain a sense of highly-pitched tension throughout.

Here's the thing, though: No, *Siege* isn't as effective as *Assault on Precinct 13*, but it may be *more* socially responsible. It would be easy enough for a movie with this logline to glorify the kind of rugged survivalism so often exalted in action movies of the '80s. "If only everyone were more prepared for this kind of trouble," it could easily say, "think how differently this could have gone."

Except that the people who fare the best are, in many ways, those who are the least prepared. Indeed, *Siege* is a movie that feels like it has a lot to unpack when it comes to masculinity, and the connection between machismo and using violence to get what you're after, whether that's intimidating people who (let's be honest) intimidate you, like the right-wing militia at the beginning, or just making it through the night, like the survivalist member of the besieged apartment-dwellers.

After all, the folks in the apartment would have had *more* bullets for that rifle had he not fired them off at the beginning of the police strike. And it seems not for nothing that Chekhov's sleeve-knife ultimately goes unused when it is most needed.

What really helps to establish *Siege* as a more socially-conscious take on the material, though, is in the identity of its bad guys. I've argued before that *Assault on Precinct 13* is not really interested in a "cops and robbers" type storyline. That the silent, implacable, multiracial gang that terrorizes the precinct (staffed with mostly civilians) are really a force of nature, sharing more in common with Romero's ravening hordes of flesh eaters than any real-world outgroup.

Which is a long way of saying that, while on its surface *Precinct*

*13* looks like yet another movie lamenting society's collapse into lawlessness in the wake of the Manson Family murders and the failure of the Summer of Love, it's actually not terribly interested in being about that, and is just using it as the set dressing to tell a cosmic horror tale about individuals assailed by a carnivorous cosmos, pretty much.

*Siege*, on the other hand, foregrounds the motives of its villains. They are here to "send a message" to the patrons of the gay bar they terrorize at the beginning of the film. "Being a homo is not a normal way of life," one of them tells the bartender, shortly before the latter is dead on the barroom floor.

Nearly forty years later, the right-wing fascists at the heart of *Siege*—with their bullying and their bigotry, their cowardice and their fetishization of firearms—are unfortunately familiar. In the last few years, we've seen their ilk rise to prominence in various ways, from the so-called Proud Boys to Kyle Rittenhouse, the 17-year-old murderer described by the AP as a "police admirer" who gunned down two people during a Black Lives Matter protest, to the insurrection of January 6, 2021. *Siege*'s spate of villains could have been any one among their number.

The flick saves perhaps its most damning indictment for the stinger, however. This is a movie that's only about a decade shy of having been around for half a century, but it's also one that's seldom seen. So, if you haven't seen *Siege* and what I've already written is enough to make you want to check it out cold, stop now, because I'm gonna spoil that ending sucker punch.

As easy as it would be for *Siege* to glorify a kind of self-made survivalism, it would be even easier for it to lionize police. There's a reason why all of this is happening during a police strike, after all, right? Oh yes, there absolutely is, but not necessarily the one that you might think.

Sure, the police never come during the night's long standoff, in part because they're on strike, in part because the phone lines are cut in short order. But as someone watching the film in 2021 and looking backward, you have to wonder whose side they would be on, if they *did* show up. The movie doesn't wonder, though. It *knows*, and it makes no bones about it in that stinger I mentioned.

Once the last of the assailants are finally done in by the defenders of the apartment, save one who flees because of his injuries, the view cuts to a picturesque scene of a mother and her daughter playing ball in the park, along with titles telling us that the police strike has ended. The ball rolls to a stop at the foot of a police officer and, as the camera pans up, it is probably no surprise that it reveals the cop in question to be the one surviving member of the militia group.

Drop mic. Roll credits.


**Author's Note:** Around September of 2021, I apparently got a lot of flicks for review that were outside my usual bailiwick, but that were all pretty damn good. This is the best of them.

**Originally published October 2021**
*Downright Creepy*

# *THE SPINE OF NIGHT* BRINGS COSMIC HORROR BACK TO SWORD AND SORCERY

Before I start talking about *The Spine of Night*, I need to disclose some conflicts of interest. Phil Gelatt—one half of the directing duo behind this new animated feature—is a good friend of mine. He blurbed my second collection of short stories, we co-hosted movies together at the NecronomiCon in Providence, and I've slept in his house. So I'm not exactly an unbiased party here.

Also, I've actually seen *The Spine of Night* before. I watched a rough cut while it was still in post-production. The animation wasn't entirely finished, the story was organized somewhat differently, and there were chapter headings breaking up the film's various time points. Yet, the essence was already there, a beating, bloody heart beneath the unfinished animation and the jumbled story beats.

So, watching *The Spine of Night* in its finished form hit differently for me than it probably will for a lot of other people. It was like watching something grow up. A film that I knew to be a passion project, something that, the last time I saw it, was still sometimes in bloody pieces, actually taking steps and not just walking but running. Rather like the characters in the picture, who are often alive one minute, breathing and fleshed out and ready to have a whole narrative centered on them, only to die gruesomely and ignominiously the next minute—and sometimes return again later, alive once more.

***

Now we can talk a bit about *The Spine of Night*. For those who don't know, *The Spine of Night* is animated using a technique called "rotoscope." More than a century old, rotoscope was first invented by Max Fleischer in 1915 and has been used in numerous projects over the years, perhaps most prominently—at least for our purposes—by Ralph Bakshi in films like *Wizards*, the animated *Lord of the Rings*, and *Fire and Ice*, which, along with 1981's *Heavy Metal*, is probably the most obvious touchstone to understand what you can expect from *The Spine of Night*.

In rotoscope animation, animators draw over live action, allowing the animation of more realistic and fluid action scenes, at least in theory. In practice, rotoscope—like stop-motion and other methods of filmmaking—tends to produce a unique feel that is immediately identifiable, and in many ways that feel, as much as anything, helps to establish *The Spine of Night* on a continuum with films like *Fire and Ice* and *Heavy Metal*.

If it didn't, the movie would still let you know what to expect in short order. One of the first images we see is of a fully nude woman—Tzod, voiced by Lucy Lawless—trudging through the snow. From there, we will be treated to no shortage of full-frontal nudity, gruesome disembowelments, and sundry other, extremely R-rated visuals and themes.

Indeed, one would be hard-pressed to name a film in recent memory that is more bloody or grim than *The Spine of Night*, which exhibits brutality on a scale that would require a blockbuster budget to accomplish in live action. Yet, there is more going on here than blood and mud.

The fantasy subgenre of sword and sorcery has always been kissing cousins with weird fiction and cosmic horror, but that often takes the form of little more than mumbo jumbo, unspeakable cults, and nonsensical names. *The Spine of Night* reaches for something bigger, juxtaposing the violence and petty cruelty of human ambition against the very concept of infinity, the scope of a universe that expands both outward and forward, through space and through time.

Something else that cosmic horror on screen rarely taps into well is also mined here to good effect: the idea that this vastness can be as comforting as it is horrifying. There's a scene near the middle of the movie, where two individuals come together around a campfire after the loss of their homes, to look up at the stars and speculate, suggesting that the night has its back turned, and that human lives are just embers blown up from distant campfires; pinpricks of light dying away as they burn.

It would be one thing if *The Spine of Night* merely trotted out these ideas, put them in the mouths of its characters, but it also tries to represent them in its very structure. As I said earlier, when I watched the rough cut of the film, chapter breaks split it up, dividing the movie into a variety of discrete chunks. Those are gone now, yet *The Spine of Night* still covers vastly more territory than any other fantasy epic twice its length would convey in a trio of films or more.

We begin with Tzod, as her swamp home comes under attack from a nearby despot. We are introduced to an array of characters, enough to anchor an entire film longer than this one. And yet, within a short time, most are dead, or gone from the movie forever. As the film jumps ahead, from one period to another, we see generations pass, connected by the bloom that Tzod brings from the swamp and, eventually, finds again atop that snowy mountain—and by the repercussions that come with the bloom's ill-use.

By the end of the picture, centuries have passed. Technology has advanced considerably. What were once ramshackle buildings of wood barely pulled from the mud have been replaced with vast metropolises of steel and stone from which flame-spewing airships hunt. We have met numerous characters who could have been our protagonists, only to see them fall or vanish away.

The scope helps to sell the cosmic scale of the enterprise. Rather than telling one story—no matter how epic—we instead get several, anchored by shared themes and at least one unifying character, but spread across hundreds of years, so that the rise and fall of something as mighty as what we are shown feels much more grounded and real, even while the ultimate lesson is that even a centuries-spanning empire is just another ember burning away in the dark.

I'm not here to say whether *The Spine of Night* succeeds in its ambitions—I am, as I said, too close to the material and the people behind it—but it *is* ambitious, and that counts for a lot. Whether you like it or not may depend on your tolerance (or appreciation) for bloody and brutal rotoscoped animation, but if you're someone who likes to stand under the stars and feel impossibly small, then it's at least worth a look.

**Author's Note:** It was actually *because* of my relationship with Phil Gelatt that I was asked to write about *The Spine of Night* for *Downright Creepy* when it premiered—a task I was more than happy to undertake.

**Originally published October 2021**
*Unwinnable*

## "I WANT TO PIONEER THE ART OF TOUCHING."—
## *BLIND BEAST* (1969) ON BLU-RAY AT LAST

Twice, recently, I have been tasked with reviewing films by Yasuzo Masumura, and have found myself writing *around* the only film of his I had ever previously seen, *Blind Beast*. Once, the disconnect was pretty profound—though acerbic as hell, *Giants and Toys* is a far cry from the depravity of *Blind Beast*. With *Irezumi*, however, the parallels were more striking.

*Blind Beast* is a film that I had been meaning to watch for decades, ever since I worked in a video store. It wasn't Masumura's name that let me know I needed to see it back then, though. It was more the name of the writer whose work the film is adapted from, "Japanese Poe" Edogawa Rampo.

Even that wasn't *really* it, though. Rampo has, after all, been adapted to film numerous times—with more than 60 credits on IMDb—and I've seen hardly any of them. No, the real thing that tweaked my curiosity about *Blind Beast* was the reputation of the eponymous blind sculptor's studio, a phantasmagoric funhouse of oversized female features cast in papier mâché. Breasts, sure, but also noses, eyes, ears, lips, and two giant reclining bodies, stretching the length of the room.

Knowing that the reveal of the studio was coming, and having seen stills of what it contains for years before I actually sat down with the film for the first time not that long ago, I was still stunned by the sequence in which we are first introduced to it. It is disorienting and eerie in a way that only films from this era seem to ever manage, while also feeling vastly ahead of its time.

An extremely weird and striking set will only go so far, however, even if the vast majority of the film takes place within it. Fortunately, like the other Masumura films I've reviewed recently, there's more going on in *Blind Beast* than what it says on the tin. What begins as a conte cruel about a sculptor who kidnaps his "muse" gradually becomes something much more twisted and symbolic, as the two slowly fall into a relationship that is mutually self-destructive.

It is this that keeps *Blind Beast* from becoming the generic exploitation flick that its logline makes it sound like, even while it is probably also this that led a contemporary *Variety* review to call *Blind Beast* a "sick film." In the booklet that accompanies the Arrow Video Blu-ray of *Blind Beast*, with a gorgeous cover by Tony Stella and lavishly illustrated with stills from the film, Virginie Selavy explores Masumura's "complex idea of perversity."

In several of Masumura's films, she argues, "the perversity of deviant individual desire is pitted against the ingrained perversity of the oppressive, hypocritical social order. The outcome is never straightforward: although collective perversity is always excoriated, individual perversity in Masumura's cinema is a double-edged sword, often simultaneously emboldening and degrading, liberating and destructive."

Such is certainly the case in *Blind Beast*, where Michio, the blind sculptor, and Aki, his victim, find a kind of ecstatic liberation in the throes of their "new art of touching," while at the same time devolving in a self-destructive, sub-animal existence. This is expressed through dialogue that reads a little like decadent poetry, a little like cosmic horror, as Aki compares their degeneration within the lightless studio to insects, amoeba, and jellyfish.

The film opens with images that suggest where it is headed. The first things we see are artful images of nude forms in bondage, credited in the film to a Mr. Yamana but actually filmed during a 1968 exhibition by underground photographer Akira Suzuki.

Mako Midori, who plays Aki in the film, was one of Suzuki's actual models, leading to a disorienting sensation of falling into a fictionalized world even from the opening credits.

Just about everything in *Blind Beast* is exaggerated, suggestive, symbolic, grotesque, subjective, and gorgeous. The fictional version of the photographic exhibition that kicks off the film is called "Les fleurs du mal," named for Baudelaire's famous book of poetry, itself scandalous and frequently censored at the time of its original publication.

In 1969, *Blind Beast* was likely shocking. Today, after more than half a century filled with films geared specifically to shock, it has lost much of its power to scandalize, but the "dark, dank" depths of its central abyss are still such that few other films since have dared to plumb them, for good or ill.

**Author's Note:** The other films by Yasuzo Masumura that I mentioned at the beginning of this review aren't necessarily appropriate subjects for a book on the horror film, but they are well worth tracking down and checking out, even for those who primarily like their pictures a little on the scary side.

**Originally published October 2021**
*Unwinnable*

# THE INADVERTENT SCI-FI OF UNIVERSAL'S ORIGINAL *MUMMY* SEQUELS

Unlike *Dracula* or *Frankenstein*, the original Universal *Mummy* movies of the '30s and '40s—resurrected by Hammer in the '50s and '60s and rebooted by Universal not once but twice in recent decades—didn't have a single ur-text from which to draw. While mummies were omnipresent in the anglophone public consciousness, thanks to highly publicized finds like the (re)discovery of the Tomb of Tutankhamun in 1922, no specific narrative formed the backbone of mummy-related fiction.

There was Bram Stoker's 1903 novel, *The Jewel of Seven Stars*, which formed the partial basis for a number of later films, but the earliest known account of a mummy coming back to life is in Edgar Allan Poe's satirical short, "Some Words with a Mummy," from 1845.

Poking fun at, among other things, the notion that the Western world was, at that time, the height of scientific and intellectual advancement, the story is far from horror. The mummy, when revived, merely chastises the gathered men for their abuse, and shares with them cigars and wine while they engage in the eponymous conversation.

Film rarely, if ever, followed Poe's tack. With the exception of the suave and sinister Imhotep, played by Boris Karloff in Universal's first foray into mummy movies, most of the mummies on film were somnolent, shambling, and silent for many years. Even when they started talking again, in later decades, they tended to have resurrection of one sort or another on their mind, more than the casual conversation of Poe's story.

Unshackled from a particular narrative, the Universal movies of the '30s and '40s were free to make up whatever mummy stories fit their fancy. In 1932, that consisted of an individual, Imhotep, who had loved the wrong woman and, as punishment, been buried alive. Resurrected by an over-eager archaeologist translating and reading the words of a life-giving scroll, Imhotep spends ten years integrating into modern life as a historian named Ardeth Bey, while he attempts to find the woman he believes to be the reincarnation of his forbidden love, Princess Anck-su-namun—most of which should sound fairly familiar to anyone who has seen the 1999 reboot starring Brendan Fraser and Rachel Weisz.

Notable for our purposes here, the original Universal *Mummy* movie was made in 1932 and begins in 1921 before jumping ahead ten years, meaning it was set roughly contemporaneously to when it was made. The same is true of the film's first sequel, which was both shot and set in 1940. *The Mummy's Hand* deviates from the plot of the original 1932 film to instead introduce a new mummy, one that will dominate the rest of Universal's *Mummy* cycle.

This new mummy is named Kharis. Kharis also fell in love with a princess (Ananka this time) and was buried alive, without a tongue. Members of a secret sect come to visit his tomb every full moon, feeding him a brew made from (fictional) "tana leaves" to keep him alive. In the event that someone disturbs the tomb of the princess, they're supposed to add more leaves to the brew, restoring movement to the mummy.

Because Kharis has no tongue, he's not the eloquent villain that Karloff's Imhotep was, and is, instead, the wordless, dragging, indestructible mummy that modern audiences tend to associate with the term. In *The Mummy's Hand*, he's played by Tom Tyler, though the later films in the franchise all feature Lon Chaney, Jr. under the wrappings.

Filmed on what was described as a "modest" budget, reusing extensive footage from the 1932 film and pretty much the entire score of *Son of Frankenstein*, *The Mummy's Hand* was also the last of the films to take place in Egypt. At the end of the picture, our protagonists have successfully looted the tomb of Princess Ananka, despite the mummy's best efforts, and are heading back to the States in triumph. It is here that the rest of the films in the series will be set, and here that *our* narrative really picks up.

While *The Mummy's Hand* was set the same year it was released, 1940, *The Mummy's Tomb* was released in 1942, but set thirty years after the events of the previous film. Dick Foran, the lead from the previous film, is now the mummy's first victim, played under old age makeup, as it follows him and his family to the fictional town of Mapleton, Massachusetts. More to our point, setting the film thirty years after the events of the previous one mean that *The Mummy's Tomb* effectively takes place in 1970.

It's a detail that the filmmakers obviously didn't take into account for any number of reasons—1970 looks, in every respect, exactly like 1942 and, indeed, in once scene, exactly like the graveyard in *Frankenstein*. This means that, when our white bread protagonist gets word that he's gotten a commission in the military, we're probably meant to assume he's going to fight in World War II—never mind the chilling implication that World War II might still be going on in 1970. But maybe we're supposed to think he's going off to Vietnam, instead, and the filmmakers were just expert prognosticators, rather than simply not thinking about the math as hard as many of us nerds have in later years.

It is in *The Mummy's Ghost*, released in 1944, that the films begin to retcon certain elements of the previous pictures. The high priest, played by George Zucco, who has already died twice in the last two movies, is back alive again at the beginning of this one, once more passing on the secret of Kharis' resurrection to a new disciple, this time played by John Carradine. (The last film at least had its obligatory sinister Egyptian played by Austrian-born actor Turhan Bey, who was of Turkish descent and vastly more charismatic than any of the film's ostensible leads, mummy included.)

At the same time, the secret sect has been renamed Arkam, in what is possibly the first-ever cinematic nod to the writings of H. P. Lovecraft, though there's nothing else in the film to support such a reading. The mechanics of Kharis—not to mention the whole rigamarole of reincarnated souls and whatnot—is all familiar, though, even if the explanations have been subtly reworked. This time around, Ananka was a priestess of Arkam, besides being a princess, and it's *her* soul that's cursed, which is why Kharis has to keep tabs on her.

The film ends with Kharis being pursued into a swamp, a motif that will be recycled, in various forms, not just in the next Universal picture, but in the first Hammer *Mummy* movie and other places up to even 2002's *Bubba Ho-Tep*, so much so that mummies and swamps are almost as inextricably linked as mummies and ancient Egypt.

Unless you count 1955's *Abbott and Costello Meet the Mummy*, which features a familiar-enough plot but a different mummy played by a different actor, then *The Mummy's Curse* is the last of the original Universal *Mummy* films. It picks up 25 years after the previous film, with the Southern Engineering Company trying to drain the swamp where the mummy vanished last time. Here's the thing, though: *That* swamp was emphatically, canonically in Massachusetts, while this one is just as emphatically in Louisiana. Also, because 25 years have elapsed since *The Mummy's Ghost*, this final film would be taking place around 1995.

It's obvious that this unintentional glimpse at a speculative future is just that. In all likelihood, the filmmakers just didn't think too hard about what it would mean if a movie was set thirty years after a movie that had been set contemporaneously. These films were made quickly, for relatively small budgets. They were turned around in a hurry, destined to play double-bills, and never meant to be considered too carefully—witness the fact that both *The Mummy's Ghost* and *The Mummy's Curse* hit screens the same year. This was also decades before the advent of home video, meaning that these films were generally meant to be seen once or twice then never again.

Just as everyone was expected to accept that a swamp in Massachusetts could turn into a swamp in Louisiana between pictures, no one was expected to put much thought into just what year it actually *was* in the film they were watching. They were meant to be distracted by the mumbo jumbo and the Spanish moss, the swooning women and the mummy.

Yet perhaps it says something about America in the 1940s that we would imagine—even accidentally—a future some half-century distant in which everything still looked and felt exactly like America in the 1940s.

**Author's Notes:** This has always been one of my favorite bits of trivia related to old 1930s monster movies and, despite the amount of ink that has been spilled over those movies across the years, one that doesn't actually seem to get discussed very often. It doesn't really go anywhere in the films themselves, but it's a fascinating thing to remember when you're watching them—and hopefully in this essay for *Unwinnable*, I did some of that fascination justice.

**Originally published November 2021**
orringrey.com

## "GOBLINS ALL OVER THE PLACE."—

## *FRANKENSTEIN 1970* (1958)

Not that long ago, I wrote about the original Universal *Mummy* sequels of the 1940s for *Unwinnable*. Specifically, I wrote about the odd fact that they are (inadvertently) set in the future. You can read the beginning at that link and buy the issue to get the whole story, but the short version is that the first sequel is set contemporaneously, and then the subsequent ones jump ahead by about a generation every movie or two, meaning that, by *The Mummy's Curse* (1944) it would be around 1995.

I love that shit, so imagine my surprise when I discover that there's a movie from 1958, that's set in 1970, starring Boris Karloff as an aging descendent of the original Baron Frankenstein, who was tortured and disfigured by the Nazis during World War II and who is now continuing his deceased forebear's experiments. Now compound that surprise with the fact that the movie's plot concerns a film crew who are shooting a TV special to commemorate "the 230th anniversary of *Frankenstein*," and who are using Karloff's castle so that he can afford to buy an at-home nuclear reactor, which is definitely a thing we had by the '70s.

If that sounds like a lot, well, you're not wrong. Crammed into 83 minutes, fully 40 of which are Karloff flipping switches and looking at dials, *Frankenstein 1970* feels, at times, like three or four screenplays, none of which were even remotely finished, all jammed together into one movie and then still not finished. I loved it.

What the hell is Karloff's character's plan? It is unclear, at best, and he never seems to have even the beginning of an endgame. At one point, when his creature doesn't yet have eyes, he apparently sends it out to fetch somebody for him and is then disappointed when it brings back the wrong person.

"You fool," he says, or something to that effect, "I sent you to bring me Row."

"Boss," I wanted the monster to reply, "maybe you forgot, but I *don't have eyes.*"

Several times in the film, there are what seem to be missing scenes that might illuminate *some* of the confusion, but unlikely anywhere near all. The 1970 conceit is meaningless outside the existence of at-home nuclear generators, and, frankly, so too is the film crew conceit. Any excuse—up to and including the old saw of their car breaking down in a storm—to get some fresh bodies into the Baron's castle would have served as well.

Yet, the film crew thing is great, and not just for the metatext of it all. There's a nicely-shot cold opening that could only ever end with the director shouting cut, in-movie. As for the 1970 idea, it could have been any year at all, including 1958. In fact, working titles for the film included *Frankenstein 1960* and *Frankenstein 2000.*

As it stands, everything looks just like 1958—or, rather, like 1958's idea of what an old castle would look like, using sets mainly leftover from John Barrymore's house in *Too Much, Too Soon,* the biopic of his daughter Diana, adapted from her memoir.

Karloff, of course, steals the show, reminding us of his range as he is as sadistically sinister here as he has ever been warm and grandfatherly in any other picture. Under some impressive facial makeup and performing a dramatic limp and hunch, he oozes just enough charm to allow you to maybe buy that people wouldn't just run screaming, while still casting a long, dark shadow over every scene he's in.

And as for the monster, it's the coup de grace. Before I even knew that this movie existed, I had seen a shot or two of the monster, and that's what ultimately made me dig up the further information that was more than enough to justify a purchase. Played by 6' 8" actor Mike Lane—who also plays the actor *playing* the monster in the movie they're making within the movie—the monster looks a bit like the mummy of an astronaut.

Always depicted in head-to-toe bandages, wrapped around a piece of headgear that makes it look like a robot, the monster is *very* different than any other Frankenstein monster you've ever seen. Lane's considerable height, towering over even Karloff, certainly helps. Also helping this along is the fact that the Baron apparently just lets it wander around, eyeless, which seems like a very poor way to keep your elaborate secret.

But then, see above about the Baron not being really amazing at planning.

"We got some goblins that'll kill you, man."


**Author's Note:** As you can probably gather, when this was originally published on my website, it included a link to the *Unwinnable* article that I wrote about the inadvertent sci-fi of the Universal *Mummy* sequels. Fortunately, while the link obviously doesn't work in book form, now that they're in a book together, and conveniently right next to each other, you can just skip back a few pages to read that essay, if you're reading these out of order and haven't done so already.

**Originally published December 2021**
*Exploits*

## THE SNAKE GIRL
## AND THE SILVER-HAIRED WITCH (1968)

Before we talk about how much I LOVED *The Snake Girl and the Silver-Haired Witch*, we need to discuss Kazuo Umezu. When trying to summarize who he was to someone ignorant of the form, I described him as "like the Jack Kirby of horror manga," and I feel like that'll do the job well enough.

Many of Umezu's best-known works were published in the 1960s, which also saw the first of many adaptations of his oeuvre to the big and small screens. In this case, that adaptation was *The Snake Girl and the Silver-Haired Witch*, helmed by Noriaki Yuasa right in the middle of his long-running *Gamera* series. (In this way, it can be seen through a similar lens with Ishiro Honda's *Matango*, an adaptation of William Hope Hodgson's "The Voice in the Night," released in the midst of Honda's *Godzilla* pictures.)

The result is a film that I described on Letterboxd as "a children's gothic easily the equal of any of the ones del Toro has done, that turns into a William Castle flick in its last legs." The plot follows an orphan named Sayuri who learns that her birth parents have been found and goes to live with them in their big, dark house across the street from a high-rise construction site.

Of course, in short order, she discovers that all is not well in her new home. Sayuri's new mother has amnesia, the day she arrives the maid unexpectedly drops dead, and someone is watching her through a hole in the ceiling. Before long, it is revealed that Sayuri has a secret older sister, one confined to the attic. And the sister has secrets of her own, including that she might actually be a snake!

The ultimate resolution of the plot may be more the Scooby-Doo variety frequently employed by Castle in his shockers from the '60s, but the lead-up to it is pure surreal spookiness, with classic Japanese ghost story motifs standing in for the trauma of an abused child, all beautifully executed through flashes of lightning, things in jars, and even elements of modernity (like that construction site) standing in for the medievalism of the traditional gothic.

**Author's Note:** Every now and then, I will buy a Blu-ray sight unseen, because the movie is something that I really want to check out and the Blu-ray seems like the best way to do it. Of all the various times I've done this, *The Snake Girl and the Silver-Haired Witch* is certainly one of my very favorites.

**Originally published February 2022**
*Exploits*

# WHAT WE NEVER SAW

Matt Wagner's legendary *Grendel* series of comics began with Hunter Rose, a successful author who moonlighted as the masked assassin known as Grendel. By the time *Grendel: War Child* was released in 1992, the comics had seen a variety of characters assume the mantle, with the most recent being Orion Assante, who conquered the entire planet and became the ruler of Earth. So, what was once the reviled name of a heinous murderer becomes the most respected name in the world, and the villain is now the ruler of the entire planet.

What does this have to do with the *Saw* franchise? I direct your attention to the poster for 2010's *Saw 3D*, the seventh film in the saga, which depicts an enormous statue of Jigsaw, the antagonist who imprisons people in elaborate supervillain traps in order to punish them and test their will to live. The statue is under construction, girded with scaffolding and welded by enormous machines. It also *towers* above the cityscape behind it.

When I saw that poster, my immediate thought was of *Grendel: War Child*. What if the *Saw* franchise had gone that route? What if, by the seventh movie, the entire *world* was on Jigsaw's side? What if the *Saw* films went from a tiny picture with a budget of around a million dollars that took place almost entirely in a grimy bathroom to a movie about a world that had entirely embraced Jigsaw's grim methodology, one in which the villain was now the hero? A world where giant statues were erected in honor of a man who killed people by sealing them in reverse bear traps.

The *Saw* movies *don't* go there, of course. I've never seen most of the *Saw* sequels, but I don't have to watch *Saw 3D* to know that it's not the story of Jigsaw's ascendancy to world domination. Yet, I know enough about the events of the films to know that while such an escalation may be outside their purview, the similarities are nonetheless *there*. While the original Jigsaw killer is played by Tobin Bell, the figure of Jigsaw is also represented by an array of accomplices, copycats and disciples. His cult may never span the globe, but it certainly *grows*.

Another film that plays with this same idea is the 2019 slasher *Trick*, which begins with a bullied teen taking bloody vengeance. Though seemingly shot to death, his body subsequently vanishes. Every year thereafter, new murders occur that mirror the first. The final reveal is that the slasher is not *just* the teen from the beginning of the movie, but a cult-like gathering of devotees who work together to keep the legend alive from year to year, with members placed in positions of local government and police.

Again, it's nowhere near the globe-spanning Grendel cult of *War Child*, but it's a start in that direction. Something that looks at the way we form cults of personality—even around the most reprehensible of figures—and transform the objects of our adoration into something mythic. Sadly, it doesn't take much looking to find people doing it in real life, and I don't recommend digging too deeply into the (thankfully small) subset of individuals who regard Charles Manson or Ted Bundy as saints.

While the idea of a series like *Saw* ever going anywhere nearly that big is probably far out of reach, if anything ever convinces me to watch the rest of the films in the saga, it will probably be imagining them continuing to expand until they become something as strange and far-reaching as *Grendel* eventually did.

**Author's Note:** In addition to the short, 350-word essays that headline each section of an issue of *Exploits*, each issue also has a longer "meta-essay" that can be about pretty much anything. This is the only one of those I have written, to date, about my disappointment regarding the poster for one particular installment in the *Saw* franchise, and Matt Wagner's *Grendel* comics—a succinct example of the kind of freedom that *Unwinnable* and *Exploits* give to their contributors.

*Originally published February 2022*
*orringrey.com*

# HERE BE DRAGONS

Due to an unrelated project, I recently fell down a rabbit hole relating to depictions of western dragons in film. For creatures so ubiquitous in the rest of popular culture, they're surprisingly thin on the ground in the movies—especially prior to the 21st century.

This led to a Twitter thread in which I explored the early history of dragons in cinema. Oddly enough, the first dragons in film don't look much like what we've come to associate with the term here in the west. 1924 saw, as far as I am aware, the first two dragons ever to grace the screen—certainly in a feature-length project.

One was in the Douglas Fairbanks version of *The Thief of Bagdad*, which I initially forgot about while making the tweet thread, while the other was in the first half of Fritz Lang's diptych *Die Nibelungen*. Both looked more like dinosaurs than the winged dragons we're familiar with from *D&D*. In fact, the first winged dragon that I know of didn't show up on film until 1936, where it made its debut in an unlikely spot: a 16-minute Popeye short called *Popeye the Sailor Meets Sindbad the Sailor*.

*Popeye Meets Sindbad* was bundled with two other shorts, also inspired by the *Arabian Nights*, and released as "A Popeye Feature." Ray Harryhausen would later acknowledge that the cartoon was a major inspiration for his *7th Voyage of Sinbad*, which also features a dragon of its own, albeit again, a wingless one. As in *7th Voyage*, the dragon is far from alone in the Popeye short. Sindbad's island is also home to loads of other monsters, including a roc, an ettin, and more. It's dragons we're here to talk about, though…

Even though the short was combined into a feature, it doesn't really count as a feature film. In fact, for a winged dragon to make its debut on American screens in a feature, we had to wait until 1959, when Disney introduced one of the screen's most iconic dragons. The House of Mouse had already put animated dragons on screen before that, notably the eponymous character from the mixed live-action/animation oddity *The Reluctant Dragon*, in 1941. But in '59, they gave us the dark fairy Maleficent in *Sleeping Beauty*, who took the shape of a massive black dragon who breathes green flame.

Maleficent wasn't actually the first winged dragon to hit screens, though. The Russians had beaten America to that punch, with the three-headed Gorynych, who showed up onscreen for the first time (that I know of) in *Ilya Muromets* in 1956. That flick made its way stateside as *The Sword and the Dragon* in 1963, where it was eventually skewered by the crew of the Satellite of Love on *Mystery Science Theater 3000*.

Since then, dragons on screen have increased in frequency as the years have rolled on and these days they're relatively commonplace, by comparison. Early on, though, dragons on film were as rare as they often are in the earliest stories about them—beasts both singular and strange, representing humanity's desire to subdue a chaotic world. Which, in this case, takes the form of creating elaborate special effects to represent big, magical lizards.

**Author's Note:** The "unrelated project" that I mention in this brief essay was connected to copyediting Stu Horvath's delightful history of the tabletop RPG, *Monsters, Aliens, and Holes in the Ground*, from MIT Press. At the time of this writing, that book was still a secret. Now, it's available in print, so you should definitely pick it up.

**Originally published April 2022**
orringrey.com

# "You got to suffer to be born again."—
# *The Unknown Terror* (1957)

What feels like a lifetime ago but was, in actual fact, only a decade, Silvia Moreno-Garcia and I co-edited a little anthology called *Fungi* that was about, well, I think the title makes it fairly clear. This was the culmination of a pretty much lifelong fascination with fungal creatures, on my part, and was specifically kicked off by Silvia and I chatting about *Matango*.

As part of the process of putting *Fungi* together, we created a database (now likely lost to the mists of time) of fungal stories, movies, and so on. It contained a few of my favorites, including William Hope Hodgson's germinal short story, "The Voice in the Night," as well as various adaptations of same, such as the aforementioned *Matango*. It also included more obscure favorites, such as the "moldy corpses" of *Castlevania: Portrait of Ruin* alongside things I had never read or seen.

Of those latter, the one that jumped highest on my personal list was *The Unknown Terror*, which has the distinction of maybe being the earliest fungal horror film, even beating the "Voice in the Night" episode of *Suspicion* by a year. What's more, the fungal horror of *The Unknown Terror* is far from incidental. Not only is there a fungus-filled cavern, there are *multiple* fungus people, before all is said and done.

But we're getting ahead of ourselves. *The Unknown Terror* was directed by Charles Marquis Warren, a guy best known for making Westerns. In fact, most of his other feature film credits occupy that genre, and he also helped to co-create the TV series *Rawhide*. Before he became a director or a screenwriter, though, Warren wrote stories for the pulps—a place where the plot of *Unknown Terror* would have been right at home.

Warren didn't write this picture, however. The sole screenwriting credit belongs to Kenneth Higgins, whose only other horror credit is the jokey 1943 flick *Ghosts on the Loose*, starring Bela Lugosi and the East Side Kids. Nowhere in the film's credits or background is any reference to Hodgson, and yet any story that involves fungus turning people into *things* owes something to "The Voice in the Night."

Though it was released as the front-half of a double-bill (with *Back from the Dead*, also directed by Warren), *Unknown Terror* was always going to be a B-picture. It was a product of Robert Lippert's Regal Pictures, a production unit under 20th Century Fox created exclusively to shoot B-movies in Cinemascope, as a way to assure theatre owners that there would be plenty of features in that format.

As such, *The Unknown Terror* spends an unfortunate amount of its time on colonial fears of "native superstitions" or on lengthy caving sequences that call to mind *MST3K* jokes about rock climbing. Once they *do* finally reach the fungus cavern, however, it's pretty great. Not only is the cavern itself full of cobwebby fungus that's delightfully rubbery, it's also home to several fungus people, who look sort of like lumpy Morlocks.

And all of that is *before* the fungus itself begins pouring down. It seems that the villainous doctor character, played by film heavy Gerald Milton, has discovered a type of fungus that grows incredibly fast. So fast, in fact, that you can watch it happen, represented in the movie by what look like thick soap suds being poured down the cave walls in what is actually one of the better set-pieces in all of '50s horror.

The other interesting thing about *The Unknown Terror* comes far from the fungus cave, at the very beginning of the film, when we are treated to performances (including a theme song of sorts) by the "King of Calypso," Sir Lancelot.

Lancelot Victor Edward Pinard, better known by his stage name Sir Lancelot, will be familiar to longtime readers and vintage horror fans for his appearances in several of Val Lewton's classics from the 1940s, perhaps most notably *I Walked with a Zombie*. Here, he is performing a similar role more than a decade later, doing much of the heavy lifting required to convince us that this film takes place in the Caribbean while also providing exposition about the MacGuffin at the heart of the narrative.

"Down, down, down in the bottomless cave," Lancelot sings, "Down, down, down beyond the last grave / If he's got the stuff of fame / If he's worthy of his name / He may get another chance but he's never more the same / He's got to suffer to be born again."

**Author's Note:** One of the things I live for as an aficionado of vintage horror films is getting to see a great one for the first time. It may be a stretch to call this one great, but it was so high on my personal list—for all the reasons enumerated above—that it really felt like an event.

**Originally published May 2022**
*Unwinnable*

# "STRANGE THINGS HAPPEN THERE": TWO EARLY MEXICAN HORRORS

Many of my favorite Mexican horror pictures are from the heyday of the 1950s and '60s, when luchadors regularly went up against a variety of classic movie monsters, to be sure, but we also got more serious-minded gothics like *The Witch's Mirror* (1962). Despite this, I had not seen much of the country's earlier output until now, when Indicator—one of my favorite distributors of especially older films on Blu-ray—brought new life to a pair of extremely early horrors from the very beginnings of Mexico's output of sound film, lovingly restored and newly released on region-free Blu-rays.

> "They claim that the death of this individual was caused by the sight of a ghost at midnight."
> —*La Llorona* (1933)

Mexico's first talkie horror film—its first sound film was the melodrama *Santa* from the year before—*La Llorona* was considered lost for nearly a half-century before a badly-abused 16mm print surfaced, from which Indicator sourced this scratchy, unusual Blu-ray release.

While it was one of the first films to tackle Mexico's legendary "crying woman," it was far from the last. Indeed, American theaters and streaming services saw not one but two major releases with the ghost in the title in the last few years. *The Curse of La Llorona*, a sort of stealth entry into the *Conjuring* franchise, and

Guatemala's own *La Llorona* were both released in 2019, and both showcase the *extreme* variety of uses to which this well-known spectral figure has been put over the years.

Even as early as 1933, however, director Ramon Peon was already deconstructing and reimagining the classic tale, which, as the documentation that accompanies Indicator's handsome Blu points out, was kind of the norm for the crying woman. "The details of her legend depend on the storyteller," Emily Masincup writes in the booklet accompanying the disc, "contingent not only upon what version(s) of the story they have heard, but also on their own motivations for sharing this story with others."

That's certainly true of Jayro Bustamante's 2019 version, and I think it's probably equally true here, even if their ultimate motivations are pretty different. Masincup makes a good case that the motives of Peon were most likely heavily invested in not only selling the idea of sound pictures, but in specifically selling the idea of them as vehicles for horror. Hence, the first voice we hear in *La Llorona* is not a person talking, but the menacing and yet piteous wail of the eponymous specter—actually supplied by a puppeteer named Carlos Vallejo Espinal.

No one reading this should be terribly surprised that I'm a huge fan of movies from the '30s and '40s, but even I am the first to admit that, for various reasons, you have to approach them differently than if you're watching a movie that came out yesterday—and, of course, vice versa. Nowhere is that more true than with *La Llorona*, which has the added stumbling block of that worse-for-the-wear 16mm print I mentioned earlier.

Even as these sorts of things go, I was not a huge fan of this *La Llorona*, which still has one foot rather awkwardly planted in the silents that preceded it. But that's really beside the point, in this case. It is a piece of history—not merely Mexican cinematic history, not merely horror history, but a broader snapshot of a period in time, and the changes that were happening around it.

As that, it is fascinating and, perhaps more to the point,

*important*, whether you find the end result entertaining or not. It is the recovery and distribution of movies like these that make physical media so vital, and to that end, labels like Indicator are doing the proverbial lord's work in helping to make them accessible to the general public, while also providing a wealth of context, not merely for the film's production and release, but for the state of the print that the Blu-ray was restored from—and why all of that matters.

"Shadow was born in the monastery and has never left it."
—*The Phantom of the Monastery* (1934)

Now *this* is more like it! Though released only a year after *La Llorona*, *Phantom of the Monastery*—also known as *The Phantom of the Convent*—shows a big step up in the evolution of talkie horror filmmaking. Not as beholden to the silent films that came before it, *Phantom* looks and sounds, at least in some ways, more like what we had already come to expect from the horror movies coming out of Hollywood in the '30s. And yet, like *La Llorona*, it is also uniquely Mexican in many ways.

According to prolific screenwriter Juan Bustillo Oro—one of a handful of names credited in the screenplay of *Phantom of the Monastery*—producer Jorge Pezet proffered the nugget that formed the basis of the film. "He wanted a horror movie," Oro recalls in the booklet that accompanies the Blu, "but his sketch was very vague. It was only clear that some lost travelers found a hidden monastery, where they suffered a night of terror among the mummies abandoned there."

The mummies in question are in many ways at the heart of the film, even if we don't actually see them until virtually the final shots. When we do, they are *real* mummies—the ones that inspired Pezet's idea, in fact. The dozen mummies which are *still to this day* on display at the Museo de El Carmen in Mexico City.

According to Oro, he took Pezet's rough sketch and created "a simple story, which I don't know if I can qualify as my own at all." He wanted to avoid "the common places where Yankee cinema went," including things like "the disappointments of shadows of pretend monsters" and the "animation of the mummies." In its place, he proposed a sort of morality play about a trio of friends—a married couple and their traditionally more macho companion. "A guilty passion would be incubating between the friend and the wife," Oro wrote, which would become the meat of the film's conflict.

Citing disappointments with previous collaborations, Oro was not present for most of the filming, and says that Fernando de Fuentes directed the picture "without a great deal of imagination, as was his way, but with good taste, efficiency, and dramatic success." While perhaps that lack of imagination was true compared to what Oro had in mind while writing the screenplay, it's hard to lay such a claim at the feet of *Phantom of the Monastery*, which is full of expressionist shadows, eerie sounds, haunting images, and compelling camera moves.

In fact, prior to the release of this Indicator Blu-ray, I had seen precisely one frame of *Phantom of the Monastery*, a shot of the protagonist Eduardo reaching up to touch the shadow of a bat on the wall, which was more than enough to sell me on the film as a whole. And while that scene is, indeed, one of the more striking pieces of imagery in the picture, it is far from alone.

Much of the visual poetry of *Phantom* is achieved with the help of some well-chosen location shooting. As an essay by Maricruz Castro-Ricalde points out in the booklet that accompanies the Blu, the first of these locations was "an abandoned Jesuit educational complex" north of Mexico City. The complex itself, which provides both interiors and exteriors for the film, is described as a "jewel of seventeenth century churriguresque art," named for Spanish architect Jose Benito de Churriguera. Of equal interest are the paintings inside the building, which are said to have been created by the "indigenous Otomi people of the region."

The other significant location is equally important though less widely used—the former convent of El Carmen in Mexico City, where the real-life mummies were photographed and where they can still be seen today, in a space not unlike the one where our protagonists view them in *Phantom of the Monastery*.

These all give the film a classical feeling, but the marketing department was not above resorting to a little ballyhoo at the time, either. The booklet also includes a brief, contemporary piece on the promotional efforts that attended the film's premier, including displaying a "collection of mummies" in the "windows of the main shopping malls" in Mexico City. These were not the real mummies that were used in the film, but they nonetheless generated "much gossip and interest."

Perhaps even more evocative was a more mobile advertising campaign. "Every day a 'giant ghost' has been walking the streets of the city," describes the anonymous essay, originally published in *El cine grafico* before the film's release in 1934, "wrapped in a long, black robe, with his hands crossed on his chest and his face—a skull—horribly contracted into a painful grimace. On his back is a sign that reads *The Phantom of the Monastery*."

The essay goes on to describe how the "ghost" is constantly followed around by a "legion of children who delight in his appearance" and, I've gotta say, I'd be right there with them…

**Author's Note:** Sadly, we do not have the resources to reproduce a bunch of film stills in this volume, but that still of Eduardo reaching up to touch the bat shadow is well worth tracking down online.

Originally published June 2022
Weird Horror

## GREY'S GROTESQUERIES:
## YOUR EYES WILL LEAVE YOUR BODY:
## COMING LATE TO *ULTRA Q*

"For the next 30 minutes, your eyes will leave your body and arrive in this strange moment in time." So begins one of the Rod Serling-like voiceover intros to *Ultra Q*, a show I had never even heard of until just the last couple of years.

Like a lot of people my age, I grew up with Godzilla. The big lizard was probably my first favorite monster which, given that John Langan once called me "the monster guy," seems like a big deal. I watched Godzilla's exploits in flicks that were broadcast on some local channel Saturday mornings; owned VHS copies of *King Kong vs. Godzilla* and *Godzilla vs. Megalon*; pored over images of Godzilla and their foes in those orange Crestwood House monster books; even begged my parents to buy me a knock-off Godzilla toy from the gift shop at the Wichita Zoo—a toy that still sits on my shelf to this day.

Even then, though, the Godzilla films I watched were being beamed to me from another age. The ones I was exposed to were primarily from what is known as the Showa Era, the earliest batch of Godzilla pictures, made between 1954 and 1975, while I was watching them in the '80s.

With that background, I can't tell you when I first became *aware* of *Ultraman*, but it must have been early. I never watched the show when I was young, though. Ultraman's sleek, humanoid design appealed less to my child's sensibilities than Godzilla's spiny, squamous, reptilian silhouette. I think that, as a kid, I probably saw Ultraman himself as too much of a "good guy." He *fought* monsters; Godzilla *was* one.

That said, I probably *would* have watched *Ultraman*, and gladly, perhaps voraciously, had it been available, but we didn't get a channel that showed it. I wouldn't see an episode until *many* years later, after most of the events of this column had already unfolded.

Fast-forward a few decades from that kid eagerly crouched on the deep-pile of my parents' living room watching Godzilla movies on a big, wood-paneled TV, and I see a black-and-white gif on Twitter. In it, a man hugs close to a rock face as the glowing eyestalks of a giant snail slowly rise to tower over him. It was basically everything I ever wanted to see in a show, all contained in the few repeated frames of that gif.

A little digging told me that the image was from a series called *Ultra Q*; a Japanese tokusatsu show that had originally been broadcast in 1966. Created by Eiji Tsuburaya, the special effects pioneer who was partially responsible for Godzilla, the show featured plenty of kaiju—which were, of course, popular in Japan at the time—but was intended to ape American sci-fi shows like *The Twilight Zone* and *The Outer Limits*.

Unlike *Ultraman* and the rest of the half-century-long (and counting) franchise that would follow it, the protagonists of *Ultra Q* were just regular folks—recurring characters included a couple of pilots and a female reporter, played by Hiroko Sakurai, who reappeared as a different character in *Ultraman* that same year.

In the course of the series' 28 episodes, these regular people encountered decidedly irregular events—the original title of the series was going to be "*Unbalanced*." Often, these events involved giant monsters—usually, but not always, from outer space—but they also ran afoul of gigantic primordial plants, honey that caused creatures to grow to abnormal size, a girl who could astrally project, and, in perhaps the show's most overtly horror-themed episode, the abandoned mansion of a baron who had transformed into a giant spider.

From that gif on Twitter, I tracked down *Ultra Q*, first on DVD from Shout Factory, later on Blu-ray from Mill Creek. Finally watching the series, which was thrown together under tight time constraints, often repurposing suits and props that had previously been used in feature films, was a decidedly mixed bag. Some episodes were too childish or grating, but when the show was at its best, it hit all of my buttons in a way perhaps no other television series ever has. Here was something combining the speculative thoughtfulness of *The Twilight Zone* with the rubbery antics of early tokusatsu cinema, not to mention a team of unlikely paranormal investigators.

In just about every episode, I was guaranteed some kind of weird monster, many of whom later reappeared and entered *Ultraman* lore, but I was also treated to some surprisingly ambitious concepts. Take, for example, the time-jumping alien invaders in "Challenge from the Year 2020" or "The Disappearance of Flight 206," which essentially prefigures Stephen King's *The Langoliers*, with an extradimensional walrus in place of the chainsaw-jawed Pac-Man monsters of that TV mini-series.

*Ultraman* entered production at the same time as *Ultra Q*, and the two series premiered the same year. It's obvious, looking back across decades that are filled with subsequent *Ultraman* shows, which one took off the most. I picked up a bunch of the *Ultraman* series that Mill Creek has been releasing, too, but, at the time of this writing, haven't watched more than a few episodes. It's not that I don't enjoy them—I like the monsters and the models, all the tokusatsu stuff—but they aren't, for me, what *Ultra Q* was.

Part of it is that there's just something about the old black-and-white footage of shows like *Ultra Q* and the American sci-fi series it was emulating. Not just the stark, noir-ish chiaroscuro of shadow and light, but also that sense of looking at something from another time. Something beamed to you from the past and yet made to live in the here and now; the antiquarian bent that so typifies the ghost story.

Ultimately, though, it may be the very *presence* of that superheroic central figure which ensures that *Ultraman* and all those series that follow it will be something altogether *different* from *Ultra Q*. In the *Dark Horse Book of Monsters*, first published in 2006, there's a loving paen to the classic Jack Kirby monster comics of the 1950s—another phenomenon that I came to late and that was, in fact, being published almost contemporaneously with *Ultra Q*—penned by Kurt Busiek and Keith Giffen.

In it, retired adventurer Riff Borkum is relating the story of his last thrilling escapade—traveling to the Himalayas in search of "Kungoro, the Monster of the Snow," while back home in New York, a different kind of story is unfolding.

The conflict with the strange monster is ultimately upstaged by the arrival of superheroes, making diegesis of what was happening in the actual comic book marketplace, as the popularity of tights and capes comics edged out stories like the Kirby monster tales.

"Now the wonders *are* the heroes," Borkum says, in the story's melancholy final pages. "Saving the earth from despots, alien races and more. And mankind ... mankind just watches. And sometimes applauds." Words that may have been reflecting on a past gone by but that feel uncannily prescient more than a decade later, when superhero movies dominate a box office once controlled by other fare.

The sentiment echoes one of my favorite lines from any film, the one that gave my second short story collection its title. Boris Karloff, playing a thinly fictionalized version of himself in Peter Bogdanovich's *Targets* (1968), another near contemporary to *Ultra Q*, laments that, "My kind of horror is not horror anymore. No one's afraid of a painted monster."

There's a wistfulness to both speeches, but not necessarily condemnation. The world moves on, and we're lucky enough to be able to come late to some things, even if we didn't grow up with them.

I have no doubt that I'll have fun with *Ultraman* and its various spin-offs, and there's no denying which series was more popular and influential. But, just as some part of my monster-loving heart is always with Kirby's four-color creatures and Karloff's "painted monsters," some part of me will always be traipsing through the black-and-white sets of *Ultra Q*, waiting for my eyes to leave my body and arrive in that strange moment in time…

**Author's Note:** One of only two of my Grey's Grotesqueries columns that are reprinted here, even then it is a bit of a stretch to claim that this one is about horror *cinema*, concerning, as it does, *Ultra Q*, possibly my favorite television show of all time. However, I think there's enough overlap with Godzilla movies, *Targets*, and other aspects of horror film to justify its inclusion.

Originally published October 2022
*Unwinnable*

## Stop/Motion: Ray Harryhausen and the Magic of Stop Motion Monsters

A few years ago, I was dying, though I didn't yet know it at the time. For months, I had been lowkey sick with something the doctors struggled to diagnose. Then, in October of 2017, I finally got a CT scan—and, from there, I was sent directly to the emergency room.

It turns out that my appendix had ruptured some months before and had been rotting inside my torso all this time, poisoning me. I was in surgery for hours and awoke in the most terrible pain I have ever experienced. Recovery was a long, slow thing, and by the beginning of that December I was still far from returning to anything like normal.

However, that December I took a trip, the first time since my surgery that I'd left the house for much more than to see a movie. It was thanks to my spouse, who arranged for me to travel from Kansas City to Oklahoma City to see a Ray Harryhausen exhibition at the Science Museum Oklahoma.

The exhibition consisted of actual models, maquettes, armatures, and so on from his films, as well as extensive illustrations and other ephemera. Though it's trite to say such things, there are few experiences in my life that have been quite as magical as getting to see these items in person—an experience heightened, most likely, by my own recent brush with mortality.

At the entrance to the exhibit was a quote from Ray Harryhausen, written on a black wall in big, white letters: "If you make things too real, sometimes you bring it down to the mundane."

***

I would argue that Harryhausen may just have been the greatest creature designer in the history of cinema. But this is more than just a function of how he drew or sculpted his monsters—it was in how he understood them. Watching a Harryhausen creation move on screen is like watching a real creature. His monsters have a life to them, a heart and a soul.

A part of this comes from that tension, that push and pull between realism and fabulism that is contained in that quote. Harryhausen, in a way that few other creature designers ever did, understood how these creatures should move and act. He studied real animals, watched how they moved not merely when they were engaged in what would be "action scenes" in a movie, but how they acted when they were bored, restless, frightened, waiting.

He also knew when to ignore that stuff. He understood the fragile alchemy that means the difference between verisimilitude and bringing something "down to the mundane." Harryhausen's monsters feel like real creatures, but they also feel like real monsters—even when they *are* just mundane animals like the elephant that fights Ymir in *20 Million Miles to Earth*.

***

Part of this comes from the fact that Harryhausen was doing stop motion. Indeed, if anyone can be said to have perfected the form, it was probably him. Plenty of others have worked in the medium both before and since—Harryhausen himself learned at the feet of Willis O'Brien, who created the stop motion effects in *King Kong*, in many ways the "big bang" of the monster movie qua monster movie.

I have argued and will continue to argue that stop motion may be the greatest of all special effects techniques—though I don't think anyone, even someone like Harryhausen, would ever argue that it should be the *only* one. This is not because stop motion is the most "realistic." Indeed, you would never mistake a stop motion creation for a real animal. No matter how studied their animations, the *way* that a stop motion creature moves is unique to it—nothing else, alive or special effect, moves in quite the same way.

No, what makes stop motion so perfect is that it *feels* real, even when it doesn't look real. There's a reason why old tokusatsu pictures have a charm that Hollywood's recent Godzilla movies can't match. At the end of the day, they're people dressing up in monster costumes and playing with toys. There's something wholesome about that, even (and maybe especially) when it doesn't feel remotely realistic.

Similarly, stop motion animation feels like what it really is—toys that seem to be moving on their own. I think we have all, at one point or another, imagined our toys coming to life, moving under their own power when we weren't watching. And despite what *Toy Story* would tell us, I think we all know that, if they did, they would move like a stop motion creation.

*That* is the real magic of stop motion animation. Not only does it allow for creatures (and robots, and other things) that can do things no other technique—prior to the advent of CGI—could accomplish, but it contains that sense of wonder because, even when you don't buy what's happening on the screen, it still feels, deep down, like your toys are coming to life.

\*\*\*

Ray Harryhausen passed away back in 2013, and it would be easy enough to believe that stop motion animation died with him. These days, computer animators do what stop motion once accomplished, in a manner that is perhaps less painstaking, though probably no less complicated. But the artform isn't entirely dead, as evinced by the 2022 release of Phil Tippett's thirty-years-in-the-making stop motion opus *Mad God*, an almost impossibly elaborate cacophony of shit and noise and, yes, endless stop motion monsters.

*Mad God* is a masterpiece of grime and ugliness, in many ways the antithesis of everything Harryhausen did—and yet, brought to life with the same techniques, and the same amount of love and dedication. And it isn't even just the people who are carrying stop motion ahead into the future where its influences can be felt. There's a story that Guillermo del Toro tells on the commentary track for the 2004 *Hellboy* movie, about how he tried to hire Harryhausen as a consultant on the film.

Ultimately, the stop motion maestro passed, citing the film as "too violent"—which, again, he probably would have hated *Mad God*—but the influence of his vision is still apparent in the way that the computer-animated Sammael creatures in the film move, or the scene when Sammael is being reconstituted from salt "gathered from the tears of a thousand angels."

Whenever we bring monsters to life, whether it's on screen or even in prose, there is room for the influences and inspirations of stop motion. It's there in the juddering motion of pale specters in modern ghost movies, and it's there whenever a monster on screen feels like more than just a monster, but a genuine part of its environment.

It can even be there in fiction, where the monsters are only in our imaginations, after all. As I said before, there's a way that stop motion creations *move* that is not quite like anything else, and most of us have seen at least one or two of them in our lives. A writer can at least *try* to capture that odd form of movement, that sensation of a creature at once alive and artificial. It's certainly something I've done in my own stories, time and again.

***

The first—and, to date, only—novel I've ever published was a piece of licensed fantasy fiction set in the world of the Iron Kingdoms, a setting I've done work-for-hire writing in frequently, most recently creating large swaths of the 5e-compatible *Iron Kingdoms: Requiem* roleplaying game. That first novel involved, among other things, a hydra, and knights fighting gigantic armored creatures like dinosaurs. I dedicated it to Ray Harryhausen.

Though it's the only such dedication, it's far from the only time Harryhausen (and other stop motion animators) have appeared in or on the fringes of my work. They're there in "Baron von Werewolf Presents: *Frankenstein Against the Phantom Planet*," my love letter to (among other things) Willis O'Brien's unmade *King Kong vs. Frankenstein* film. And they're also there in less obvious places, in the diorama monsters of "Doctor Pitt's Menagerie," in the uncanny title creature of "Mortensen's Muse."

Unsurprisingly, my house is filled with monster toys, and when I look at them, as often as not, I'm imagining them lurching into lifelike (but not *quite* lifelike) stop motion. So long as there are those of us who dream of monsters—even as we dream of our toys coming to life—there will be a place for such old-fashioned techniques, and their legacies. They'll stay around in our dreams, even after they've departed from movie screens altogether.

**Author's Note:** I've always loved monsters, for as long as I can remember. It doesn't have an origin point that I'm aware of. But few creators have influenced the shape that love would take more than Harryhausen. When I was a kid, I had a copy of *Clash of the Titans* recorded off TV, and seeing that movie for the first time was definitely a formative moment.

As I said in the essay above, the experience of going to the Harryhausen exhibit in Oklahoma City was also something that felt truly special and magical, and I was glad to get to pay tribute to it for *Unwinnable*.

**Originally published January 2023**
*Signal Horizon*

# "I KNOW ENOUGH ABOUT STRANGE THINGS NOT TO LAUGH AT THEM."
# THE LEGACY OF *THE DUNWICH HORROR* (1970)

The *Dunwich Horror* is not the first movie ever adapted from the works of H. P. Lovecraft. Indeed, it is roughly the fifth or sixth, depending on how you count. It isn't even the first to be released under its original title, though most people can be forgiven for forgetting *The Shuttered Room* (1967). Yet, I have a feeling—based on absolutely no evidence whatsoever—that it is the earliest one with which many fans are familiar.

This claim—again, supported by no actual data—may have as much to do with the fact that *The Dunwich Horror* is one of the first Lovecraft films to feel "modern" in its depictions of sex and occultism, meaning that it, more so than previous films in the canon, feels like it could play on a double-bill with Stuart Gordon and Brian Yuzna's later forays into the Old Gent's work, with their copious rubber monsters and equally copious nudity.

The first H. P. Lovecraft adaptation to hit the big screen was Roger Corman's *The Haunted Palace* back in 1963. Ostensibly a part of Corman's "Poe cycle," the film borrowed only its title from Poe, and was instead a fairly straightforward adaptation of Lovecraft's posthumously published novel *The Case of Charles Dexter Ward*. Daniel Haller, who would later direct *The Dunwich Horror*, worked as an art director on that film, as he had on virtually all of the "Poe cycle" pictures.

For those who have seen those amazing Technicolor gothics, I don't need to tell you that Daniel Haller was a bravura art director capable of wringing some truly unforgettable sets from relatively meager budgets. In case you *do* want to know more about it, though, the booklet that accompanies the new Blu-ray from Arrow Video features a lengthy essay about Haller and his background as an art director.

Haller made his directorial debut in 1965, helming the second or third (again, depending on how you count) cinematic adaptation of H. P. Lovecraft to ever hit screens, the dramatically titled *Die, Monster, Die!*, a loose adaptation of Lovecraft's "The Colour Out of Space." There, his background as an art director was already apparent, and the film looks every bit of a piece with the "Poe cycle" movies that came before.

By 1970, however, things were changing, and *The Dunwich Horror* brought something that had been absent from the "Poe cycle" films. Namely: hippies. It wasn't the first time that sexuality had made its way into Lovecraftian cinema. Even as far back as *The Haunted Palace*, the unfortunate female lead is offered as a "mate" to one of the Old Ones, while 1968's *Curse of the Crimson Altar* brought in BDSM imagery and a decidedly swinging '60s vibe.

*The Dunwich Horror* felt modern in a way that those films hadn't, though, while also staying truer to the original story than *Crimson Altar* and bringing in New Age-y dream sequences and psychedelic effects to represent Wilbur's invisible twin—who, when we *do* finally see him, looks something like a Beholder made out of spring snakes. Normally, I am all about showing the monster as much as possible, but in this case, the camera's negative effects might actually have been a good call.

Dean Stockwell's smirking, corduroy-clad Wilbur Whately could not feel more early-'70 if you paid him, while his love interest and female lead is played by none other than *Gidget* herself, Sandra Dee. They bring the (relative) youth to the proceedings, while older character actors like Sam Jaffe and Ed Begley (in one of his final film roles) round out the cast.

While all this helps to explain the modern "hipness" of *The Dunwich Horror*, Haller's background as art director is still plainly visible, and no place more so than in the Whately house itself, which looks on the outside like the Sawyer clan from *Texas Chain Saw Massacre* decorated for Halloween, and on the inside like Dr. Strange's Sanctum Sanctorum.

Unlike some other films from the era, *The Dunwich Horror* has remained relatively well-known (and well-preserved) throughout the years, so there have been plenty of previous opportunities to watch it, even before this Blu-ray release. And most of those prints have been in fairly good repair, so while it has never looked better than it does now, the restoration is not such a triumph as some others that have been done before.

Of course, film quality is not the only thing that an Arrow Blu-ray tends to bring to the table. *The Dunwich Horror* also offers a unique opportunity to appreciate Les Baxter's otherworldly score, which gets its own featurette on the disc, not to mention new commentary tracks, interviews, and so on. The release also boasts a reversible sleeve, with new artwork by Luke Preece, as well as the original poster art by Reynold Brown.

And if anything is truly responsible for the longevity of this film in the public consciousness, it might be that poster, featuring a chimerical beast that the movie's meager effects could never hope to replicate.

**Author's Note:** I once found a full-size original copy of that *Dunwich Horror* poster at a local thrift shop, where it was folded up and tucked inside a medical biohazard bag—which feels appropriate, anyway.

**Originally published March 2023**
*Unwinnable*

## THE TWO EARLIEST FILMS STARRING THE SILVER MASKED MAN

"I have to confess that I don't really know anything about Mexican wrestlers," Mike Mignola wrote in the author's notes to *Hellboy in Mexico*. "I've never seen any of the movies, but I sure like the idea of them."

That was me, pretty much, until a few years ago. Everything I knew about lucha libre came from secondhand cultural osmosis, and the closest I had ever come to any of the films was the *Mystery Science Theater 3000* episode featuring the K. Gordon Murray dub of *Santo contra las Mujeres Vampiro*—the seventh of an *extremely* long line of films featuring El Santo, easily the most famous luchador enmascarado of all time.

Which brings us to the present. Things have changed a bit since then. I'm still not going to act like I know very much about lucha libre but I *have*, at least, seen a few more of the movies, including *Santo in the Wax Museum*, *Santo and Blue Demon vs. the Monsters*, and even the occasional non-Santo lucha libre film, such as *Curse of the Aztec Mummy*, which features a wrestler character called "the Angel" that is pretty obviously intended as a stand-in for El Santo.

My experience in this realm is still much less robust than I would like it to be, however. So I jumped at the chance to tackle this release from Indicator, a Blu-ray double-feature of the first two movies to star El Santo himself, both originally filmed in 1958 and released in 1961.

> "These scientists don't get much rest."
> —*Santo vs. the Evil Brain* (1961)

The first Santo film has almost no Santo in it. Let's just get that out of the way right up front. In fact, it's about 40% scenes of cars driving slowly around, and another 20% establishing shots of docks. The remainder of the film is made up of a mix of people having dinner, musical and dance numbers, and an occasional wrestling match. Also, Santo spends the vast majority of the film hypnotized by the mad scientist villain and therefore serving the bad guys.

And yet, Santo is introduced in such a way that we in the audience are obviously intended to already know who he is. He's given no origin story or background, with the police lieutenant referring to him, at one point, as "one of our best agents," and everyone who sees him, from the bad guys to the heroes, immediately knowing who he is and what he's about. And Rodolfo Guzman Huerta, the man who was El Santo, with almost no lines, nonetheless demonstrates his stage presence, even if he is not yet an actor.

When Santo is hypnotized, his movements and bearing change. The characters call him robotic, but today we would see him as more like a mix between a zombie and an ape. Even the way he sits changes. The hypnotized Santo slouches and slumps in a way that the legendary Silver Masked Man never would. There's also *another* masked wrestler in *The Evil Brain*, one whose presence is every bit as significant as Santo's.

In the film, this is a fellow agent of good called El Incognito, who actually gets to accomplish a whole lot more than Santo ever manages, thanks to the title character's aforementioned indisposition throughout most of the picture. What is noteworthy, however, is that El Incognito is played by fellow wrestler Fernando Oses, who co-wrote this and many of the other Santo movies, and appears, in various roles, throughout them.

Though not released in Mexico until 1961, both *The Evil Brain* and its companion picture in this set were filmed in Cuba during the revolution, with crews made up primarily of Cuban technical personnel. The booklet that accompanies the Blu-rays recounts an anecdote told by Joaquin Cordero, the actor who plays the villainous mad scientist in *Evil Brain* and the heroic Joaquin in *Infernal Men*, that the crew were cautioned to "crouch down when they heard shots." Cordero goes on to state that the filming was over in a hurry, and that they "left the island just an hour before Fidel Castro entered Havana."

Perhaps this goes some distance toward explaining the rather slapdash nature of the two films, what an essay in the booklet calls their "careless execution." More likely, the state of the pictures can be attributed to the fact that they were the first of their kind, filmed simultaneously, on a shoestring budget and in quite a hurry. As a result, both films feel like a patch-up job, with large sections seemingly shot silent with sound then dubbed in later.

They also feel like something that is still finding its footing. While the opening credits of *Evil Brain* point out that it is the first "cinematic presentation of Santo," it was not until the third Santo film, *Santo vs. the Zombies*, in 1962, that the Santo character was officially registered by the Film Production Workers' Union.

*Zombies*, the earliest of the Santo films to be re-dubbed and released in the United States—as *Invasion of the Zombies*—also feels more of a piece with the more than fifty films that were still to come in Santo's filmography, which see the masked wrestler going up against Martians, monsters, ghosts, vampires, head-hunters, the mafia, mummies, inquisitors, werewolves, Dr. Frankenstein, La Llorona, and many more.

"We had to take a big detour."
—*Santo vs. the Infernal Men* (1961)

Reusing *numerous* shots—not to mention cast and crew—from *Evil Brain*, Santo is barely in this movie, either. Indeed, he might play an even more minor role in *Infernal Men*, acting as a phantom that haunts the edges of a straightforward story about an agent who goes undercover to infiltrate a group of smugglers.

Even as the plot is less ambitious, however, the movie is possibly more so. While watching the two in order is tedious, as probably a full reel of film is reused between them, the scenes likely fit better here than in *Evil Brain*, and while Santo is just as scarce this time around, his presence feels more like what we're used to from later films. He shows up in a convertible to save the day, and operates on the fringes of what is basically a secret agent plot filled with notes passed via matchbooks and secret messages written on money.

*Santo vs. the Infernal Men* may have precious few set pieces, but the few it does have are at least marginally more exciting than those of its sibling film, as well. There's even a chase through part of an abandoned Coney Island amusement park, which the booklet describes as "an unimaginative imitation of the famous conclusion to *The Lady from Shanghai*."

In spite of these improvements, there's still not a lot to recommend *Infernal Men* except as a historical curiosity. As Santo movies go, much better ones are still in the offing. This set from Indicator is less about two movies that you'll want to put into your regular rotation, however, as it is about giving audiences access to films of historical note that might otherwise be lost to time. These may not be much fun to watch, but it's extremely nice that we get the opportunity, nonetheless.

With Santo himself largely absent, the story in *Infernal Men* instead focuses on the heroic undercover officer, played by Joaquin Cordero, who had the bad guy part in *Evil Brain*. It's even got a halfhearted attempt at a framing story, as we see the film's climax at the beginning, and then flash back to how things ended up that way. Ultimately, both pictures end with the same footage of an airplane taking off, ostensibly ferrying two different newlywed couples to new lives together, guarded by one or two masked wrestlers who are along for the ride.

Both also end with variations on the same monologue from Enrique Zambrano, the other half of the films' co-writing team, explaining to the audience why the Masked Man (or men) keep their identities a secret: "They are citizens of the world. Their duty knows no borders. They use masks to hide their identity for the good of all mankind."

**Author's Note:** A topic I return to again and again is the importance of physical media in keeping films like this around, and I'm always grateful for imprints that help to preserve these bits of film history, regardless of how I feel about the films themselves.

**Originally published March 2023**
*Signal Horizon*

# "THESE ARE THINGS THAT CAN HAPPEN IN A WOMAN'S LIFE." DARIO ARGENTO'S *PHENOMENA* (1985) IN 4K

*P**henomena* is not the best Dario Argento movie. It's not the most significant, the best-known, or the most widely seen. Yet, it boasts a singular accomplishment that few other films can match: If it were not for *Phenomena*, we very likely wouldn't have the *Clock Tower* series of video games, a franchise that is, itself, often considered to be the genuine classic that many might argue *Phenomena* is not.

At one time, I might have been among that "many." *Phenomena* was the first Dario Argento film I ever saw, and I was not prepared for it. While I enjoyed my time, it didn't win me over the way something like *Suspiria* later would. And yet, each time I return to *Phenomena*, I seem to love it more.

That early reticence can't be laid entirely at the feet of my relative inexperience with Argento, either. Looking on Letterboxd, one can find plenty of devoted fans of Italian horror who dismiss or deride *Phenomena*, calling it, for example, "by far the worst movie of Argento's otherwise untouchable '75-'87 run" or even "fake Fulci horseshit."

There are also giallo purists who will lay out a very strict set of definitions regarding what is and is not covered by that peculiar subgenre. They will tell you that expressly supernatural films such as *Suspiria* and *Inferno*—which were not the direct predecessors of *Phenomena*, but pretty close—don't count. I don't know how those individuals feel about *Phenomena* but, for my purposes, it also doesn't really matter.

Whether it truly *is* one or not, *Phenomena* is, in so many ways, practically the ur-text of what many of us think when we think of giallo—and of Italian horror from this period more generally. There's a little bit of everything (perhaps, some would claim, too much) in this flick set at a girls' boarding school in a region that the film assures us is called the "Swiss Transylvania."

Naturally, there's a killer on the loose, knocking off young women using a knife on the end of a long metal pole that snaps together. There's also a very young Jennifer Connelly—a year before *Labyrinth*—playing the daughter of an absent movie star who comes to stay at the boarding school and who has a psychic rapport with insects (you heard me). There's Donald Pleasence with a Scottish accent as a wheelchair-bound entomologist who is helping the police to try to catch the killer.

There is ominous wind, said to "cause madness." Portions of the school, which is on grounds once owned by Richard Wagner, are abandoned and unsafe. There's sleepwalking and music cues that at once flout the normal approaches of score deployment and, at the same time, define and structure the scenes in which they occur. Before all is said and done, there's a deformed killer, a creepy life-sized doll, a gross pit filled with corpses, more than one unlikely decapitation, and a chimpanzee armed with a straight razor. When we get the killer's motive—to the extent that we ever do—it hinges upon what is essentially a pseudoscientist's understanding of psychology.

It is, in sum, an Argento movie. And while it may not be the *most* Argento movie he ever made, it's probably the one that I think of the most, when I think of his work, even while it lacks certain trademarks such as the Mario Bava-esque lighting of *Suspiria* or *Inferno*. In the grand traditions of the best of the form, it is both beautiful and grotesque, lurid and poetic, potent and nonsensical. It is not what the kids these days might call "pure vibes," but it either works for you or it doesn't, and very little that I can say is likely to change anyone's mind.

Shot on film, released in a variety of cuts over the years, heavily reliant on soundtrack and atmosphere, movies like this are basically what fancy Blu-ray and 4K editions were made for, and *Phenomena* has been released a number of times on home video in various forms. This new 4K Ultra HD release is only the latest upgrade even from Synapse, who previously rolled out a features-loaded Blu.

I'm not an expert on film restoration or sound mixing or any of that, but I can say that, to my untrained eye and ear, the movie has never looked better. What's more, the two-disc 4K set is just as features-packed as previous Synapse releases and boasts what I think is every major cut of the film, including the 116-minute Italian version, with a mixture of English and occasional Italian dialogue, the 110-minute "international" version, and the much shorter, R-rated, 83-minute U.S. cut, under the title *Creepers*.

So far, I've only watched the longest cut on this edition, but I'm told that all three boast new 4K restorations, including lossless soundtrack restorations. Various additional material includes a feature-length documentary originally produced for the Arrow Video release of the film. If you already own *Phenomena* in high definition from one of its numerous previous releases, the question of whether the upgrade is worth it will probably come down to how strongly you feel about the film. But then, if you feel strongly enough about it, like I do, there's probably not really even a question to begin with…

**Author's Note:** Thanks to the fact that *Phenomena* was the first Argento film I ever saw, combined with its influence on *Clock Tower*, it remains to this day the aesthetic that I most closely associate with the giallo, even though that is… pretty inaccurate.

**Originally published March 2023**
*Signal Horizon*

# "WHATEVER I DO HERE IS NO DIFFERENT FROM WHAT IS DONE AT ANY OTHER SCHOOL."

## *THE HOUSE THAT SCREAMED* (1969)

### AND THE HORRORS OF FASCISM

Ballyhooed as one of Spain's first horror movies, *The House That Screamed* is barely that until its closing minutes. Despite a couple of grisly and well-shot scenes of violence, most of the horror of *The House That Screamed* is the horror of repression—although, of course, repression is itself a type of violence, a fact that is ever boiling just beneath the surface of the film.

Released in Spain in 1969, under the title *"La residencia,"* aka *The Finishing School*, the picture was later brought out in the States by AIP in 1971 as *The House That Screamed*, the title for which it is better known. By then, however, it was already a box office hit in its native country, where it became the highest-grossing movie up to that time, raking in the equivalent of roughly a million U.S. dollars. It did not perform as well Stateside, where it had about ten minutes trimmed from its running time and somehow received a GP rating (at the time the equivalent of PG-13) despite the film's heavy psychosexual themes.

The new Blu-ray from Arrow offers both the original Spanish cut of the film, which clocks in at around 104 minutes with the original title, and the AIP *House That Screamed* cut. Like a great many European films of the time, *The House That Screamed* was shot with a combination of actors from different countries all speaking their own native languages, then re-dubbed as needed for export. This means that both versions are here in English, with only some of the characters dubbed and others not.

Indeed, the film's star is undoubtedly Lilli Palmer, a German actress who transitioned to Hollywood in the 1940s. She received a Golden Globe nod for her role in the 1959 Clark Gable comedy *But Not for Me*, though horror fans are more likely to recognize her from the 1971 version of *Murders in the Rue Morgue* or the Nazi clone thriller *Boys from Brazil*. Here, as the school's sadistic yet "profoundly human" headmistress, she does an admirable job of holding the screen, even as she is surrounded at all times by nubile young ingenues in various stages of undress.

Critics and film scholars have compared the film unfavorably to *Psycho*, which is fair only if all you watched was the last five minutes or so. Despite a couple of stabbings which occur first at about the midway point of the film, this overt horror ending feels almost tacked on by comparison to the rich gothic melodrama of the rest of the picture, though it is executed no less artfully for all that, and comes as quite a punch, even when you can't help but know that it's on its way.

Sure, there are a handful of murders and the expected whippings and psychological torments that you won't be shocked to see in a girls' boarding school movie, but the real horrors of *The House That Screamed* are taking place outside the walls of the house itself—and, indeed, outside the time period in which the film takes place. Introducing a screening of *The House That Screamed* at the New Beverly Cinema in Los Angeles, Marc Edward Heuck wrote that, "Some clever Spanish filmmakers found a means to tell the world about the ravages and effects of living under totalitarianism, while still working under the strict dictates of the state, and that was through making horror films."

Though *The House That Screamed* is a period piece set in 19th-century France, it is pretty clearly meant to evoke the horrors of fascism, under which Spain was suffering at the time the movie was made. The ease with which the psychosexual politics of the boarding house can be read as a microcosm of national fascism is rendered particularly striking when you realize that the film was made in Francoist Spain.

It comes as no surprise, then, that Guillermo del Toro has singled out *The House That Screamed* as a favorite, calling it a "deranged, Freudian gothic melodrama" and a "keystone of Spanish horror." Its influence can be seen throughout del Toro's filmography, from the psychosexual dynamics of the orphanage in *The Devil's Backbone* to the gothic opulence of *Crimson Peak* to del Toro's own extensive metaphors (and outright depictions) of Franco's Spain. You can even see the ghosts of *The House That Screamed* (which has no ghosts of its own) in some of the films that del Toro merely produced, such as *The Orphanage* (2007).

The debut feature of Narciso Ibanez Serrador, the director, was already a household name in Spain by the time he released *The House That Screamed*. This was thanks to the Spanish-language horror anthology series he created and helmed, *Tales to Keep You Awake*, which was a huge hit on Spanish television in the 1960s and has, itself, recently been released on Blu-ray by Severin.

In spite of its box office success, *The House That Screamed* was one of only two feature films that Serrador would ever direct. The other is probably much better known, at least among American horror fans—the 1976 cult hit *Who Can Kill a Child?* Fortunately, with this new Arrow Video Blu, fans can now experience this other low-key classic from Serrador, as well.

**Author's Note:** A recurring theme throughout the reviews in this book is movies I didn't expect to like but did anyway. A more unlikely recurring theme is the fascism of Francoist Spain.

Originally published March 2023
orringrey.com

## HORROR IS WHERE YOU FIND IT

The other night, we watched *The Sea Hawk* (1940) for the first time. We watched this for several reasons, among them because Grace loves the old swashbuckling novels like the one this picture was adapted from. Books by folks like Rafael Sabatini (who wrote this one), Alexandre Dumas, Frank Yerby, and a variety of others, especially Samuel Shellabarger, who wrote one of Grace's favorite books of all time, *Prince of Foxes*, itself adapted into a movie in 1949 starring Tyrone Power, Orson Welles, et al.

While I also like these old Hollywood movies, I was excited about this one for a particular reason. Like *The Adventures of Robin Hood* (1938), another all-timer that we watched for the first time last year, this was directed by Michael Curtiz. While Curtiz is probably best known for *Casablanca*, and perhaps only slightly less well-known for swashbuckling fare like this, when I think of him, the first two movies that spring to mind are two of his only horror pictures—and two of my favorite horror films of all time: *Doctor X* (1932) and *Mystery of the Wax Museum* (1933).

I've written about those two films at some length in various other places, but for those who are just hearing about them for the first time, know that I recommend them, especially *Doctor X*, as heartily as I possibly can. Not only are they two of the only surviving films shot in what's known as "two-strip Technicolor," lending them a lurid and unmistakable palette, they are also just dynamite examples of the horror films of Hollywood's golden age—and horror films in general.

On those two films, and several others, Curtiz worked with

Polish art director and production designer Anton Grot, who, for my money, may have been one of the best who ever plied that trade. The incredible look of both *Doctor X* and *Mystery of the Wax Museum* owes at least as much to Grot's work behind the scenes as to Curtiz's work behind the camera.

Grot and Curtiz are working together again on *The Sea Hawk*, and while the sets here are not as filled with expressionistic horror or pulpish shadows and angles as those of *Doctor X*, they are no less impressive, or integral to the mood and function of the piece. From possibly the most impressive ship-to-ship battle I have ever seen, which opens the film in dramatic fashion and for which Warner Bros. had to build a larger sound stage to accommodate the full-scale ships, to minor touches in quiet scenes, the production design and art direction here is always top of the line.

In fact, there's very little in *The Sea Hawk* that isn't a shining example of Golden Age Hollywood operating at the peak of its powers. The actors, including Errol Flynn, Claude Rains, Brenda Marshall, Alan Hale, Una O'Connor, and many others, all acquit themselves nicely, while Flora Robson as Queen Elizabeth is an absolute force of nature. But the human elements may be the film's weakest links. Everything from the score (by swashbuckler stalwart Erich Wolfgang Korngold) to the costumes (by the prolific Orry-Kelly) to the scope and scale of the film itself is absolutely top-drawer Hollywood, as they only did it back in those days.

Earlier on, though, I was talking about horror, and I want to address the horror bonafides in *The Sea Hawk*, which absolutely has them, even if we discount the involvement of Curtiz and Grot. One of the things that really sets *The Sea Hawk* apart from a number of the other cutlass-and-tights flicks of the era is the way in which it deftly handles a variety of disparate moods, from swashbuckling adventure to throne-room intrigue to romance to tragedy to tension and, yes, horror.

Each of these transitions is handled at once dramatically and dynamically, with touches that are often both small and ingenious.

Take, for instance, the sequence of the film which takes place in the New World, where the standard "silver screen" black-and-white of the rest of the picture is replaced with a sepia tone that captures perfectly the changed feel of the setting.

This extends to the film's few moments of genuine horror. The galleys of the Spanish ships, where slaves are whipped into pulling heavy oars, are rendered in an expressionistic scale that calls to mind the great German silent films, while an attempt at escape late in the movie is suffused with more genuine tension than most entire thrillers can ever manage. The desperation of a slog through the swamps of the New World is rendered suitably oppressive, but the real star of the horror show comes when the escaped crew of the *Albatross* attempt to return to their ship after an ambush.

Worn down and desperate, they row toward what should be their salvation, but even before they reach the ship, it is clear that something is very wrong. As they climb aboard a ship that should be bustling with the rest of their crew, all is silence and the grim creaking of the rigging, a setting as haunting as any ghost ship ever put on film. The real bravura touch, however, comes as they move to explore the deck, and the camera suddenly switches to a top-down shot from high in the rigging, one that expertly conveys the isolation and the unknown danger of the situation in which they find themselves.

These are only a few brief moments of horror in a film that otherwise moves effortlessly across a variety of other tones and moods, but they are no less deftly deployed for all that and for me, at least, they served to heighten what was already a most enjoyable experience with a classic film of yesteryear.

**Author's Note:** While I watch more horror films than any other kind, I watch and enjoy all kinds of movies, especially those from the so-called golden age of Hollywood. Watching *The Sea Hawk* was a particular pleasure, and I was compelled to put my thoughts about it onto my website, especially as it relates to the horror film.

For those who do primarily watch horror pictures, it is well worth your time as a detour.

Previously unpublished

# THE DARK SÉANCE: MIDNIGHT SPOOK SHOWS AND THE GIMMICK FILMS OF WILLIAM CASTLE

If you're a horror fan, odds are you've seen ads for the midnight spook shows that were once incredibly popular entertainments in the '40s and '50s, even if you have probably never attended one yourself. These ads, with their ballyhoo about spooks on the loose and monsters invading the audience, show up often in the fringes of even modern horror culture, from trailers played in movie pre-shows to decorative elements found on Etsy shops.

For as long as I can remember, I've loved the *idea* of these spook shows, even while I never really knew what they truly entailed, until I read the 1991 book *Ghostmasters*, by Mark Walker. The now sadly out-of-print book contains a heavily-illustrated history of a unique tradition that is otherwise largely lost to time, preserved only in the form of those advertisements I already mentioned.

At the height of their power, these spook shows sold out theaters and commanded massive audiences. The book includes photographs of crowds stretching around the block waiting to get in and be shocked, mystified, and, perhaps above all, scared.

Just what *were* these spook shows, though? They varied from one to the next, of course, but they had a sort of common structure. Almost always held at midnight, fundamentally they were little more than simple magic shows, with a spooky theme. Most preceded a short feature film. Always a horror picture, sometimes thematically chosen to match the show.

The highlight of the spook shows was a brief interlude that occurred usually between the normal magic routines and the start of the film. This was called the Blackout or, more evocatively, the Dark Séance, and it is something we could probably never get away with today, thanks to stricter fire laws and more cautious liability insurance.

The lights in the theater were shut out entirely. Which, given that the auditoriums were packed to capacity with rowdy midnight crowds, was probably already chaotic enough. But then the magician and their assistants would introduce various spooks and monsters to the mix.

Sometimes this meant a person in a monster suit, running down from the stage just as the lights were extinguished. Sometimes, it meant pelting the audience with fake rubber insects or anything else that felt creepy and crawly. In one humorous anecdote, Walker's book recounts the story of an enterprising spook show operator who intended to introduce live bats but, unable to acquire them, substituted pigeons instead. Unfortunately, the pigeons took a liking to the inside of the auditorium and proved impossible to displace for some weeks after the show.

By far the most common element of these Blackouts were glow-in-the-dark ghosts and skeletons that were paraded across the stage, swung out over the audience on what were essentially fishing poles, or otherwise made to appear to "float" in the air above the crowd.

One can't help but imagine that such theatrics would be pretty effective, even now, and they must have been absolute show-stoppers in their heyday. Unfortunately, as I mentioned, not much remains to mark this moment in horror history except for lots of vintage ads making bold promises that go far beyond what any crowd was ever likely to have experienced.

There are rare photographs that capture elements of these shows, but even books like Walker's *Ghostmasters* are often out of print and sell for exorbitant fees online, so most of us are shut out from these experiences. The closest we can come is perhaps the 1965 film *Monsters Crash the Pajama Party*, which was made to be part of one of these spook shows, with a baked-in interval in which costumed "monsters" would appear to exit the film and snatch a "victim" from the audience.

\*\*\*

Fortunately for all of us, these midnight spook shows were not left entirely in the realm of hearsay and record. Though the shows themselves ended and were lost to time, they had an inheritor. A director who carried their spirit, if not their substance, into a string of popular "gimmick" horror movies released between 1958 and 1965 (give or take).

William Castle was born in New York City in 1914, and by the age of 15 he had dropped out of high school to work in the theater, after meeting Bela Lugosi during the Broadway production of *Dracula*, which presaged the legendary 1931 film version. According to Castle's autobiography, Lugosi recommended the young man as assistant stage manager for the play's road company, and Castle took the job. The rest, as they say, is history.

By 1943, Castle was directing low-budget movies for Columbia Pictures. By 1958, he had already directed dozens of mostly forgotten B-pictures, but he wanted something more. As he put it in his autobiography, "I wanted to scare the pants off audiences." In '58, he took his chance, mortgaging his own house to finance his first independent feature, *Macabre*, inspired by the French classic *Les Diaboliques*. *Macabre* also featured Castle's first gimmick, a $1,000 life insurance policy from Lloyd's of London for anyone who should die of fright during the film.

*Macabre* was a smash hit, making an estimated $5 million from a budget of around $90,000. The success of *Macabre* and its gimmick paved the way for the run of films (and gimmicks) that would make Castle famous. Over the next decade, Castle would bring audiences floating skeletons, vibrating seats, "ghost viewers," and many more.

Here's the thing, though. Castle's gimmicks were nothing new. They were (brilliantly wrought) echoes of the very same things that the spook show pioneers (Walker's *Ghostmasters*) had used to put audiences into seats—and then scare them out of them—in decades prior.

The places where Castle's indebtedness to the "Dark Séances" of midnight spook shows are most obvious are in the first two movies to follow *Macabre*—which are also probably Castle's two most famous pictures as director. *House on Haunted Hill* and *The Tingler* were both released in 1959, and both starred Vincent Price.

The gimmick in *House on Haunted Hill* was called "Emergo," and it consisted of a skeleton that sailed out above the audience on wires during the film's climactic moments. The parallels between this singular spook and the many glowing apparitions of the spook show "Blackouts" are obvious, with the chief one being the way that "Emergo" seemed to come out of the film itself and enter the audience proper, breaking down the fourth wall and transforming the members of the audience from viewers to participants. At the same time the skeleton was being propelled over the audience on wires, a skeleton was emerging from a vat of acid to menace Carol Ohmart on screen.

"Percepto," as the gimmick for *The Tingler* was called, may be the most infamous that Castle ever dreamed up. The movie is about an eponymous creature that looks rather like a larger, rubbery centipede. It is created inside the human spine whenever we are afraid, and it can only be destroyed by screaming. The gimmick involved a number of military surplus airplane wing de-icers, which Castle purchased and had attached to the undersides of certain theater seats.

These de-icers worked by vibrating strongly. When the mechanisms were activated, the seats would shake, giving the person sitting in it a "tingling" jolt. Not electricity, as has often been erroneously averred—merely vibration. Like an early version of a Playstation DualShock controller.

While the "Percepto" gimmick served a similar function to "Emergo"—that of bringing the film off the screen and into the audience, just as the monsters and ghosts came off the stage and into the audience during a "Dark Séance"—the *real* part of *The Tingler* that echoes a spook show "Blackout" comes in the film itself.

The plot of the film involves the proprietor of a silent movie theater, who uses the titular critter to frighten his deaf and mute wife to death in their apartment above the theater. Afterward, however, the tingler gets loose and makes its way into the theater. This is where the "Blackout" begins. As the tingler gets into the projection booth, Price's character shuts off the lights and advises the audience not to panic but to "scream, scream for your lives" because "the tingler is loose in this theater."

At the same time that Price's character was killing the lights in the theater on the screen, the screen itself went black, plunging the actual theater, where people were watching *The Tingler*, into darkness, and his exhortations to the film's diegetic audience seemed equally applicable to the audience in the real-life theater, now plunged into an effective "Blackout."

These two films were followed by several others, all of which incorporated gimmicks that mirrored the stunts of the midnight spook shows less and less as time went on. *13 Ghosts* brought audiences a "ghost viewer," which let them either see or remove the ghosts from the screen, depending on which lens they looked through. *Homicidal* had a "fright break" before the ending, during which time you could "chicken out" for a full refund, though to do so, you had to endure the shame of walking to "Coward's Corner." Here's how John Waters described it:

"A yellow cardboard booth, manned by a bewildered theater employee in the lobby. When the Fright Break was announced, and you found that you couldn't take it anymore, you had to leave your seat and, in front of the entire audience, follow your footsteps up the aisle, bathed in yellow light. Before you reached Coward's

Corner, you crossed yellow lines with the stenciled message: 'Cowards Keep Walking.' You passed a nurse (in a yellow uniform? ... I wonder), who would offer a blood pressure test. All the while a record was blaring, 'Watch the chicken! Watch him shiver in Coward's Corner!' As the audience howled, you had to go through one final indignity—at Coward's Corner you were forced to sign a yellow card stating, 'I am a bona fide coward.'"

While these gimmicks grew less involved as time went on, they all, up until the last ones in films like *I Saw What You Did*, which installed seat belts in some seats to "keep patrons from being jolted from their chairs in fright," served a similar purpose: they brought the movie off the screen and into the audience, a proper sendoff to the "Blackout" antics of the popular spook shows of yesteryear, which had already begun to fade into obscurity by the time Castle was releasing his gimmick pictures.

**Author's Note:** It would be fair to say that this was written expressly for this volume, but it's more accurate to say that the timing just worked out. I had been cooking on this essay ever since I read the *Ghostmasters* book that I mentioned in it, and realized the connection between Castle's gimmick pictures and the spook shows. That said, I think it makes a good endcap for this book, and I'm happy to say that it appears here for the first time.

**Previously unpublished**

# 100 MOVIES TO SEE AFTER YOU DIE

It felt weird to publish a book like this without including at least one recommended movie list, especially since the movies reviewed here are so scattershot, from old favorites to new encounters, from movies I loved to movies that are not really my thing, even when they are very good.

In putting this list together, I held myself to a few requirements. I avoided listing any movies that I covered extensively elsewhere in the book, no matter how much I might love them, and I tried to eschew obvious classics and movies that you've likely been told to see many times before, even if you haven't seen them yet. Here and there, I may have made exceptions to both of those rules, but that was the guiding principle. Finally, I cut the list off at 2010, the year after which the writings collected in this book would have begun.

As I mentioned many times throughout this book, I'm not interested, as a critic, in telling you which movies are "good" and which are "bad." As such, this (extremely non-exhaustive) list is not, by any means, a list of the "best" movies. It is simply a list of movies I find interesting, and hope you will, too. Also, in order to keep the list at a manageable length, I had to leave off innumerable films that I would otherwise have loved to include. Still, this should help get you started.

The title here comes from a joke I posted on Twitter some time ago, in response to seeing yet another of the many "X number Movies to See Before You Die" books or online lists.

*The Cabinet of Dr. Caligari* (1920)
*Haxan* (1922)
*The Magician* (1926)
*Island of Lost Souls* (1932)
*Murders in the Rue Morgue* (1932)
*The Old Dark House* (1932)
*Night of Terror* (1933)
*Mad Love* (1935)
*Mark of the Vampire* (1935)
*The Invisible Ray* (1936)
*The Cat and the Canary* (1939)
*The Ghost Breakers* (1940)
*Cat People* (1942)
*Night Monster* (1942)
*The Undying Monster* (1942)
*I Walked with a Zombie* (1943)
*Return of the Vampire* (1943)
*The Uninvited* (1944)
*Dead of Night* (1945)
*Hangover Square* (1945)
*The Spiral Staircase* (1946)
*Valley of the Zombies* (1946)
*The Maze* (1953)
*The Quatermass Xperiment* (1955)
*Attack of the Crab Monsters* (1957)
*Curse of the Demon* (1957)
*The Monolith Monsters* (1957)
*The Monster That Challenged the World* (1957)
*The Four Skulls of Jonathan Drake* (1959)
*The Manster* (1959)
*Caltiki: The Immortal Monster* (1959)
*The Brides of Dracula* (1960)
*Mill of the Stone Women* (1960)
*The Ship of Monsters* (1960)

*The Curse of the Crying Woman* (1961)
*The Pit and the Pendulum* (1961)
*Night Creatures* (1962)
*The Haunted Palace* (1963)
*Matango* (1963)
*Blood and Black Lace* (1964)
*The Gorgon* (1964)
*Curse of the Fly* (1965)
*Die, Monster, Die!* (1965)
*Planet of the Vampires* (1965)
*Island of Terror* (1966)
*Plague of the Zombies* (1966)
*The Ghost of Sierra de Cobre* (1967)
*It!* (1967)
*Viy* (1967)
*The Devil Rides Out* (1968)
*Yog, Monster from Space* (1970)
*The Brotherhood of Satan* (1971)
*Night of the Devils* (1972)
*Whoever Slew Auntie Roo?* (1972)
*The Legend of Hell House* (1973)
*Messiah of Evil* (1973)
*Phantom of the Paradise* (1974)
*Sugar Hill* (1974)
*The Devil's Rain* (1975)
*House* (1977)
*The Pyschic* (1977)
*The Medusa Touch* (1978)
*Death Ship* (1980)
*Next of Kin* (1982)
*One Dark Night* (1982)
*The Deadly Spawn* (1983)
*C.H.U.D.* (1984)
*Razorback* (1984)

*Making Contact* (1985)
*Return of the Living Dead* (1985)
*The Stuff* (1985)
*Chopping Mall* (1986)
*Anguish* (1987)
*Dolls* (1987)
*Evil Dead Trap* (1988)
*Lair of the White Worm* (1988)
*The Spider Labyrinth* (1988)
*I, Madman* (1989)
*Witchtrap* (1989)
*Nightbreed* (1990)
*The Boneyard* (1991)
*The Resurrected* (1991)
*Subspecies* (1991)
*Doctor Mordrid* (1992)
*Ghostwatch* (1992)
*Wax Mask* (1996)
*Event Horizon* (1997)
*Deep Rising* (1998)
*Lake Placid* (1999)
*Pitch Black* (2000)
*Uzumaki* (2000)
*Brotherhood of the Wolf* (2001)
*From Hell* (2001)
*She Creature* (2001)
*Noroi* (2005)
*Reincarnation* (2005)
*Dead Silence* (2007)
*The Mist* (2007)
*Occult* (2009)
*Triangle* (2009)

# ABOUT THE AUTHOR

Orrin Grey is a skeleton who likes monsters, as well as a writer, editor, and amateur film scholar who was born on the night before Halloween. You can find him online at orringrey.com.

Milton Keynes UK
Ingram Content Group UK Ltd.
UKHW030746071024
449371UK00006B/495